A FAN FOR ALL SEASONS

D.A. Shaw
Aug 2023

Jon Harvey

A FAN FOR ALL
SEASONS

A Journey Through
Life and Sport

YELLOW JERSEY PRESS
LONDON

1 3 5 7 9 10 8 6 4 2

Yellow Jersey, an imprint of Vintage, is part of the Penguin Random House group of companies whose addresses can be found at global.penguinrandomhouse.com

Penguin
Random House
UK

First published by Yellow Jersey in 2023

penguin.co.uk/vintage

A CIP catalogue record for this book is available from the British Library

ISBN 9781787290587

Typeset in 12/15pt Minion Pro by Jouve (UK), Milton Keynes
Printed and bound in Great Britain by Clays Ltd, Elcograf S.p.A.

The authorised representative in the EEA is Penguin Random House Ireland, Morrison Chambers, 32 Nassau Street, Dublin D02 YH68

Penguin Random House is committed to a sustainable future for our business, our readers and our planet. This book is made from Forest Stewardship Council® certified paper.

MIX
Paper | Supporting
responsible forestry
FSC® C018179

To Dan

Contents

'We all have our time machines, don't we? Those that take us back are memories . . . And those that carry us forward are dreams.'

H. G. Wells

'There's always a story, bro.'

Daniel Harvey

1

Walk the Line

L et's start at the very beginning. The starting point of all
starting points.

It was 2016 – the year everyone called a bad one before all
the worse ones that were yet to come – and I was sweating my
way through a hot summer's day at the Home of Sport. That's a
title to which a fair few venues might like to lay claim: Wembley calls itself *the Home of Football*, Lord's *the Home of Cricket*,
St Andrew's *the Home of Golf*. But none of those quite cut the
mustard as being the home of Sport with a capital S. There's
only one landmark on the planet worthy of that accolade. It's a
long oblong of dusty earth, surrounded on all sides by gently
rising grass banks and fringed on its horizon by the green hills
of the western Greek Peloponnese. Bare but beautiful. Humble
but historic. Birthplace of one of humanity's most gargantuan
inventions. It's the ancient stadium at Olympia. The most precious site in world sport. And I had the place to myself.

Or what's left of it, anyway. In AD 394 the Olympic Games fell
victim to an early version of cancel culture, when the Christian
emperor Theodosius cracked down on pagan festivals and
banned them. That decision sentenced the sacred site to nearly
2,000 years of looting, neglect and decay, and the Olympia I
was looking at had melted into nature. For acre after acre, meek
marble stumps of once-mighty temples rose with the weeds out
of the crumbling, sun-baked earth. But here used to pulse the
quadrennial heartbeat of the Mediterranean. In its heyday this
was the hottest of tourist hotspots, boasting not only the Games

but also one of the Seven Wonders of the World: a vast and astonishing Statue of Zeus. These days both the colossus and the beautiful temple that housed it are long gone, shattered by time into smithereens, and there's a distinct Ozymandias vibe to the few slabs that remain. But while the complex that staged the Games may have been been reduced to rubble, the flame it ignited burns brighter than ever. Thanks to the efforts of William Penny Brookes and Baron Pierre de Coubertin, since 1896 the Olympics have returned to inspire and enrapture billions of lives. Including mine. I'd come here because I wanted to see this sporting crucible for myself and feel its history, its essence. More than that, I needed to.

The ruins of Olympia are imbued with two key things that make sport tick: the glory of winning, and the honour of taking part. And locked within the surviving stones that scatter the site are exotic stories and incredible truths. Of these, the most powerful and poignant is that, all the way back to its origins, sport has gone hand in hand with death. That might sound surprising, but you only need to think back to the Gladiators for proof. Remember how every time Wolf appeared on screen he looked as if he was about to have a heart attack? And turning the clock back further than Saturday teatimes in 1995, or even AD 95 at the Colosseum, historians have traced the origin of competitive sport back to the eighth century BC, when the Greeks invented it as something to do at funerals (presumably because they didn't have smartphones for distraction.) It was out of this funerary tradition that the ancient Olympics, first recorded as taking place in 776 BC, grew. And they were full of death. Never more so than in one of their favourite events, the pankration, which was basically Ultimate Fighting meets Mortal Kombat. Absolved from almost any rules, participants in this all-out slugfest were encouraged to bite, gouge, twist scrotums (NB: each other's) and pretty much anything else besides, and one contestant is even on record as having torn out his opponent's intestines. Peculiar as it might seem to us, this is how competitive sport on Earth began. Just as birds are descended from the dinosaurs, so it turns out that snooker is descended from an ancient Greek wrestler ripping out another bloke's duodenum. Death, glorious death, permeated the crusty soil on which I was standing.

And it wasn't just the occasional defeated competitor who perished here and bit the Olympian dust. Also running the gauntlet in antiquity were the thousands upon thousands of fans who'd routinely flock to the Games. For a start, the food on offer was always a bit of a gamble. In *Naked Olympics*, Tony Perrotet itemises the takeaway fare at the early Games as including 'suspicious sausages, rock-hard bread and dubious cheese, to be washed down by throat-scalding resinated wine'. You may, like me, have copped an unfortunate hot-dog or two at a sports event, but this was next-level stuff. Rumours used to swirl around the ancient world of spectators finding 'human flesh and knucklebones in their stew'. Back then, if you caught yourself eating someone's spleen, there was no TripAdvisor on which to vent yours.

But dodgy food was the least of their problems. Disease was so rampant that on-site priests would routinely pray to Zeus, the 'Averter of Flies'. There was no fresh water, nobody washed, riverbeds were turned into giant latrines, every inch of space was taken up by camping and afterwards it could take days to get home. Basically it was Glastonbury without the rain. Or, mercifully for them, Coldplay. If there was a laurel wreath to be won for poor hygiene, ancient Olympia would have strolled to victory every time. More dangerous still was the heat. A Greek philosopher named Thales once wrote that water was the most precious gift in nature, an insight the twenty-first century is rapidly bearing out. But Thales was way ahead of the curve, and on a visit to the Games he emphatically proved his point by dying from dehydration. Conditions were so notorious that one ancient Greek man is recorded as threatening his disobedient slave with a ticket to the Olympics. But nothing could put fans off going. Even back then, the magic of sport transcended logic.

It crosses the language barrier, too. Eager to avoid the same fate as Thales, I stopped off at a snack van in the archaeological park for a bottle of water. The vendor pointed at my London 2012 souvenir T-shirt: 'English?' After confirming I was, I discovered that the only other words this cheery Greek and I shared were the names of some Premier League football teams.

'Manchester United!' he exclaimed as he handed over my drink, his smile revealing his allegiance.

I shook my head, then put my thumbs up. 'Tottenham Hotspur!'

The merchant replied with a smile and one further word of English. 'Who?'

In many ways, sport as we now know it is a universe away from the athletic contests that once graced these ancient fields, and for good reason: nobody in their right mind is crying out for the pankration to be an exhibition event at Paris 2024. But as well as inventing the idea of competition, the Greeks were masters of sports administration, and they could teach the International Olympic Committee (IOC) a thing or two about how to run the show. A relic of one of their best ideas endures at Olympia to this day. Lining the path to the old stadium is a row of modest, unadorned stone pedestals, each of which once supported a small bronze statue of Zeus. Together they were known as the Zanes. But it wasn't the statues themselves that were remarkable. It was their purpose. They were funded from the proceeds of fines that had been issued to any athlete who was found to have broken the rules of the Games. And, pointedly, on the plinth beneath each Zeus was written the name and home city of the guilty party, to secure the miscreant's place in eternal infamy. It's thanks to the Zanes that we know about the likes of Eupolus of Thessaly, who in 388 BC bribed three boxers to lose fights against him. Sorry, Eupolus; we still haven't forgotten. If everlasting public disgrace wasn't enough, offenders were likely to be beaten and banned from future Games too. The message of the Zanes was stark: don't cheat. And the small number of plinths (only sixteen survive) suggests that it mostly worked. It's a brilliant idea, and if there's a single aspect of the ancient Olympics that could do with being brought back, it's the creation of a Hall of Shame for disgraced athletes. The only hitch would be getting planning permission: nowadays it would need to be very long indeed.

It's only a short walk past the Zanes and through a small stone arch to the stadium itself. The Big Bang of world sport. Where I was now standing. It was rush hour, when hordes of tourists can be expected to pour onto the track. But by sheer luck I'd managed to turn up during a gap between coach parties, and the arena was empty. Silent. Serene. Down at my feet was the original starting line, marked by three parallel rows of thin white blocks. For centuries this was the exact point where sprinters from across the Greek empire and beyond would assemble in their bid to be crowned the fastest human in the world. Now, after who knows how many other millions before me, it was my turn.

On your marks.

Why was I lining up on the starting blocks at ancient Olympia? Because of something that had happened one year earlier in Kensington Olympia. Because of sport and death. Because of Dan.

2

The Day It All Changed

Some of my favourite stories finish with death. At the end of the *Star Wars* trilogy Darth Vader dies. At the end of *Ghostbusters* the Stay-Puft Marshmallow Man dies. At the end of the *Back to the Future* movies, the DeLorean dies. At the end of the last *Jurassic World* movie, the integrity of the franchise died. But this story is going to go against the grain and start with death. Because for those of us left behind, that's how it happens. Death strikes first, and then we have to pick up the pieces and learn to cope. I want to tell you about my older brother, and my oldest friend.

Dan and I grew up together in Croydon. (That's not the sad bit.) He was nine years older than me, which was old enough to be almost like a second dad as well as a sibling. We had a lot in common, including a passion for movies, politics and comedy. More than anything, we shared a love of sport. And by that I mean the arduous, energy-sapping side of sport: being a fan. Playing's for wimps. It's the watching that's the hard part. He was the biggest Crystal Palace FC supporter in the world, which wasn't ideal for me, being a Tottenham fan. But to be fair to Dan, there are much worse things an older brother could be into. Just ask Prince Edward.

We loved all sport and any sport, from kabaddi highlights on Channel 4 to the traditional new year's treat of *World's Strongest Man* (you can't beat an Atlas Stone). If that's not esoteric enough, as kids we'd lap up shows like *Junior Kick Start*, which was a mad BBC series hosted by Peter Purves that ran through the Eighties, involving children racing on motorbikes over logs, oil drums, walls and cliff faces. (It was often followed in the schedules by *Junior 24 Hours in A&E*.) We even used to adore the Royal Navy Field Gun Competition at the Royal Tournament. In case it passed you by, until 1999 that was an insane annual race between two teams of sailors in front of a packed house of thousands at London's Earl's Court, televised by the BBC. And what they had to do was this: disassemble a piece of heavy artillery, fly it over a chasm on a zip wire, take it through a tiny door, then reassemble it, fire it, and then do the whole thing in reverse, in the fastest possible time. They don't do it any more, because the Royal Navy doesn't have any guns, and without the guns it was basically just a stag weekend at a Go Ape centre. But Dan and I wouldn't mind. We'd watch *anything* sporty together. Until the morning of Tuesday, 9 June 2015.

It's just before 9 a.m. and London is looking glorious, the way it does when sunlight bathes the city in gold and optimism. A perfect summer's morning. Except in my head, where everything else has been evicted by fear. I'm making the short walk from Earl's Court Station to Dan's dinky studio flat on Ifield Road, trying not to think about what's going to happen next. Clinging to hope but weighed down by dread. Nothing feels real. I'd distract myself by listening to music, but I can't think of anything appropriate. Instead I try to focus on my surroundings. Little details are magnified: the birdsong in the trees, the whisper of leaves on the breeze, the soft hum of a Hoover wafting out of a pub, the gentle clank of empty swings swaying in a playground. Normal things. But normality is a universe away right now, because I'm on my way to find Dan, and I'm very scared.

What's now a terrible, unremitting despair started thirty-six hours ago as a nagging concern. We'd all been due to meet up at my mum Linda's house in Croydon for Sunday lunch: my younger sister Lucy, her husband David, Mum, me and Dan. It's not something we often do, but Lucy had taken the initiative to get us together for a bit of family quality time, which sounded like just the ticket. Dan had been having a difficult few months. He'd quit his job with the London Borough of Kensington & Chelsea, possibly after suffering some workplace bullying he was keeping coy about. If that wasn't enough, the council had been continuing to pay his salary in error, which had enabled him to survive financially – until they'd realised their mistake. Now they were demanding their money back and he didn't have a bean. He wasn't exactly a picture of health either. He was forty-three years old, a squat man with a head of short bushy black hair, unfashionable glasses and a slow, shuffling walk due to the obesity he'd carried for his whole adult life. Nothing too notable about any of that in twenty-first century Britain, but since the new year he'd been putting on more weight, and from time to time complained of leg pains.

Through this period Dan had been in touch with me a fair bit, but not because he wanted to chat about his problems. Quite the opposite. What Dan wanted to talk about was sport. Any sport. All sport. It was a crutch he could lean on: diversion, salvation and an unbreakable bond between us. It was his lifeblood. Of course, in the grand scheme of things sport is unimportant, but for us it was the most important unimportant thing in the world – what Stephen Fry calls 'that glorious distraction'. (Although Stephen's a Norwich fan, so in his case it's mainly just distraction.) By sharing with Dan a common language of off-side in football, leg-side in cricket, Grand National winners, decathlon disciplines and so much more, I'd been able to – gently – broach the trickier subjects: money, diet, health.

I'm not proud to admit it, but over the course of the previous weeks and months these cares had begun to drain me too, and I'd felt stalked by worry and stress. At the same time, I'd respond to the onset of these emotions by telling myself, 'If it's bad for you, how do you think Dan feels?' Thankfully I wasn't on my own. Mum and Lucy were there for him just as much as I was, and it was Lucy who'd helped him apply for the state benefits to which he was entitled. (He'd have struggled to navigate the forms on his own.) If he'd been leaning especially on me, it was because they didn't have the same hinterland into which he wanted to go deep and escape.

That Sunday morning I travelled to Mum's place in Selsdon, on the southern edge of Croydon, and I'm so glad I did, because it turned out there was a specific reason for the get-together. It was the happiest news: Lucy was pregnant. For the first time she'd be a mum, our mum would be a grandma, and Dan and I would be uncles. Sunday lunch was suddenly a celebration, and we shared a toast. But as time ticked on – the roast dinner untouched and going cold – there was no sign of Dan.

This wasn't entirely out of the ordinary. Dan had a habit of going off-grid and not replying to messages, and his timekeeping was erratic at best. (Unless Crystal Palace were involved. In a quarter of a century he barely missed a kick-off). Given he hadn't been on top form recently, it wasn't hard to imagine he might prefer to spend Sunday resting at home rather than trekking across London. Still, we thought, he said he'd be here, and he loved a roast. If he changed his mind he'd usually let us know. Maybe he was sleeping? He'd developed a habit of nodding off regularly when we watched TV together, so an unscheduled nap wasn't out of the question. Maybe he was cross about something? But what? The afternoon passed and the silence continued. More texts were sent; no replies came. Perhaps his phone had given up the ghost? After all, he did use a battered old 'dumb' model which had to pack up sooner or later. All these harmless explanations. We hadn't begun to consider the alternatives.

Dan had never been officially diagnosed with any mental health issues, and as a kid I just thought he was a bit unusual. A touch of paranoia. Talking to himself in the bathroom.

Compulsively checking he'd shut the front door, pulling so hard it seemed he might take the handle off. Carrying incongruous objects around with him. (Only a couple of months earlier I'd spotted an old 1980s telephone poking out of his bag. When I asked him why, he simply smiled a guilty smile and zipped the bag up.) With twenty-first century eyes, perhaps this could have been identified and understood as neurodiverse behaviour. But during our childhood years, society too often ignored this kind of thing or brushed it away as eccentricity. Dan was part of a generation whose mental well-being fell through the cracks of the system, or what then passed for a system. How many middle-aged men and women (Tens of thousands? Hundreds of thousands? More?) must be living now with conditions never treated, understood, or even acknowledged, without professional support? My brother's case was exacerbated by a cruel double whammy: he craved privacy, yet he didn't really know how to look after himself. Sometimes I wonder how he managed as well as he did. This unusual chemistry of character traits could manifest itself in Dan not responding to calls or messages for a couple of days. But while his silences weren't usually alarming, that Sunday afternoon it felt odd.

The next day, Monday, we all tried to carry on as normal. In the evening I even went on a Tinder date to see a play, which ended in a kiss by the ticket barriers at Leicester Square Tube. But my mind was running away elsewhere. (Sorry, Daisy.) Home at this point was my best friend Tom's place in Wood Green, where I'd been taking refuge after a thirteen-year relationship with my ex-girlfriend Sarah had broken down the year before. It was a happy house in an unlovely neighbourhood that I shared with Tom and our housemate Jules. I'd nearly got back from the date when Mum called. It was 10.30 p.m., which was very late for her to be up. 'I'm worried,' she said. So was I. We needed to find Dan. I tried to keep us both calm and offered to go over to his flat straightaway if she thought that was best. But if everything was OK, as we obviously hoped it was, then he'd probably be asleep and wouldn't hear me knock-ing. So what if instead I went over there first thing in the morning? Mum agreed and we said goodnight.

Half of me stayed rational, refusing to entertain dark thoughts. The other half was racing. When I got home I told Jules what was going on. Ever a voice of reason, she did all she could to offer reassurance, but the words just bounced off me. Come dawn I found myself sitting on the loo, shaking and Googling 'What to do if you find a dead body'.

Now it's nearly 9 a.m. on Tuesday morning and I've reached the front of number 43, Ifield Road. Slap-bang in one of London's richest areas, on a street filled with million-pound houses, Dan's minuscule second-floor studio flat is an aberration, like a pim-ple on a supermodel. I'd barely been back since I'd helped him move in nearly a decade ago. That day we'd celebrated complet-ing the heavy lifting by watching a World Cup 2006 group game in a nearby café. (It was the cabbie and I who did the heavy lifting. Dan wasn't a picture of fitness even then.) It's a tiny memory that's fluttered back, stained with guilt. Should I have done more to reach out over the intervening years? He never wanted me to meet him here. He'd always say he was in the mid-dle of 'doing some sorting' – code for his flat being a complete tip – but by accepting that boundary had I failed him? Could I have tried more? Would there be a chance to try again?

Right now I just need to get up to his flat, and to do that I'm going to need someone from one of the other apartments to let me into the building, except – wait – the front door is ajar. Weird. It's a quirk of fortune I'm grateful to receive. I run in and pound up the stairs; bang on his door; call out his name.

No response.

I phone his mobile and push my ear up against the door to listen. I can hear it ringing. And ringing. 'I'm here, bro!' I shout out. 'I'm calling 999. If you can hear me, help's coming.'

No response.

11

I dial emergency services and explain the situation, my voice dry and breaking. The operator tells me police and an ambulance are on their way.

Until they come I don't really know what to do. My brother may or may not be on the other side of this thick wooden door, and he may or may not be alive. All I can do is wait. I head back downstairs, wedge the house door open with a phone book, and sit on the steps outside. I feel very small.

It takes an hour, an excruciating hour, before the police arrive. (The ambulance never does.) At last two constables turn up: one is young, tall and friendly. Probably new in the job. He introduces himself as PC Evans. The other is older, pony-tailed, short and grizzled, hanging back and offering no greeting. Before I can ask anything, Constable Noname gets a message on his radio: 'Negative from the hospital.'

Damn. Until now I'd been allowing myself the briefest glimmer of hope that maybe Dan is just ill and he'd gone to A&E without his phone – that would explain everything. Make the panic end. But now, in just four words, that faint possibility has been extinguished. I swallow hard and tell the officers what I know, and they follow me upstairs. Between the two policemen hangs a portable battering ram, and they ask me to stand aside. A brief smash, and PC Evans forces his way in.

'Is he in there?' his colleague asks.

'Yeah, he's here.'

3

A Wake's Progress

Do you have someone special with whom you share your favourite passion? Who'll text you when the winning horse he picked in the 1992 Grand National passes away; who you'll phone on Saturday night to pore over the classified results; who'll text you when the winning horse you picked in the 1994 Grand National passes away; whose shared highs, lows and near misses bind you together with atomic force? Until that morning I had Dan.

Picture him as two parts Danny Baker to one part Ronnie Corbett. He had a nervous manner, a slightly rasping voice and a lexicon that was ingrained with Eighties and Nineties television. (His shorthand for me, 'bro', wasn't an attempt to sound cool – Dan had taken it from an obscure sketch in an even more obscure early Nineties comedy show called *Paramount City*.)

There was another distinctive trait to how he sounded. He used to love joining in with Crystal Palace chants at Selhurst Park, or with *Top of the Pops 2* at Christmas time, but he had an uncanny ability to do it in musical keys no other member of the human race had previously discovered. In my very first music lesson at secondary school, I remember the teacher Mr Vincent looking across at the whole class and proclaiming to us that there was no such thing as being tone deaf, and that in his professional career there was never a single boy he hadn't been able to teach to sing. Then he turned to me and said, 'Except your brother.' It was a kind of fame, and I was kinda proud. I studied my piano grades; Dan's choral skills were weapons grade. I can still hear his undulcet tones loud and clear in my head. But I'd swap everything to hear them for real. A sound more endearing than any actual music could ever be.

Most distinctive of all, he had the happiest happy-face I've ever seen, soundtracked by the cackliest laugh. Dan was the only friend I'd known my whole life. It wasn't remotely long enough. He was a keystone in my Jenga tower, and now he was gone I could feel my whole edifice teeter. He'd been taken away by diabetes, but we weren't to know that for weeks, as he'd never been formally diagnosed and was on no medication for it. At the time of the funeral, we still didn't know the details of what had happened. When exactly had he passed? How preventable was it? Might he even have taken his own life? We were in the dark. And the darkness.

Nobody's first wake should be their own brother's. There was only one place in the world for it that would do.

I'd been to the Palace so often I'd lost count. This was different. I stepped out of the car and edged towards Selhurst Park's main entrance feeling weary and punch-drunk. The legions of devoted Eagles fans who flock here on match days must know that sensation well, but for them it tends to descend as they leave the ground if the team has taken a hammering. I was on my way in. Selhurst is the home of Crystal Palace Football Club: Dan's alma mater, pater and every other relation besides. We'd been there together dozens of times. But this afternoon I wasn't being funnelled up the imposing slope of Holmesdale Road or through the creaky turnstiles of the Arthur Wait Stand. Instead a new eeriness was radiating from the main entrance.

For most football fans the plushly upholstered VIP suite is simply not for us. But here I was with what was left of my family, taking hesitant steps inside the club's inner sanctum. Lucy and David took the lead; I followed, holding Mum's hand, head buzzing. Jostling with the unsavoury mix of sadness and adrenaline

14

that had been fuelling me all day was an undeniable curiosity. It felt uncouth to admit, but I actually wanted this rare peek behind the curtain, to catch a glimpse of the forbidden Palace. I just ached beyond measure for Dan to be sharing it with me. Since 1986 I hadn't entered this stadium without him; never even let the thought of doing so flash through my mind. And yet here we were, because of him, at his spiritual home, saying goodbye.

Sandwiched between two mighty yet spindly TV towers and hemmed in by residential streets as only the best traditional grounds are, Selhurst Park has really grown on me over the years. When I was a kid, this ramshackle old cauldron never made much of an impression: it would flirt with life as a top-flight venue while the team yo-yoed between divisions, and its higgledy-piggledy shape didn't look like the great arenas beloved of TV cameras such as Anfield, Old Trafford or St James's Park. Besides, we'd pass it every weekend in the car on the way to Dad's office nearby, so over the years it became more and more familiar, and less and less cool. It was hard to see Palace as much more than the butt of constant family jokes, not just because they were the local team but because they were *Dan's* team. Since then, though, time seems to have woven a spell on the place. As old grounds across the country are sold off and smashed to bits, replaced by identikit Americanised bowls on the edge of anonymous ring roads, so the strange lustre of Selhurst has grown. To us, it felt as much Dan's place as Crystal Palace's. I always assumed my brother would bring me back here again. But never like this.

We climbed the staircase to the function room, and in the hiatus before other mourners arrived from the funeral we made final preparations. Lucy tied two balloons to each table in Palace colours, one red, one blue, matching the clothes she'd picked specially for the occasion; I hitched my phone to speakers and a playlist of Dan's favourite music began to percolate through the room, throwing a thin and invisible comfort blanket over us.

*

Football's coming home... 'Three Lions' isn't exactly a profound piece of music, but it contains a kernel of what Dan and I had in common. Two wonderful things: sport and comedy. Together, I like to think, they explain why he loved Crystal Palace. But they had also helped immeasurably in those detestable days between his death and funeral, when time seemed to stand still and I found myself sucked into grief's whirlpool of emotions – incomprehension, confusion, sorrow, regret, fear, frustration and occasionally plain boredom. I'd reacted by retreating to the sofa with some comfort TV, binge-watching our favourite old sitcoms and the 2012 Olympics DVD box set (my copy of which was as yet unopened: 'Break cellophane in case of emergency', it seemed to implore). Memories erupted like fireworks. And I cried. Difficult tears. Necessary tears. By celebrating Dan's loves, here at least was the smallest of rafts on which to float through those bitter first weeks.

Guests began filtering in to join us in the Palace Suite. In the vanguard was my octogenarian great-aunt Sheila, who'd grown up in the Blitz and remained a tower of strength to us, even now as she walked with a cane. How many painful deaths must she have mourned? My dad's ten years ago, his mum's in childbirth before that, now Dan's, and many more. I snatched a breath and put away the thought. Soon a thrum of conversation filled the room as groups of friends and family clustered, chatted and commiserated. The scene was warmer and more welcoming than I could have imagined or hoped. I'd been dreading the special mix of grief and awkwardness which a wake threatens, but instead wherever I looked there were people sharing stories, strangers meeting for the first time, and old friends reunited. Everyone was sad, but there were smiles and laughter too, which twinkled across the room like flashbulbs at a 100 metres final. I wanted to be everywhere at once, hearing each story and wrapping myself in the warmth of it, but just to see all this love was a tonic. It's odd that our culture reserves such unalloyed displays of affection for someone for after they've gone. If Dan could have seen how much he meant to us all, might he have looked after himself better?

That was a question for another day. For now there was far too much to take in. I was surrounded by people celebrating the things Dan stood for, his zeal for the things he adored, and his offbeat wit. His intense privacy had masked a real fondness for his work colleagues at Kensington council, and it filled my heart to see it mirrored here in their memorial mirth. Death can snuff out so much, but not love. The defiance of it was fortifying. I dwelled on this for a moment before joining their conversation, whereupon they revealed that next month was the annual staff outing to Sandown Park, which as a racing nut Dan would have been looking forward to with relish. In fact, that's putting it mildly. He would have been poring over the form guide weeks in advance. Would Mum, Lucy and I like to join them at the races in his stead? We gladly accepted. Dan was loyal to his core – there's no other explanation for his twenty-five-year Palace season ticket – and there was something reassuring in seeing how this quality had outlasted him into the future, through such a touching invitation from his friends. What's more, it felt fitting to keep the flame of his passion burning by experiencing more of his beloved sport. It was too soon to realise, but a seed had been planted in my head.

Meanwhile the past kept prompting new pangs. I realised I was probably standing in the same room from twenty-eight years earlier, on my first visit to Selhurst, when I'd been a guest at a birthday party for the then-chairman Ron Noades's son and seen Palace thump Birmingham City 6–0. (I can't claim to be a friend of the Noadeses. They'd invited the whole class of six-year-olds along, who obligingly overran the place like gremlins after midnight.) I'd always imagined that I'd watched that game from the other side of the ground, but now I could see how I'd misremembered. I wanted to text Dan right now and quiz him about it – had I got it wrong? And had there really been four disallowed goals that day? It almost felt as though I could ask him: nowadays we live our lives through our phones, and it's often through such devices that our loved ones primarily exist – in the ether, not with us, but always available. It can play havoc with the first stages of bereavement. When the ether stays silent. When the answer never comes back.

Wakes are exhausting, even when the buffet food is surprisingly good. (Palace have definitely never served a bhaji *that* delicious on a match day.) Eventually I found a polite juncture to take a breather and stepped out of the executive suite into a corridor, to be confronted by something that stopped me in my tracks. If this had been a movie a chorus of sonorous female voices would have suddenly struck up. There, in all its splendour, was the Crystal Palace trophy cabinet. I felt as Indiana Jones must feel when he happens upon one of those relics in between the really important ones: the ones which nobody bothers fighting him for. It was an unexpectedly large display, containing an obscure stockpile of silverware: League play-off victories, the old Second Division Championship title, and the pièce de resistance, the 1991 Zenith Data Systems Cup. Oh, for Dan to be here now, so I could royally take the piss out of that. Over the years I'd got so much mileage out of mocking this kooky competition and Palace's typically atypical success in it that I'd come to treasure it. In fact, right now it meant more to me than it did to Palace. It was one piece of brotherly history that wasn't just in my head but shining in front of me, resplendent and real.

I took one last look at the cup and continued along the corridor, emerging into the arena itself by the team dugouts. My friends James and Will had got there first, and they'd made the most of the opportunity by pretending to be managers in the middle of a touchline row. It's exactly what Dan would have loved to see (and do), and it made my heart sing. I joined them for a while and took the Palace boss's seat for a quick glance from the best view in the house, despite (and a little bit because of) being told not to by a steward. The close-season pitch in front of me was cordoned off and jaundiced, more sand than grass, as the groundsmen were busy growing new turf for next season. But seeing the old place without her make-up on just added to her aura. Win, lose, draw, or no game at all, a sports stadium is always a magic realm.

The hours passed, the wake thinned out, and soon it was time for our final duty of the day. Lucy led the way clutching a handful of balloons while Mum held Dan's wreath, also decked out in the club's colours, as we walked over to the most sacred place in the ground, in the central lower tier of the Holmesdale Stand: Dan's seat. I didn't know what to think. But I did at least discover that movies and television shows have got funerals spectacularly wrong. They're always portrayed as dank, overcast occasions, maybe even mid-thunderstorm (if the production can afford a rain machine). What confronted us instead was the polar opposite. It was 25 June, and the solst*ish* sun was blazing in a deep blue sky, scored by cursory wisps of cirrus. To have fine weather was the smallest thing, yet it made a difference: a clear day has always made me feel better about what might be on the horizon, and that afternoon it was lighting my darkest hour.

We placed the wreath on Dan's seat, and took some photos to capture the desperate but symbolic image. Then I sat there myself, and the totality of what Dan had witnessed over thirty-five years hit me in a torrent. I found myself recalling one of his favourite movies – a little-known festive TV film by Richard Curtis called *Bernard and the Genie* – in which the Genie, who once upon a time had been friends with Jesus, tells Bernard, 'When you're looking through that old Bibble [sic], and it says, "And the multitude gathered," remember one of them is a very good friend of yours.' Well, whenever I see a clip of Gazza's goal against Scotland, Cantona's kung-fu kick, Dwight Gayle snuffing out Steven Gerrard's Premiership dream, Ian Wright as a Wembley super-sub, Hedgehunter winning the Grand National, Gareth Southgate's missed penalty at Euro 96, the hundredth Test match at Lord's, the London Paralympics closing ceremony, or the very first game at the new Wembley, I will always remember that one of the fans in the crowd was more than a very good friend of mine. He was my brother.

What would I do next? How could I even start? Thankfully, in a sporting sense at least, Dan had the next steps mapped out in advance. There was racing at Sandown for starters, followed by tickets to the Rugby World Cup in the autumn, and the World Cycling Championships the following March. Yes, while he'd lived a very day-to-day existence, when it came to sport – and only sport – my brother could make intricate plans years in advance. And there was something else too, that eclipsed all other considerations. Dan was quite a frugal soul, so he hadn't left much behind in the way of material goods. But there was one object he passed on to me that changed my life. In the midst of grieving for him, one day an envelope flopped through the letterbox and onto the doormat: his Crystal Palace season ticket.

I know what I'd have been telling him if he could hear me: that was a fate worse than death. The idea of paying nineteen trips to Selhurst Park in a single year to watch the Eagles had never been an ambition of mine. But I couldn't just let his season ticket go. This was Dan's prized possession, his Golden Fleece, his precious. Plastic seat number 133, Row 26, Block G. Just when I needed support in my life more than ever before, sport seemed to be offering a scaffold from which to rebuild. So I decided to take his place, and entered into a sporting version of *Withnail & I*: I became a Crystal Palace supporter by mistake.

Up in the Holmesdale Stand, Lucy, Mum and I joined hands, and together we let the balloons go, watching them soar up and away until they merged with the sky. When the last red one finally faded from view, I looked back down to the pitch and thought ahead to August. In just six weeks I'd be back here, cheering on the Eagles in raucous voice. And I'd need to. The team didn't know it, but they were starting the new season a man down.

4

Ashes to Ashes

Nobody looks forward to a funeral. But, crushing as saying goodbye to Dan had been, the outpouring of love for him at the wake had coddled me in its afterglow. It was energising, even; a pale beacon in the gloom. Over the next couple of weeks, though, its comforting light faded, eclipsed by a new sensation of agonising indefiniteness. Living through that weird interval between death and the service had been tortuous, but at least it had to have an end point, even if it didn't always feel that way. Now the future was a vast expanse yawning open in front of me, and I didn't have a map.

No one prepares you for this side of grief – when your bereavement is no longer news and everyone else has slipped back into normal life. The wound's no longer fresh, but you can't help staring at the scar. Nobody tells you about the admin, either. It's maddening. A seemingly never-ending flow of emails, forms and phone calls from the insurance company, the bank, the home clearance firm, the council, another bank, and so on. It turns out Death isn't just inescapable, he's a petty bastard too. We all know about the scythe he wields in one hand, but he hides a fat roll of red tape in the other.

I wanted the world to stop turning. Just a quick timeout. Give me a break. Then life could start rumbling on again and I'd have a go at finding a way to manage. Wouldn't that be fair? But Time doesn't cut deals, and heaving into view were invitations, engagements, duties. Life. I tried to delay the inevitable, like the ten-year-old me sitting on the edge of a swimming pool, reluctantly contemplating the act of sliding in. (As the forty-three-year-old me still does.) But there was one event that couldn't be missed, and which drew me out into the world: race night with Dan's old colleagues.

Wednesday, 22 July 2015: Horse Racing

I arrived at Sandown Park alone, feeling none of the excitement that usually bubbles inside me when I arrive at a new sporting landmark for the first time. Apprehension had crowded out everything else. But no sooner had I joined our group – a dozen of Dan's friends, plus Mum and Lucy – than the negative thoughts unloosed their grip and flew off, to give me a night off from the pain. To see the smiles and comfort of Dan's friends was bracing all over again, and I realised we were all co-starring in a mini sequel to the wake. It was a balmy evening and the setting was beautiful, encapsulated by the sight of runners and riders thundering past us silhouetted against the dipping sun. The sport was secondary. And no, Dan, I'm not just saying that because I didn't pick any winners. What mattered was the opportunity to revel in the kindness of strangers, who made us feel so welcome when they didn't have to. Some of them really knew their gee-gees too. Ant told us he was on a mission to visit every racecourse in Britain, a challenge that Dan would have loved to take on one day. Jon K. recalled how on a previous work trip here in 2012 he'd been chuffed to back three winners, but his feat had been eclipsed by Dan who'd correctly picked six out of six. 'I can still see his face that night. He was so over the moon.' I bet. Warmth spread inside me as I imagined my brother's glee. At the same time a question mark sloshed around in my head. I didn't remember this lucky streak. Had Dan told me about it at the time? If he hadn't, should I be wondering why? Or would it be a good thing, a sign of how his life had been ticking along merrily at points in the past? On the other hand, if he had told me about it all those years ago, was it bad that I'd forgotten? This was grief talking. It makes you question everything, from the profound to the placings of horses at nondescript National Hunt meetings. Synapses were busy firing thoughts in all directions, but for now they were subsumed by joy at this snapshot of bro's happiness, preserved by a friend sharing a memory.

The celebratory mood outlasted the racing and spilled out into Sandown's post-sport entertainment, which was provided by a Take That tribute act. Their billing boasted that they'd had rave reviews from none other than TV personality Ricky Tomlinson *and* Jason Orange's mother. It's the sort of thing I'd usually risk an asthma attack to avoid. But we were swept up in the ebullience of the occasion, and in the oddest of circumstances, among people I hardly knew, I felt an unlikely euphoria as we all danced along. The group's name sadly wasn't *Fake That* but *Rule the World*, which would soon turn out to be a sporting omen staring me in the face: less than a year later, a horse with that name would win the Grand National.

'And did you put a bet on?' Dan's voice goads me now. 'No, you didn't, did you? How easy do I have to make it?'

At the end of the evening, the fifteen of us gathered in a circle in the shadow of the grandstand, each holding aloft a can of Coke – Dan's favourite tipple – to toast him. It was a strange symbol for sure, given the role diabetes played in his death. But now was a time for defiance, not diet, and we chorused, 'To Dan!'

Aside from the sojourn to Sandown, I had little appetite for going out. Fortunately the desolation of those long July days hid a peculiar kindness, by playing host to a more welcome absence. In the world of football, summer heralds the period known as the 'close season'. It's the ever-shrinking temporal perineum between league campaigns, when the national game briefly disappears from the back pages. For most fans it's a hateful hiatus, spent swallowing bitter disappointments and recharging the hope-batteries for August, when battle will be joined once more. But it's not all bad. To quote those timeless philosophers Beavis and Butthead, you need the bits that suck to make the bits that rock rock harder. And for any football fans' loved ones who don't share this obsession, the close season is bliss. It's a chance for them to breathe a sigh of relief and thank the deity or expletive of their choice for a break from having their weekend plans foiled by the footy. Magnifying the ceasefire, 2015 was one of those fallow years that fall between World Cups and European Championships, when international tournaments shorten the lull even further.

As trivial as it sounds, a full two months without football was a blessing. It gave me a chance to compute my new Danless world before the leviathan of his number one passion loomed back on the horizon. Confronting *that* beast could wait. For now I had enough on my plate dealing with the pain. It was always there. An extra shadow. I craved consolation, distraction, escape. Then, slowly, creepingly, sport began to come to the rescue. Soccer's retreat to the wings wasn't just serendipitous in itself; it gave something else the chance to shine, and a chance to help me. That something was cricket.

Wednesday, 5 August 2015: Test Match Cricket

For as long as I've known what it is, I've always thought an Ashes summer is special. For starters it stands out for being the longest event in the longest version of the longest sport in the world. OK, a quick Googling reveals that's not precisely true. It's outdone in sheer length by the 1984 Anatoly Karpov v Gary Kasparov chess match, which lasted five months and forty draws until it was abandoned for health reasons. But excluding life-threatening board games, no rivalry is as evocatively named or more fiercely fought than the one between England and Australia on the cricket pitch, when they do battle for the famous urn. And summer 2015 played host to the next instalment in this centuries-old epic.

Cricket is the first sport my parents remember me being into as a kid. Apparently as soon as I could run I enjoyed nothing more than flinging tennis balls in the garden, usually at Dan, imagining he was a moustachioed Aussie batsman and I was Ian Botham on the warpath. I have hazy memories of this, and they reside in that bit of the brain where your own recollections and the stories you've been told about the younger you blur together into a warm nostalgic smudge. So I can't accurately confirm quite how Bothamesque my bowling was, but I'm sure my performances and Beefy's were equally deserving of a place in the House of Lords. Not that I appreciated back then how lucky anyone is simply to have a garden. Childhood for us proved to be a rocky affair, and in the first eleven years of my life we lived in eleven different properties, several without the luxury of grass. Cricketers are judged on their average, and by that standard our family's figures of one home a year for over a decade, as we zigzagged all over Croydon, constituted a piece of world-class nomadism. Why such promiscuity in property? That would be the same reason I got into watching cricket: Dad.

So far I've only mentioned him in passing, in reference to his passing. But while John Donald Harvey isn't the subject of this book, in some ways he's the root cause of it. He was the fun-loving, gregarious, creative character who first instilled in me the pleasure of writing. He was the sideburn-sporting, polo-neck-wearing eccentric who sowed the seeds of sport and comedy that blossomed into the full-blown adoration which Dan and I shared. And he was an alcoholic. A really bad one. Like so many heavy drinkers he'd crawled inside the bottle to find a refuge from pain. In his case it was the loss of his mum, Lilian, who died in childbirth in 1958 when Dad was just eleven years old. I don't think he ever recovered from that tragedy, and way before I was born in 1980 drink had long since defined him. When he was sober he was cheerful, supportive, loving.

He was Dad. But when he was drunk he could be a monster, never physically abusive but verbally poisonous. Corrupted by chemicals, a spiteful fountain of hate. When you're a tiny kid, the idea of a baddie is supposed to be Megatron or Skeletor, not the overweight lump in the living room glowering at the TV and yelling obscenities while the rest of us cower upstairs until he falls asleep, conked out and exhausted by his own rage.

As if that wasn't bad enough, the morning after an episode he'd wake up not remembering an iota of it. I can still see his eyes: jaundiced, translucent, bloodshot, filled with a mixture of pain, sadness and confusion. If we'd been growing up now we'd have just filmed him and shown him the truth of his tirades. But this was the Eighties and Nineties, when smartphones were the stuff of *Star Trek* gadgets. So instead we'd have to spend countless hours recounting Dad's antics to him in minute detail to make him accept he could have done anything wrong, let alone apologise. He was Jekyll and Hyde sponsored by Strongbow. For decades we tiptoed around his Hyde because we deeply loved his Jekyll. We wanted to believe it was worth it for the good times. In ever decreasing circles it was. Like so many children with an alcoholic parent, we suffered it as a secret shame, unaware of just how common the syndrome is. It burned us: I stayed teetotal into my thirties until I started to believe I might not be doomed to repeat Dad's fate; Dan, who'd had nine years' more experience of the devils that drink could unleash, never let a drop of alcohol pass his lips.

Dad's life is a saga of its own. His CV included spells as a policeman, bus conductor, teaching assistant, estate agent, security guard, even a publican. Yes, two of my first eleven homes were flats above pubs, during a stint at the start of the Nineties when Dad ran the establishments below. That went just as well as you can imagine. I remember sitting in the back of the car in a Caterham side street when he told the whole family about this new master plan, and how my ten-year-old brain actually looked upon it with hope. After all, Dad's problem had always been getting hold of a drink. Maybe, just maybe, if the prospect of his next pint was no longer a challenge, it would make everything all right? I learned the hard way that my tweeny logic was very flawed. Dad and the keys to a bar formed a potent cocktail, and he'd have drunk that too given half the chance.

Nine months and two pubs later the experiment was abandoned, brief but not nearly brief enough. All we had to show for it was Max, our pet Alsatian: an RSPCA rescue dog descended from a Crufts champion, and surely the only guard dog in history with the power to sleep through burglar alarms. But Max was a binding force for the family, and adopting him made the whole pub episode worth it. I confess my initial reaction was somewhat different: aged ten I was scared shitless of dogs, and when Dad first brought him into the pub I shot upstairs faster than you can say *An American Werewolf in London*. But pretty soon Max was one of the Harveys, and he became a Dan's best friend. They were the Scooby Doo and Shaggy of Selsdon, just with an even larger appetite for snacks.

Speaking of which, it was Dad who laid the breadcrumbs that drew first Dan and then me into the labyrinth of sport-watching (as opposed to playing), and when it comes to cricket a couple of early memories are lodged in my brain. They come from the summer of 1989, just before pubs went from being somewhere we tried to coax Dad out of into somewhere we called home. I remember regular trips to the Croham Arms, one of his regular watering holes, where Dan, Lucy and I would slurp Coke and take on the Chase HQ arcade machine for as long as a couple of 50p pieces would allow. Festooning the pub's interior were branded posters and beer mats advertising the dates for that year's Ashes series. The words didn't mean anything to me – Edgbaston just looked like a spelling mistake – and I was yet to twig that it was all connected to the ball game we used to play at home when we had a garden. But over the next few weeks and months the Ashes seeped by osmosis into my developing brain, until one day it all clicked.

I was with Dad, passing Selhurst Park as we drove home from his office in our trusty blue Fiat Regatta. Crackling out of the radio was an incessant burbling sound I couldn't make head nor tail of. 'It's sport', Dad explained. It didn't sound much like sport to me. It was just a bunch of old men rambling on about something or other, punctuated by the odd clonking sound followed by a ripple of polite applause. This, it turned out, was *Test Match Special,* or TMS. Together with the TV coverage which Dad switched on when we got home, it *never* seemed to end.

'What's going on?' I pleaded.

'Just stick with it. You'll see.'

By the end of the day's play I was hooked, just like the juicy long-hops being offered up to the Aussies by England's hapless bowlers.

From that point on, my happiness has always risen a notch when the Ashes are on. Thanks, Dad.

Spooling forward to summer 2015, I was facing my first Ashes series without Dan, and I needed a pick-me-up more than ever. On the morning of Thursday, 6 August, cricket delivered.

I'd taken a day off work for the first day of the Fourth Test and was home alone, ready to wrap my bruised heart in a bit of sporty comfort. If the weather gods allowed. Over in Nottingham indecisive clouds were languishing above Trent Bridge, deliberating over whether to wash away the fervour of a sell-out crowd. Meanwhile, I faced my own dilemma: to BBC or not to BBC? That is the question every armchair cricket fan faces in the twenty-first century. Even for those of us who don't fork out for a regular Sky Sports subscription, the tantalising carrot of watching the live action is constantly dangled in front of us thanks to the temptations of pay-per-view and – if you know where to look – nefarious, unlicensed Internet streams. Bombarded with video options as we are by the modern media climate, it's a marvel that an institution as venerable as *TMS* has survived, let alone thrived. All those years since Dad exposed me to the programme, the personnel may have changed but it's essentially still the same. It's the radio equivalent of Trigger's Broom, still going strong after decades with a little help from seventeen new heads and fourteen new handles. If only we could catch a particle of the fairy dust with which *TMS* sparkles and examine it under a microscope . . . Well, that morning I did.

Like so many great discoveries it happened by accident. As the teams took the field at 11.05 a.m., after a short cameo by the Nottingham rain, I remained in a quandary. The cosy, blanket-like feel of Jonathan Agnew & Co. was enticing, yet I couldn't escape the nagging doubt that without watching the action I'd somehow be wasting the day. Frankly, it's ludicrous that we should have to choose. As recently as 2005 you could do both at once: the telly was free and analogue, so it was easy to synchronise *TMS* with live television. Instead, the so-called advances in media technology have since robbed us of this simple pleasure – in Britain's digital paradise it's nigh-on impossible to match Sky's pictures with the BBC's words, thanks to DAB radio, satellite TV and online streams all being transmitted with different amounts of delay to real time. Tim Berners-Lee needs to get out of his hammock and sort this out.

Until then, if you're ever faced with the same crisis in cricket consumption, I can vouch for the temporary solution I stumbled upon that August morning. I based myself by the kitchen radio and switched on the cumbersomely named BBC Radio 5 Live Sports Extra. But I also shelled out £10.99 for a week's pass to NOW TV in the living room. This created two separate time zones in the house, with the latency between audio and video just long enough for me to be able to hear anything noteworthy on the radio first, then run around the corner to see what had happened on the telly, before returning to the warm sanctuary of *TMS* for the next ball. It was a good work-out, but more importantly it enabled me to compare directly the merits of watching and listening to live cricket when at home. And that's how I discovered the secret.

The choice of new-ball pairing to start a Test match is always a crucial decision – and not just on the field. That morning's BBC team selection blessed us with Henry Blofeld and Phil Tufnell – Blowers and Tuffers – the most entertaining commentary box duo of recent years. To steal a Blofeldism, they were both in mid-season form as they welcomed us to Trent Bridge while the pre-match formalities frothed in the background. Above the wafting strains of Blake's 'Jerusalem', we learned that England's songstress-du-jour Laura Wright was wearing a striking mauve dress which Stuart Broad's sweater could beat on length. 'It's a magic ground, small,' mused Blowers as the England fielders took the field to cheers. 'The most perfect cockpit for cricket.'

A crescendo from the crowd accompanied Broad's charge towards the wicket for the first delivery of the match, to be faced by Aussie opener Chris Rogers. The batter's effortlessness in defence was matched by Blowers, who had time not only to describe the ground's geography but also point out his first butterfly of the match, 'flittering' past at a personal-best time of 33 seconds after the first ball was bowled. Tuffers rose to the challenge. 'It's a Cabbage White,' he added, as Broad's second ball erred down the leg side and was deflected away by Rogers for four leg-byes. Australia 4 for 0. Standard stuff. Nothing to leap towards the living room for. But the thing about earthquakes is that they happen without warning.

There was an explosion of exhilaration. Rogers was out, fending the ball to first slip for a duck. Three balls gone, Australia 4 for 1! It was a terrific start for England and for Broad, who'd now reached the landmark of 300 Test wickets. In the kitchen I jumped for joy, watched through the back window by a gang of feral cats who liked to use our garden as their playground (with en suite bathroom). Blowers' antennae were up. '. . . Of course Steve Smith, here he is, in the very first over,' he proclaimed, 'walking briskly to the wicket like a man who feels: "Well, I'd better get there quickly and get it over with."' Smith clipped two runs off his first ball, and cracked Broad to the boundary off the next.

Then came a second eruption. Bigger. Wilder. 'Can you *believe* it! You can't believe it! It's quite extraordinary!' Blowers' voice quavered at Smith's demise, squared up and caught at third slip for 6. Tuffers was so excited he got a fit of the giggles. Australia were 10 for 2 after one over! Fantastic.

Over in the living room, Sky Sports was letting the pictures do the talking but, remarkable as the footage was, their coverage lacked the frisson that comes from truly masterful commentary. By contrast, the nature of *TMS* behoves its broadcasters to react more like fans and to rely on their instinct. While television is unbeatable for presenting the physical reality of cricket, *TMS* is the more accurate transmitter of its emotional reality. As listeners on that August morning, we were living it just as Blowers and Tuffers were. It was aural alchemy.

Such was the maelstrom that there was no time for Blowers to conduct his usual inventory of buses, cranes or Tina Turner lookalikes. Instead he focused on the batsman at the non-striker's end – the Aussies' pantomime villain, David Warner. 'We've forgotten about him. He's been at the other end watching the carnage – he must have thought he was in a butcher's shop!' Ever the model of BBC politeness, Blowers asked Australian listeners to forgive him for displaying his gaiety. 'Sorry. But we are English after all.'

After a change of end, the next bowler, Mark Wood, was soon springing into his run-up to deliver the second ball of his spell. A heartbeat and an inside edge later, Warner was being sent back to the pavilion, caught behind. Blowers' voice became a euphoric rasp as he struggled to be heard above the crowd: 'Unbelievable! Both openers out for nought. We've had eight balls of this match and Australia are 10 for 3! No scriptwriter in the world – Sam Mendes, all those James Bond movies – he couldn't have written this! No one would have believed it, would they? It is amazing, Tuffers!' It was not so much the words that made it poetic as the tone. Blowers was self-combusting in par-oxysms of delight, and his voice was laced with jovial surprise. He was a human lightning conductor for every England fan on the planet. I didn't feel alone.

After rushing to the living room to see the wicket of Warner replayed on TV, I was soon sprinting back to the radio to hear the drama that was fizzing over the wireless. Scarred as I am by growing up in the cricketing doldrums of the 1990s, the creep-ing sensation grew over me that England's high-water mark of the day had been reached. But Tuffers, one of the survivors of those dark times, was attuned to how near the batting side was to the precipice: 'Australia need to find something here or this could get messy very, very quickly . . .'

Meanwhile, Blowers had zeroed in on the travails of the Aus-tralian captain. 'Poor old Michael Clarke, who thought, "Going in at five, I'm going to be able to shelter myself a bit" – he's coming in to face the ninth ball of the match!' As Clarke reached the crease, the crowd were still chanting a delirious 'Cheerio!' to the dearly departed Warner.

Mere seconds later yet another Aussie victim was being dis-patched. Shaun Marsh, out for another duck. Blowers went into overdrive. 'He's gone! It gets better, and better, and better for England, and worse, and worse, and worse for Australia! What an extraordinary morning's cricket!'

'Morning?' responded Tuffers. 'We've only had a couple of overs!' This was Blowers' fourth fulmination in 18 balls, and now my exultant leaping even scared the cats away. 'Blowers was on fire there!' Tuffers reflected as Jonathan Agnew began his stint.

'I think we need a fire extinguisher to hose down his seat,' said Aggers.

It took just an hour for the innings to implode completely. Australia dismissed for 60 runs.

For the first time Dan had missed a piece of sporting history. He'd never seen anything like this, and he never would. It made me only more driven to savour the whole thing to its utmost. I was shuttling between rooms so often, I must have run more singles than the entire Australian team. It was a few minutes of ecstasy I'd never needed so sorely. The TV coverage might have been seconds behind in real time, but it was light years behind in emotion. If a new *Voyager* probe was to be launched tomorrow complete with a gold disc of sounds from planet Earth, that clip of Blowers and Tuffers should be on it.

When most people think of *Test Match Special* they think of the cakes that listeners send in, or the rain breaks, or the famous corpsing episode between Aggers and Brian Johnston when they tried to describe how an off-balance Ian Botham, accidentally hitting his own wicket, 'couldn't quite get his leg over'. But such hallmarks are united by the curious fact that none of them directly involved the live sport itself. Even the 'leg-over' incident happened during a review of the day's play rather than the heat of the action. Thursday, 6 August 2015 was different. It was all about the cricket. Eclipsing 1981, 2009, 2013 and, dare I say it, even 2005, this was England destroying the Australians more unexpectedly and more utterly than ever before – to the extent that the *Sydney Morning Herald*'s headline was simply, 'Pomicide'. It was the shortest innings in the annals of Test matches, and it was *TMS* that crystallised the passion of the moment.

I hadn't fully appreciated the power of radio sport until then, but it was something Dan knew well. Countless were the times when as a kid I used to pop to his room to say hi and find him on his bed listening to a football match. On more than one occasion it was because his little TV was broken, and he hadn't had the impetus to do anything about it. But more often he just liked to lie there, eyes closed, and let the sound of Radio 5 Live or Capital Gold wash over him, enveloping him in the action. That morning, I too discovered that sometimes in the world of sport hearing is believing.

Far higher hurdles were yet to be faced. In two days' time a new football season was set to begin, and I was going to have to come face to face with Dan's greatest love at Selhurst Park. Without him. For him. Compared to that, in my incipient battle with grief today had been a phoney war. But a single day of Test cricket had released more endorphins than a month-long holiday and, for the first time since Dan was gone, I'd had a taste of joy. A little flame had risen out of the Ashes.

.4lbW24W|.W.41nb..|...W4lb.|...11.|W.2lb...|
.4.2nb...|W.....|....1.|1...1|1W..11|2...1lb.|.4..4.|
...W1W|3.....|......|..4...|......|.....2nb.|.4W

The Australian first innings in full, Trent Bridge, 2015

5

Roller Coaster

Summer brought chinks of light, but it wasn't quite finished doling out dollops of shit. Two months on from the day when normal life had caved in, I was still wading through a sour treacle of admin. The business of tidying up someone's affairs really does carry a special awfulness. One mid-week mid-morning in August took the biscuit, when I had to visit Kensington Town Hall to collect Dan's death certificate. A kindly clerk led me from the cool, stone-walled entrance hall through a series of winding beige corridors down to a windowless room in a soulless basement. There was a damp silence to this hidden place, like the Batcave, but with interior design by Mr Bean. Inside his office, the two of us were hermetically sealed from the world. Time seemed to move more slowly. I felt simultaneous despair and hope: despair at finding myself in such an uninviting place carrying out the most horrific of duties; hope in considering how calm and ordered the clerk and his life appeared to be. There was no stench of ambition here, no sense of struggle or threat. Half of me wanted to switch places with him, even as the other half recoiled from the thought.

The clerk asked if I wanted help from the council in notifying various companies about Dan's death. Death. Hearing the word aloud and seeing it printed on paper brought a fresh stab to my heart, as once again I had to face up to the fact that this was real, and not the sick piece of interactive theatre I'd have given anything for it to be. Needing a distraction, I focused on the walls, taking in every detail like Verbal Kint surveying his interview room in *The Usual Suspects*. One item stuck out like a sore thumb: a wall calendar. It was showing the page for June: two months out of date. 'Bit lazy,' I thought. Then I focused harder. 'June 2010'. Two months *and five years* out. FFS.

The nightmare of 'sadmin' rolled on but its stranglehold slowly loosened. There was now competition for my attention, literally, thanks to the new Premier League football season. Just when I most needed a change, my whole lifestyle was about to be shunted off its axis, as I prepared to moonlight as one of Crystal Palace's newest full-time fans. Even though I used to mock Dan's obsession with Palace, I grew up in awe of it too. Watching my big brother expend so much energy on his passion was an early lesson that, if you want to get the best out of anything, dedication's what you need. (It's the same message Roy Castle used to drum into millions of kids every week on *Record Breakers*. But Dan said it with football, not tap-dancing. Thank God.) It became an early life goal to emulate him and one day hold a season ticket of my own. But not for a minute did I envisage the dreadful way it would happen. At Palace, not Spurs. And not with Dan, but instead of him.

If you like football, going to watch a match is always a wonderful thing, whether you're a grizzled fan visiting a new away ground or a complete novice getting your virgin taste of the world's favourite game. But nothing compares to a season ticket. Instead of the freshness of the occasion, it's the regularity that becomes the special ingredient. Every club in the world is a unique institution, and it's only once you've paid enough visits and shown sufficient devotion that it will begin to reveal its trove of secrets. Then and only then will you be able to appreciate the subtle flavours (beyond the pungent aromas) that roll across a stadium on a Saturday afternoon. You'll see how the ground gleams in the sunshine one week and makes rain look beautiful the next. Little discoveries will live long in the memory, like that day when you found the best place to get a burger. And the day you found the worst place to get a burger. You'll get to know the shortcut back to the railway station, and the three key pieces of music on the match day playlist: the home team's walk-out theme; the victory song that greets the final whistle if they win; and the gratingly inoffensive track that gets played when they don't. Eventually you'll even crack the code of niche references that litter the club's unofficial fanzine, the mere name of which will sound like gobbledegook to outsiders. (The gold medal for this goes to Gillingham FC for *Brian Moore's Head Bears an Uncanny Resemblance to the London Planetarium*.) In a digital world, a football club's most precious qualities remain steadfastly analogue. To feel them, you have to put the hours in.

As you go to more and more games, it's not just the club's timeless traditions you become steeped in. You start to notice nuances that shift and slip as the years go by: from the personnel on the pitch to the adulatory chants that rain down upon them from the stands, to the faces of the fans who sing them. And that's the real meaning of a football club. The fans. Together you form a collective organism far greater than the sum of its parts, whose loyalty and passion (if not always their good humour) will never waver. Within their number every year there is a slow, ineluctable churn. New members join. Old ones die. Even so, while a season ticket is many things, it's rarely something you inherit. Especially from your brother.

I felt an awe towards Dan's ticket. As I took hold of it, I felt possessed in turn by the memories locked inside. This small token was a giant symbol of a love affair between my brother and Crystal Palace that had ignited one fateful day in 1981 when Dad's friend Tony took him along, aged eleven, to see them play Manchester City. I was just a baby at the time, more interested in a different kind of dribbling, but Dan regaled me with the story many times. Throughout his schooldays, while record collecting and computer games competed for his attention, Palace were always his number one obsession. Then, as he was turning eighteen, he made the biggest decision of his life: from the 1989/90 season onwards, he joined the serried ranks of Selhurst Park and became a fully-fledged Eagle. This was back in the Dark Ages, before the Premier League era erupted in a volcano of Sky TV cash, when Barclays League Division One was far from being a worldwide object of desire. More Piers Morgan than Alex Morgan. But there were two reasons why Dan couldn't have better timed his dive into full-time football fanaticism. First, because this was the year that Palace got humiliated 9–0 by Liverpool in a league game, which gave me some excellent fuel to take the piss out of him. (To be fair, Dan saw the funny side too, and bought the commemorative full-length video of that game.) And second, because it took him to Wembley. I doubt many people know or even care what happened in the 1990 FA Cup. But for me and Dan it was the epicentre of everything that followed in the years and decades since. And it was about to emit its final shock wave.

The story begins, as many cup runs do, without fanfare, as Palace somehow mustered the capacity to beat Portsmouth in the third round. Then, as winter bled into spring, they strung together victories against Huddersfield Town and Rochdale before squeaking past the might of Cambridge United. *Whoopdedoo!* It wasn't exactly a headline-grabbing set of results, as I liked pointing out to Dan. But somehow, thanks to the luck of the draw, this quartet of wins propelled Palace into the semi-finals. The date? The eighth of April 1990. The venue? Villa Park. The opponents? Their nemesis from a few months earlier, Liverpool. It was the most important fixture in Eagles history. And Dan was there.

When match day came around, back home in Croydon the family all somewhat feared for him. The previous year's semi-finals had seen the Hillsborough disaster, the horror of which had stuck in my mind even as a nine-year-old. I remember watching *Blind Date* on TV that night with Lucy and Mum when a newsflash interrupted the programme to report on the tragedy. So we couldn't fail to be worried about Dan's safety. As a coping mechanism we shared glib speculation about how many goals Palace would get thrashed by. At the same time we knew how much this game meant to him, and how rare the experience was likely to be, so there was never any doubt he'd go. What's more, while Palace were huge underdogs, there was the faintest of hopes that they might pull off a shock. They were a young team with enormous camaraderie, marshalled by a talented tyro manager in Steve Coppell and their very own Captain Marvel in the shape of future fundraising superhero (and England shot-shanker) Geoff Thomas. Vitally, they were also blessed with an attack twin-pronged by a pair of lethal young strikers, Mark Bright and Ian Wright. The odds were still stacked against them overcoming Kenny Dalglish and his all-powerful Red Machine, but in sport you just never know.

I sat cross-legged on the living room floor, far too close to the TV, as the match see-sawed one way, then the other. When a John Barnes penalty gave Liverpool a 3–2 lead in the eighty-third minute my heart sank for Dan. The underdogs were chasing the game; the seconds seemed to be ticking faster; hope was ebbing away. But this doughty Palace side weren't finished yet. Just two minutes from the final whistle, midfielder Andy Gray craned his neck high and nodded a header past Bruce Grobelaar to equalise. Extra time beckoned, and the spotlight fell upon an unlikely hero. From a corner kick, centre-half Andy Thorn flicked a near-post header across the face of the goal, evading the Liverpool defence. It was met by a bullocking run from yeoman midfielder Alan Pardew, who bundled the ball into the net – and Palace into the final. 'It's in!' yelled commentator John Motson. 'Thorn flicked it on, and somewhere out of the crowd came Pardew!' God knows what he was doing in the crowd. Surely that's off-side? But Palace were in front. The Eagles fans inside Villa Park went wild, and the TV cameras picked out a few individual faces enjoying their instant of ecstasy. One of them had his face painted in red and blue halves, and looked a fair bit like Dan. Back in our living room we were all thrown by this. *Was that him?* We couldn't believe he would have daubed himself like that – it wasn't his style. Could it really be him? We soon got our answer. It wasn't Dan. How did we know? Because the next shot definitely *was* him. Improbably, a cameraman had picked him out. There he was, front and centre, on the telly. In raptures. The smile was the giveaway. We couldn't believe our luck at getting to see him in this zenith of happiness. Joy was beaming all over his face, and the BBC was beaming it all over the world.

Palace 4, Liverpool 3. To this day it's regarded by aficionados as one of the greatest FA Cup matches. So much so that, thirty years later, when live sport disappeared during the Covid pandemic, the Beeb chose it as one of the all-time classics worthy of a repeat airing. And it took Dan to the final, for his first visit to that most hallowed of all football stadiums, Wembley. Standing between Palace and triumph were Manchester United, led by a certain Alex Ferguson, who was in very real danger of getting the sack. Hindsight makes even the suggestion sound comical, but back then the wily Scot had failed to win a trophy in four years at Old Trafford, and their success-starved faithful were losing patience. They'd only just scraped into the final too, needing a replay to overcome Oldham Athletic. If Palace could bring down the champions-elect Liverpool, were United there for the taking?

The week before the match, the whole of Croydon went into festival mode. Every possible surface was decked out with red and blue balloons, from lamp posts lining the town centre to the window display of the local butcher's. The squad even made it into the pop charts, with a lusty (i.e. awful) recording of their theme song 'Glad All Over' by the Dave Clark Five. Or, to give them their full title, the Dave Clark Five, Crystal Palace Nil. For me, now aged ten, this was all impossibly exciting. Raised as I was on heroic stories like *Star Wars* and *He-Man*, somehow it felt as though Fate was calling Palace. (I didn't dare say this out loud in case I hexed it.) Dan might have been the only Eagles fan I knew who was going to the game, but in wanting them to beat the Red Devils, everyone in my life – friends, family, schoolteachers, shopkeepers – were, well, united.

The final itself was one of the finest games to grace the old Wembley, pitting Man United's all-star pedigree against Palace's youthful determination. With his side trailing 2–1 in the second half, Steve Coppell rolled the dice and threw on his talismanic but half-crocked striker Ian Wright, who'd had to start the game on the bench. The gamble did the trick, twice, as Wright quickly conjured a brace of sensational goals to turn the match on its head. Three–two! Palace were winning the Cup Final! But United came again, and in the eighty-third minute the outsiders' defence cracked, just as it had against Liverpool in the semis. The always potent Mark Hughes thundered a trademark volley into the Palace net, drawing the Mancunians level and forcing a replay in midweek.

A Cup Final *Replay*. How absurd that sounds now, an idea belonging to a less sports-saturated world. There's charm in the quaint notion that, when English football's showpiece occasion couldn't be decided after 120 minutes, everybody used to go home and come back four days later to try again. Even penalties are less cruel than that, not least on fans' wallets. The return match in 1990 was the penultimate final ever to be replayed, and it's something Eagles fans prefer not to talk about. Dan certainly didn't like to. It was a dour 1–0 defeat, lacking all the thrill of the first clash and settled by a winning goal from Lee Martin, possibly the least famous person ever to play for Man United. (At the time of writing, Lee's cup-winning goal isn't even listed on his own Wikipedia page.) The result left such a sour taste that the Palace away kit for that night – a new strip of yellow and black stripes – was never worn again, cast into eternal ignominy. As for the original 3–3 final, while the sands of time have piled sediment upon the game one fact still stands out. Palace were just seven agonising minutes away from seizing glory. And had they achieved it, they could have set off a chain reaction that would have changed football as we know it. Who knows how high Dan's Eagles could have flown? By contrast, Fergie would in all likelihood have left United, and their near total dominance of the next two decades might never have come to pass. I think I can speak for all non-United fans when I say: *damn*.

For me and Dan, it wasn't just the course of football history that was set by Palace's 1990 cup run. It put rocket boosters on our shared love of sport. Dan became fully scooped up in the Eagles' talons just before the whole nation went doolally for Italia 90, when Gazza's World Cup tears gushed onto the turf of Turin. My brother's excitement sparked an epiphany for me too. Granted, I was just a primary school pipsqueak, so I had to get my sporting fix mostly via TV, video games and the playground. But I could also live it vicariously through Dan, because for him it was now very real. A large part of his life was set in train, and there was barely a single home game he missed for the rest of his life. Through the club's relegations, promotions and a brief flirtation with going out of business altogether, he never faltered in his loyalty to the soldiers of Selhurst.

Now I was picking up the mantle. And I was afraid. Would the ground be forever tainted by its new association with the wake? Would my love of football be polluted by pain? Week by week, as the credit card-sized ticket buzzed me through the pleasingly rickety turnstiles, I gradually discovered that, thanks to how much this club defined Dan, it remained overwhelmingly a happy place to be. Up a few flights of steep concrete steps I'd jog, weaving between slower-moving fans who were struggling with the climb. I'd never not hurry because I'd be impatient for another dose of that special moment, when you're seized with the wonderment that comes from entering any sporting arena: the split second when the stairway ends. The fresh air hits your cheeks. The lushness of the pitch fills your eyes. It's like when you crest a hill and catch a first glimpse of the sea, or that point after take-off when a plane breaks through the clouds into the ocean of sky above. It never fails. It took only a couple of games to be swept up in the rhythm of a season. It was fortifying.

That's not to say that it wasn't also really weird. Pulling down the tip-up plastic seat for the first time, I felt like a secondary officer on board the starship *Enterprise* upon whom it falls to take the captain's chair while James T. Kirk or Jean-Luc Picard is marooned on a far-off planet. It's an honour to step up and be given the seat. But it's not really yours. The difference is that in *Star Trek* the real owner always comes back in the end. But there was an extra strangeness about this position in the ground. It wasn't Dan's old seat. For decades he'd been sitting a few blocks across from here, behind the goal that Palace liked to attack in the second half. Then, only months before his death, Dan had decided to switch to this new position. It took me a while to discover why. The crux was that he'd fallen out with a fellow fan for whom Dan had been getting an extra season ticket for a number of years. Not only that, but Dan had also been putting this second ticket in my name. So it turned out that technically I had been a season ticket holder already; I just never knew it. This was peculiar, and emblematic of the fact that, however well I thought I knew Dan, there were layers to him that I never uncovered, and which now I never would. If only I could just pick up the phone and ask him about it. Every reminder that I couldn't was another gut punch.

But this was enfolded by a far bigger thought: following in my brother's footsteps. The story of Crystal Palace in 2015/16 was to be the backbone of my life for the next nine months. And gradually it became more than that. While grief continued to buffet me with its sickening turbulence, Palace provided a surprising sanctuary. A shield. Soon there was no escaping the clichéd conclusion that football is a modern religion. Each club is a creed, its ground is the temple and every match is a service: the chants are the hymns, the believers gather in their thousands to worship, there's a panoply of crosses (some better crafted than others), and when it comes to the booze that's on offer, be prepared to queue.

My head was swimming with thoughts of mortality, so the notion of worship especially resonated. It seemed to me that on

the pitch at any one time the players were fighting not one battle but two. There was the obvious struggle to win the game,
but beyond that there was something else, less tangible but
more valuable in the long term. Every Saturday at 3 p.m. was an
opportunity for these individuals to gain a kind of immortality.
And in a way, wasn't that their quest? Not all of them would
manage it but, through a mixture of achievements, longevity
and charisma, some would in time become legends lining the
fans' hall of fame. For Palace, only the occasional star like Ian
Wright is destined to become a true household name. But cult
heroes like Julian Speroni, Andy Johnson and Chris Armstrong
are in their own way just as beloved. They live on and are celebrated through the magic of memory, as well as the honour of
having bars at the ground dedicated to them. (Speroni went
one step further and founded a restaurant in his name behind
one of the goals.) Seeing the footballing soap opera unfold
before my eyes solidified my own thoughts about how I might
chart a course through loss, and why the season ticket could
help. I needed to zero in on Dan's passions and celebrate them
as best I could. Not let them slip into oblivion. *Nessun dorma.*

Introspection was all too easy to slip into, but week after
week the action on the pitch stopped me getting sucked down
irretrievably into the whirlpool. Instead it transported me into
a shared adventure. The football was riveting, and as the weeks
ticked by it became clear that this wasn't just any season. In
fact, Palace's progress in the league befitted their avian nickname. By Christmas they'd soared up to the fringes of the top
four, with talk of a Champions' League place being gently
mooted in the press. Then they nose-dived into a relegation
battle from which they barely survived. Their escape from the
trapdoor was enthralling. Being there made it visceral.

The feeling was magnified by Dan's new choice of seat. It was
positioned at the extreme western edge of the Holmesdale
Stand, with only a brick wall separating me from the players'
tunnel. This conferred the privilege of seeing the full cast of

Premier League characters parade past me at close range, a view that transformed how I thought of footballers and managers. These multimillionaire figures are ubiquitous in our lives, plastered over adverts and the back pages of the papers, but for most of us they are usually hidden behind TV paywalls and trapped inside perpetual PR gloss. This makes them seem unreachable. Unreal, even. But when Harry Kane, Sergio Agüero, Arsène Wenger et al walked right past me they were suddenly humanised. They did exist, and not just on my PlayStation 4. It's easy to forget that they're just people, fallible and foible-ridden like the rest of us. When it came down to it, they were simply doing their day job. But what a job. And what a workplace.

The players and managers weren't the only legends I got to see up close and personal. I must reserve a word for Kayla the bald eagle, the club's official mascot. She's a real eagle, by the way, as opposed to the giant furry one who waddles around the ground to gee up the fans. (He's called Pete, as it happens.) More than once during the season Kayla came to sit right next to me, for a break between flying laps of the pitch before kick-off. Looking at her eyes, so intent, so alien, tiny spiritual questions flitted through my head. *Was there a reason she'd come to say hi to me?* And then the idea was gone again, as quickly as she was. How simple Kayla's life was, I thought. But I didn't know the half of it. Back in 2010, a Charlton Athletic fan had been arrested during a cup tie for trying to punch her. The Beautiful Game?

Not always – but often. Even the dourest fixture in the bleakest of midwinters can be lit up and rendered magnificent by a single flash of sublimity, and one goal I saw was so good it made the months of match-going worthwhile all on its own. It was for Spurs, naturally, and comprised an awesome solo effort by the mercurial Dele Alli, which *Match of the Day* went on to crown Goal of the Season. Outside the penalty area and loitering with intent, Dele caressed the ball on the volley with his first touch; flicked it impishly with his second, lobbing Palace's onrushing defender Damian Delaney; and hammered home a stinging finish with his third, kindling memories of Paul Gascoigne's brilliance against Scotland at Euro 96. It didn't matter that this piece of virtuoso play happened at the far end of the pitch. Its wizardry was crystal clear from any angle. If only I could have shown my appreciation. Instead I had to contain my delight because of the awkward fact I was in the Palace end and, even though the people around me were a good-natured bunch, it's always wise to keep schtum when you're surrounded by fans of the opposing team. In this instant of happiness I felt a sharp pang of loss for Dan, and pined for him to be able to share in the moment. He would have grimaced at the goal but he'd have acknowledged its genius too. After all, he'd been at Wembley on that sunny Saturday in 1996 when Gazza had run rings around Scotland's hapless Colin Hendry and sealed his own legend. I should have been able to hear Dan compare the two goals. It was abominable of Fate to deny us that pleasure.

The Eagles' league season, echoing Ronan Keating's life, was a roller coaster. But in the background something else was bubbling away. Slowly, quietly, Palace were embarking on another cup run. Unlike their lucky route in 1990, this time they had to face some serious opposition, which I say mainly because they had to play Tottenham in the fifth round. Dan would have laughed in my face at this proposition, particularly after the pride of South London dispatched Spurs 1–0, with defender Martin Kelly picking this moment to end a 1545-day goal drought. Sweet revenge for Dele's wonder-goal the month before, bro would have said with a satisfied nod and a cheeky dimple-studded grin. I could picture him all too clearly. The BBC sport match report began by saying the game 'ended Tottenham's hopes of a treble'. I can picture his reaction to that too. His absence was horribly present. It was my first birthday since his passing, and a new chapter of fraternal fun was being written. Just with half the pages torn out.

Each round that Palace progressed through the tournament

re-scrambled my emotional kaleidoscope. Should I let myself imagine that they were winning for Dan? Was it too hateful to contemplate that they could succeed without him? I didn't know what to think. The grief burrowed away inside me as FA Cup weeks trundled by. After downing Spurs, Palace conquered Reading and Watford and, almost by stealth, they landed themselves back in the final. After Dan had watched twenty-five failed attempts, at the first time of asking since his death they'd made it back to Wembley. Not just that, but their manager this time was Alan Pardew, the very man whose goal had sent them into the final last time. And who were the Eagles' opponents? Manchester United, all over again. The symmetry with our spellbinding Spring of 1990 was uncanny.

One thing that had changed was Wembley itself. The historic original bowl with its iconic twin towers, which had played host to the climax of Dan's first proper season as a fan, was gone. It held a special place in his heart and briefly even became a second home for him, when he snaffled a multi-pack ticket to all of England's games at Euro 96 – plus the final – for just £150. How he loved telling me about that. And fair enough: these days that would barely buy you the programme. Since that summer when football nearly came home, the old ground had bitten the dust and respawned as the hulking Noughties leviathan we know today, with its giant, crowning arch. Dan had been desperate to see the new stadium at the earliest opportunity, and wanted to share the novelty with me. So he'd bought us tickets to the very first public fixture to be held there, an inexpensive test event in 2007 featuring England's men's Under-21s against Italy. He treated me to a T-shirt that day from a merchandising stall, which I still have, along with the memories. A physical fragment of a happy day; a crumb of comfort in my clothes drawer.

Cup Final Day arrived and it was time to return to Wembley, joined arm in arm by Mum, buttressing each other for the emotional whirlwind. Mum likes sport as many mums do, not by supporting a team herself so much as supporting her kids' passions for theirs. But this time she had an extra personal interest in the Palace team: midfielder Jason Puncheon was the son of one of the former dinner ladies at the primary school where Mum was head teacher. What can I say? She moves in high circles. A slight crimp on her claim to fame was that Puncheon was starting the match as a substitute, but for me that just made our link to Dan's team all the more deliciously tenuous. Hurrying out of the Tube station, we joined the throng of fans making the famous walk down Wembley Way towards the stadium. Spread across the exterior wall facing us was a giant screen rotating the names of both starting XIs and the scores that had brought each team to the final. In between the facts and stats flashed up a slogan: 'The Final Adventure'. For Dan's story as a Crystal Palace fan, with his season ticket about to run out, it was painfully apt. I'd known in advance I would need to mark this milestone, and as we made our way down the wide boulevard I blurred into the red and blue hordes of Eagles fans more than I ever had before. For one day only, for my brother, I was wearing a Palace shirt. (He'd have pissed himself at that.)

Before kick-off, there were a couple of pre-match rituals for me and Mum to observe. First, we indulged in bro's favourite meal, burger and chips. Then, with our stomachs full of the fast food feeling – that perfect blend of satisfaction and discomfort – we detoured for a pilgrimage to the stadium's most significant landmark. The elegant statue of England's World Cup-winning captain Bobby Moore . . . stood right next to it. To Dan's stone. During his beloved London Olympics, he had come here to watch the women's football, and he'd invited two friends, Christina and Joanne, to join him. They're a pair of twins who'd been fellow Palace season ticket-holders for many years and whom Dan had known since they were kids. In return for the game the twins had bought Dan a 'Wembley Stone': one of a patchwork of small slabs lining the outside of the stadium and dedicated to fans. Engraved on it were the words, 'Special Friend Daniel Harvey'. Only a year ago I'd been here with him, on our way to watch a Harlequins v Saracens rugby match, and I'd got to see how much this present meant. It brought him to tears. *Happy* tears. One of the only times I ever watched him shed any of those. Now the stone had become much more than just a gift. It was the only physical memorial we had to Dan. Thousands of Palace and United fans tramped past us, oblivious to the turmoil in our heads and the significance of this spot. We stopped and touched the stone, brimming with love.

Observances complete, we headed inside the ground to our corner of the lower tier. On each seat was draped a foil flag, alternately red and blue, and once the Palace end was full each and every one of them was twirled with abandon. Every head was submerged beneath a sea of swaying colour, putting the United fans to shame. But that was understandable. Reaching a cup final was nothing special to them. It was everything to us. Just visible through the gaps between flags, a man was pacing about at the edge of the pitch. But his identity was unmistakable. Using a break from his media duties to have a laugh with the fans was none other than Ian Wright, the two-goal hero from 1990 and now a national treasure. He might be best known these days as an Arsenal legend (nobody's perfect), but here he was, showing his love for his old local team and sending me another fuzzy echo of happier times.

It was an excellent final. United looked dangerous with every move, while each Palace attack felt plucky but underpowered, like squirting a super soaker at the Death Star. By the seventy-minute mark it was still somehow goalless, and Alan Pardew turned to his subs' bench. It was Puncheon time. Mum gave me a thumbs-up. And in the blink of an eye she was proved right. Lurking on the left-hand side of the penalty area, Puncheon received a lofted pass and controlled the ball with a deft touch. Then, surprising every pair of eyes in the stadium, he smashed a volley past David de Gea from an acute angle that would make Marco Van Basten proud. Goal! One–nil! After twenty-six years and seventy-seven minutes Palace were winning the cup final again. Thanks to Beaumont Primary School's finest former dinner lady's son. That doesn't happen every day.

The whole stand was rocking. Three complete strangers scooped me into a group hug. It was pandemonium. Palace were minutes away from winning the cup! Was I about to witness glory? Then, as the jubilation subsided, I noticed lots of people around us staring down at their phones and sharing the screen with their neighbours, expressions of horror on their faces. I tapped Twitter to see what was going on. Had a foul been committed that might affect Palace's chances? Had an atrocity been perpetrated somewhere in the world? The answer to both those questions was: in a way, yes. Social media was ablaze with a video clip of Alan Pardew on the touchline celebrating Puncheon's goal. It was a contender for the most iconic, meme-worthy piece of dad-dancing in human history. I showed Mum and we shook our heads. It wasn't just embarrassing. It was hubris. United were going to make Palace pay for that. We just knew it.

In *The Lord of the Rings: The Two Towers*, during the epic Battle of Helm's Deep, the action hinges on a pivotal incident after the goodies have repelled wave after wave of attacks from the evil hordes. Then a single orc carrying a flaming torch breaks through the line and hurls himself into a drain that has been pre-loaded with explosives: the detonation destroys the castle barricade and turns the tide of the battle. Right now at Wembley, Wayne Rooney was that orc. And every Palace fan was the hero Aragorn, screaming for a defender to bring him down. I could just tell, even from over a hundred yards away, this was going to be the defining moment. Time stood still. So did the entire Palace defence. Rooney powered past four men, before lofting a clever cross that fell into the path of Juan Mata, who volleyed a shot through the hapless Joel Ward's legs for an equaliser. No one was more deserving of a cup final goal than Mata, a player who has been dubbed the nicest man in football. What a bastard. Palace's lead had lasted two minutes. Pardew had barely stopped dancing.

With the score tied at one-all the game moved into extra time, just as it had in 1990. But this time could they actually do it? The answer was – no, they couldn't. Not even after United's Chris Smalling caught Yannick Bolasie with a textbook tackle – in the rules of rugby union, that is – to become only the fourth player ever sent off in an FA Cup Final. Mere seconds after the red card, the outnumbered Mancunians swarmed forwards and a lucky bounce saw the ball loop into the path of mid-fielder Jesse Lingard. Once again a volley proved deadly, as Lingard's first-time strike fizzed through the air and into the side of the Palace net. Keeper Wayne Hennessey hadn't the fog-giest idea about it. Hennessey, by the way, is the player who notoriously was once caught on camera appearing to perform a Nazi salute, and explained away the offensive gesture by claiming he didn't know what a Nazi salute was. So as the ball whistled past him into the top corner, it made sense that he'd be clueless about his far right.

A sudden roar burst around us. United fans were every-where, and they'd gone berserk. Thousands of them must have bought illicit tickets and infiltrated the Palace end, but only when the second goal went in did they make their presence felt. The coup de grace had been applied on the pitch; now salt was being poured into the wound from the stands. Referee Mark Clattenberg's final whistle pierced the Wembley air and with it the Palace players crumpled to the ground, as shattered as the dreams of their faithful. Sad all over, yes, they were. With Man U chants resounding behind us, including a fair few with a Sur-rey twang, Mum and I slunk away through the bowels of the stadium and back out onto Wembley Way to begin the sombre trek home.

I wasn't sure what to make of it all. I'd have loved to see

Palace win the cup, and occasionally miracles do happen – after all, that was the season when Leicester City won the league. But maybe it would have just been too bizarre for the Eagles to realise their dream without Dan there to see it. Especially at the first time of asking. The joy would have brought pain. As it was, the FA Cup had teased, tormented and slipped away once again, chalking up another romantic failure in the annals of Crystal Palace FC. And that felt like a more appropriate coda. Close, but no cigar. So very Palace.

To put a bow on my dalliance as an adopted Eagles fan, I kept up another of Dan's traditions and in due course bought the souvenir Season Review DVD. The blurb on the back of the box read: 'Included is every kick of the final against Manchester United that saw the Eagles go tantalisingly close to claiming their first ever piece of silverware.' I know precisely what Dan would have said about that. 'They've forgotten about the 1991 Zenith Data Systems Cup!' Quite right, bro. Are they wishing away their own past? And how come I know more about this team that I don't even support than the people who work for the damn club? I guess Dan did his work well. Something had lived on.

Every football season is a wave lapping on the shore, gently rubbing away at and replacing what lay there before, and I'd been Dan's Selhurst Park substitute, watching as his time as a fan was washed into the past. It was a small but invaluable thing, to catch a final glimpse of his sandcastle. Just a few weeks after the Cup Final came the first anniversary of his death and, as distressing as that was, it was leavened just a bit by feeling that I'd been preserving his joyous ardour for sport. In that sense Dan's ticket had begun to equip me for approaching the future. Although grief couldn't be defeated, it could at least be funnelled by love. From beyond the grave he'd shaped a year of my life.

The question was: what next? Was this just the start? I'd kept up his twenty-six-year season ticket streak. Should I make it twenty-seven? Twenty-eight? Was this a life sentence?

6

Let the Games Begin

My first thought was to hold onto the Selhurst seat. It was the easy option. I'd had enough change to last a decade. And it was the safer one too: over the past year the ticket had not just outlived Dan, it had sustained me. To cut off bro's link with his club now, after all the years he'd invested into it, seemed like sacrilege. It was his one constant. The final hanging thread. I hadn't asked for it, but the burden of Dan's loyalty had passed on to me. I couldn't just let it go. This was his life.

But I had to be true to myself as well. Despite everything I was still a Spurs fan, and I wasn't exactly bouncing at the prospect of spending who knew how long watching Dan's team. At least I wasn't the only one that summer stuck in a quandary. I had everyone for company. The historic In/Out referendum on leaving the European Union fell on 23 June the same year, causing the government to implode, forcing the Prime Minister to resign, and leaving the UK at odds with itself. (I'd won £200 betting on the outcome. Brexit 6/1 in a two-horse race? It was a gift horse, more like. Again, here was the Dan in me shining through.) While I wrestled with my own dilemma about maintaining an uneasy membership of a quirky institution, the entire country was in the same boat.

From a sporting perspective, though, the pantomime of Brexit was just a sideshow. Because 2016 had something else to offer. Something faster. Higher. Stronger. It was time for the Olympic Games. This was another of Dan's enduring favourites I'd never had to face without him, and it added a new dimension to my grief. Up till now, the torture of missing his company had been glacial, inching through the course of a football season and the Ashes that preceded it. Compared to those slow-cooking feasts of action that marinated over several months, the Olympics were a short, sharp shot of 100 per cent-proof sport. To have to stomach the Games shorn of my brother would have been difficult in any event. But their significance was magnified exponentially by what had happened to us four years earlier, when we'd both been bewitched by London 2012.

Ah. London 2012. It wasn't too shabby, was it, all said and done? Anyone lucky enough to have been in the capital during that extraordinary time can attest to the unusual mood that briefly descended upon the city. The feel-good factor was so strong that all you needed to do was spot a volunteer in their trademark purple 'Games Maker' jacket to feel all warm and bubbly inside. Strangers on the Tube started talking to each other: it was *that* weird. The whole thing was so outstanding that after everything that's occurred in the years since, it's easy to question if it really happened at all or if it was just the mother of all group hallucinations. And let's face it, the opening ceremony did feel like that, with the sight of East London being dive-bombed by hundreds of flying Mary Poppinses, while beneath them legions of volunteers pranced and cavorted around hospital beds dressed as doctors and nurses, not knowing that just a few years later that would be enough to qualify them for front-line care duties. But it did happen. I know, because Dan and I were there. The London Games were the happiest period of Dan's life, the only thing that ever eclipsed his affection for his beloved Eagles. In fact, I think that for him it coloured everything that came afterwards. Long after the famous five rings had moved on from London to Rio, above my brother their immense shadow somehow always continued to hang. After a year without him, visiting ancient Olympia – the wellspring of all that joy – somehow felt right.

We weren't new to the party when the Greatest Show on

Earth landed on British shores in 2012. We'd always adored the Olympics. For my brother and me our shared memories went back to hazy snatches from Seoul in 1988, when we sat glued to the TV coverage of Adrian Moorhouse winning, Ben Johnson being caught cheating, and Flo-Jo winning without being caught cheating. Every four years after that, from Barcelona to Beijing, we'd gorge on as many minutes of telly as we possibly could. Any spare time after that would be spent playing the (usually rubbish) official video game, after a race of our own to the Selsdon branch of Blockbuster before anyone else rented the shop's only copy. Being the slightly more gifted brother in the art of button-bashing, I'd invariably beat Dan at these games, but he was a glutton for punishment (see also: Crystal Palace) and he kept coming back for more. If either of us had spent as many hours on mastering a discipline like archery or shooting, there's a slim chance we might have made it as Olympians ourselves. But that would have tipped the effort-to-fun scales completely the wrong way. We were fans. So when, on the morning of 6 July 2005, IOC President Jacques Rogge uttered in his beguiling Belgian brogue the word 'London', it meant *everything* to us. Not many people on the planet will ever live through a home Olympics, but Fate was sending the Games to us. It was a hundred Christmases all coming at once.

Of course, alternative opinions were available. In the weeks before the cauldron was lit most people in my social circle seemed utterly uninterested, despite my enthusiastic imprecations. When it started raining medals, pretty much everyone I knew caught the bug, but in the run-up to Danny Boyle's curtain-raising extravaganza, the only one who'd always got it was Dan. Knowing that something special was on the horizon, we both took the full fortnight off work. And this time we weren't just going to plunge onto the sofa: because by the sheer persistence of logging on dozens of times a day, we cracked the convoluted online ticketing system. It transpired that as long as you kept clicking like a maniac, you could snaffle entry to an event on almost every day of the spectacle. And at a bargain price too. We didn't care what we saw: fencing, weightlifting, table tennis – bring it on. It felt as though the sporting gods were on our side, not least when I bagged a pair of opening ceremony seats for just £20.12. We'd dreamed for seven years of seeing the world's biggest event in the flesh and incredibly, like a pair of sporting Charlie Buckets, we'd won golden tickets.

I can sum up our entire brotherly bond in a single Olympic memory. It was during the previous Games, in the middle weekend of Beijing 2008, and I was in a pickle. Thanks to an almighty diary cock-up on my part, I found myself not plonked at home in front of the TV, but traipsing through the middle of Berlin with my then-girlfriend Sarah. It was a well-meaning mistake. Months earlier I'd agreed to go on a city break to visit our mutual long-distance university friend Setareh, not realising it was going to clash with the Games. My dates had got in a tangle; now my mind was stuck in a mangle. What turned the cock-up into a catastrophe was that we'd also agreed to go out for lunch at the precise time of the Men's 100 Metres Final, one of the blue riband events of any Olympiad. I'd never missed the race before; never not seen the fastest human on the planet be crowned. Across the table from me in the restaurant, my dinner companions couldn't give a rat's arse. They didn't even know it was happening.

I was stuck in a torment that just two years later could not have occurred. For as recent as 2008 feels, it was just before smartphones invaded all our lives. So there was no way that I could sneak a surreptitious look at the race on my lap, or on my way to the loo. The 100 Metres was a mere ten seconds of action, but I needed it. And yet there was no way out. In Beijing the starter's pistol was going to fire any minute. It was time to give up, grow up, and just focus on having a nice meal. Then my mobile rang.

It was Dan. He knew I was in Germany but had no idea I wasn't watching the race. He was just phoning because he was as excited about it as I was, and he wanted to share the fun with me. I excused myself from the table, telling Sarah and Setareh the truth, the whole truth and nothing but the truth by saying it was important, and stepped outside. Dan was already setting the scene. All the hype was about Jamaica's big new hope, a 6-foot-4-inch colossus with a catchy name. Usain Bolt. Convention said this guy was too lanky to be a sprinter, but two months earlier he'd confounded that by setting a new world record of 9.72 seconds. Bolt didn't do conventional. Now it was time to find out if this precocious upstart could do it on the Olympic stage. Laying out my predicament, I asked Dan if he could give it his best David Coleman and do a live commentary. Dan was up for the challenge, and what he came up with – halting, garbled, yet oddly perfect – was more memorable than anything the BBC could dream of rustling up.

'*They're on their marks. They're off . . . Bolt's had a bad start . . . Some other bloke's winning . . . It's close . . . Now it's Bolt! Bolt! Oh, my God. Oh, my God. Oh, my God . . . No . . . I don't believe it.*'

There followed several seconds of nothingness.

I thought the line had gone dead, but it was Dan's tongue: it had been completely tied by what he'd seen.

What had happened? Had Bolt got injured? Had he clotheslined a rival to stop them overtaking him? Had the whole stadium got naked? Or nuked?

Whatever Dan had witnessed, it was *big*. I had to prompt him to give me a bit more detail, to break the silence.

Still no words followed. Instead, he broke into laughter, the distinctive high-pitched *hee-hee* that would ring out with glee whenever he was particularly tickled by something. Then, through his chuckles, he tried to explain.

'*Bolt stopped running, bro. He just stopped!*'

'What? So he didn't win?'

'No, he did win.'

'You what?'

'He just gave up halfway through. He jogged it. But he won

anyway. And it's a world record. Nine point six nine seconds.' Cue more giggling.

When I was able to catch a replay of the race later that day, I understood what Dan meant. After 70 metres Bolt was so far ahead of the field, and so confident he'd got the race in the bag, he did the unthinkable. He threw out his arms, slowed down and started showboating. During the Olympic Final. All while running faster than any person had ever done before. A world record 9.69 seconds. With his shoelaces untied! The BBC's analyst Michael Johnson, who knows a thing or two about greatness, summed up Bolt's performance like this: 'He is a global superstar now. Michael Phelps? Michael Who?'

The Beijing Men's 100 Metres Final is one of the most breathtaking sights in the history of sport. And I had it immortalised for me by Dan, whose breath was literally taken while trying to commentate on it for me. He might not have had the words to convey what Bolt had done, but he nailed the emotion of it, and that was so much better. Just as with *Test Match Special*, it was all in the hearing. At that moment the two of us weren't even in the same country, but in my heart there was nobody closer. Nobody who knew me better. Just a couple of minutes after leaving the restaurant I returned to the lunch table, where Sarah and Setareh were chatting and waiting to be served. For them nothing had changed. In a strange way, I felt full.

It was now eight years since Bolt's Beijing blitz, and four since the wonders of London. Rio 2016 provided a new chance to hook back into the summer Olympic buzz and mainline it. But it wasn't the same. The hosts were beset by a welter of issues, some simply cosmetic and others potentially cataclysmic: unsold tickets, an uninhabitable athletes' village, the newly emerged Zika virus, a diving pool whose unattractive green tinge was blamed by many on a bloom of algae. The whole thing sounded chaos.

Part of me was almost relieved by the bad news. It fitted the narrative I wanted to believe: that nothing could top *our* Games.

Of course, the reality was that it was still an Olympics, full of extraordinary triumphs, hair's-breadth defeats and Russian doping controversies. And I'd have loved to bathe in its happiness again, if not the algae. Like most people, my piggy bank couldn't stretch to a fortnight in Rio, but I needed a summer holiday and six days in Greece was much more in my price range. And it still gave me the chance of an Olympian experience, by taking a sojourn to the ancient stadium. Sport's birthplace. Where billions of people's strongest passion was forged.

Getting there isn't a doddle. After a four-hour flight to Athens, it's the same again by car along the long and winding roads of the Peloponnese. The small modern town of Olympia is dotted with references to this land's glorious mythological past, through dedications that are comically incongruous: the Hotel Hercules, Taverna Orestes and Guest House Poseidon. Once you've woven your way through a last few higgledy-piggledy blocks, you reach the archaeological complex itself. The place that launched a thousand stadiums. And now here I was, in the arena, on the starting line. With the whole site to myself.

There was only one thing for it. I had to run a lap of the track. (And by run I mean a gentle asthmatic jog.)

It was a long and crusty, grassless rectangle, like a giant's cricket pitch, and each step of my trainers caused a quiet crunch on the surface. I thought of the Greek athletes who'd graced the same spot, the cheats like Eupolus who tried to snatch immortality (and in a sense achieved it), and the armies of die-hard fans who'd risked their lives over the centuries to come and watch, filling the banks with their cries. Pacing past the exedra – a shallow stone structure at the side of the track's halfway point, where a panel of judges used to sit – I wondered if the ancient officials would ever have seen such an uninspiring sight as me. Unblessed by speed though I've always been, as I crossed the finish I offered a nonchalant Bolt-esque look to the side, exulting in how flukey it was to have solitary use of this stadium. Then, throwing a glimpse up to the azure sky, I let the thought briefly flutter past that maybe somewhere Dan had flicked a switch; arranged for me to have sole use of the place. Just for an instant. The likelihood of that was up there with the odds of successfully contacting Zeus the Averter of Flies. But if anyone had fixed it for me to have this perfect moment, whether it be Dan or Zeus or Martine McCutcheon, they'd timed it brilliantly. No sooner had I finished my lap than a platoon of Spanish schoolchildren marched off a coach and through the arch to join me. The exclusivity was gone, and the quiet with it.

But that was how it should be. Silence was out of keeping with what this place had done for the world; the children's animated chatter was far more real. Far more Olympic. I climbed up onto one of the grassy banks and sat watching the kids mill about the arena, taking their turn to time-travel in their heads. Their teachers, meanwhile, were on a mission. With admirable patience, they herded the throng of pupils into a single row of at least fifty people (and one dog) stretching across the full breadth of the ancient starting line. They were going to have their own Olympic sprint final. A couple of over-eager contenders crept forwards to gain an advantage, but were quickly ushered back to their blocks. One of the teachers let out a yell, and they were off. Leading the pack was the dog: a tiny, scrappy beast, ears pinned back, tail wagging and absolutely loving it. (He was also guilty of a flagrant false start, well deserving of a place in a newly reinstituted Hall of Shame.) The school party followed in hot pursuit, aged from eleven to fifty-odd, all springing off as fast as they could, enjoying their turn to race on the planet's oldest track.

That Spanish sprint was – to quote one of Dan's favourite comedians, Tommy Cooper – just a bit of fun. But it was Sport. Thrilling. Pure. True to what had filled my brother's soul. The act of watching these happy tourists germinated for me the seed that had been sown at the wake. Sure, I could renew Dan's season ticket, keep his streak going, and be his eyes and ears at

Selhurst Park for the rest of my days. But that would be to mimic him, not to breathe his spirit. What defined Dan wasn't a love of the Olympics. Or the Ashes. Or even Crystal Palace. It was Sport itself. He loved all of it. It didn't matter if it was Jimmy White hitting a 147 break or Jimmy Anderson bowling a hat-trick; Ruby Walsh winning the Grand National or Ayrton Senna duelling with Alain Prost. Or even a bunch of Spanish kids chasing a puppy. Sport was his lifeblood. There were so many fixtures in the calendar we'd have loved to go to together, which Fate had denied us. The Derby, the Six Nations, World Snooker, the darts . . .

I'd never get to see these with him, but I could see them for him. I could invest the money I would have spent on maintaining his seat at Crystal Palace on visiting as many top sporting events as I could in a single season. It would be a small way to keep Dan's fire flickering, and it could start right here, where the original sporting flame had been lit.

I was moving into the second year of grief, and its raw reality was getting harder. Coping without him was going to be a marathon without end. Now, just when I needed it, I'd found a map for how I might move forwards while staying connected with the precious past. It made sense to be starting out in Greece, because I was about to set out on an odyssey.

Olympia's monuments were built of marble, bronze, ivory and gold. The one I was going to build for my brother didn't require anything as grand: just shoe leather and time. I was going to build the world's greatest season ticket.

On the Olympic starting line (*top*: me; *bottom*: the Spanish race)

7

It's Football. But Not As We Know It

Although I was embarking on an odyssey, in almost every respect I was nothing like Odysseus. On his quest to return to Ithaca, the cunning Greek was twice detained on Mediterranean islands by ravishing goddesses demanding to have sex with him. I was a soon-to-be-singleton moving back in with my mum. He was known throughout Arcadia as a hero; I was known to frequent arcades to play *Guitar Hero*. He never asked to go on his long adventure; I'd devised mine. And whereas he just wanted to get home, the more varied and exciting my journey could be the better. I needed my wanderings as much as Odysseus could have done without his.

But the two of us did have one thing in common. The route of our travels was something out of human control. The King of Ithaca was sent all over the ancient world by capricious gods, and for the next twelve months my life was to be held in the iron grip of an immovable Titan: the British sporting calendar. I'd have no choice over the order in which I'd reach staging posts like the Grand National, the Open golf or Wimbledon. No say over when my diary would be full. The dates were set in stone. All I could do was let the fixtures roll up, and pick off as many as I could.

What did the next year hold? Before me lay an assortment box of action: Dave Bassett's Liquorice Allsports. Energising me most was the promise of a whole heap of new sports that Dan and I had never been able to go to. Beginning the journey in autumn meant the first one that hove into view was an unlikely event for a Brit living in London: American football. Over the Halloween weekend the capital was set to play host to a fixture between the Washington Redskins (yet to drop their racially insensitive moniker) and the somewhat oxymoronic Cincinnati Bengals. And this wasn't just some silly exhibition match. It was the real thing. The road to the Super Bowl. So I nabbed myself one of the last available tickets and set off on the first leg of my sportathlon, to see the star-spangled glitz of the NFL. You couldn't get much further from the dusty plain of Olympia than that. But while the game itself was an exotic prospect for British shores, the venue was bracingly familiar: I was heading for a return date at Wembley, and a rematch with my feelings.

Sunday, 30 October 2016: American Football

Bears. Dolphins. Steelers. 49ers. Replica shirts of what looked like every pro team in the league scrimmaged off trains and onto Wembley Way, just as conflicting emotions were doing the same in my head. Excitement versus Dread. It was just months since I'd been here for the Cup Final – for the end of a chapter of my life – and that time I'd had Mum with me for support. Today's trip I was taking alone, and it made the loss rawer. There was no small talk to hide behind. Filling the gap, my mind dived back into the past, to my last visit here with Dan. It was just a year before his death, and we'd come to watch a London rugby derby between Harlequins and Saracens.

His obesity had made the long walk to the stadium difficult that day, and frequently he'd have to stop and lean on a bollard to recover his strength, casually looking around or pointing out something inconsequential in a vain effort to pretend he wasn't tired. As usual I waited for a diplomatic juncture to ask if there was anything the family could do to help him look after himself, and plead gently with him to lose some weight. 'I know, I know': his usual refrain. Defensive. Stubborn. Hearing but not listening. As Saracens went about putting Harlequins to the sword, I'd racked my brains for answers as I'd done countless times before: how do you help somebody who won't accept help? Now in the aftermath, when I knew the end of the story, I was having to confront darker questions. Poison-tipped. Could I have found a way through to him? Had I failed my brother? I'd feared his clock was ticking, but I had no idea how fast.

On other days, such spectres would linger and stalk. Unshakeable shadows. But this afternoon was different. Arriving at a major sporting venue seemed to make the worry oxidise and disappear, at least for a while. Wembley was buoyant, the crowd multifarious and far less tribal than I was used to at a soccer match. From the accents around me, they were pretty much all British. I had no idea the UK was so full of NFL lovers, or that they could create such a swell of enthusiasm. Instead of attracting two segregated throngs of supporters, today's event had drawn fans of every NFL franchise as well as plenty with no fixed allegiance. It didn't matter that today's match was nominally a 'home' game for Cincinnati – a case of geographical elasticity that makes 'London Oxford' Airport seem reasonable. Everyone was just looking forward to a day out watching world-class sport. It was a massive Pigskin Pride party, and a sell-out to boot. I might have been alone, but there was a togetherness in this mass of people. Comfort in the cauldron. And this time I was armed with my new purpose. Today wasn't merely an ordeal to be got through. It was part of a plan: to fix my gaze on the horizon instead of down at the scars.

But were such sparks of positivity enough on their own to stop my thoughts from sinking? How could they be? Grief is quicksand in the head, always trying to pull you back in. As an extra countermeasure I'd been drawing on another, darker, impulse to help propel me forwards, one that sprang from a negative: the doubts of my nearest and dearest. When I'd mentioned the idea of my pilgrimage to friends and family, some had expressed bafflement. How was that going to help? they asked. What did American football have to do with Dan? It riled me that they didn't know. My brother's essence didn't begin and end with Crystal Palace, and I was overcome with the feeling that only I knew how far his passion had stretched. Only I could defend it and keep it alive.

Their question marks had to be quashed. No matter the sport or how tenuous the connection, at some time or other and in some shape or form, we two brothers had had a dabble. That was as true for the NFL as it was with the Olympics. I knew from the bottom of my heart how much he'd have adored being here today. He'd have been in heaven.

When we were kids American football hadn't been on TV much, so my first memories of the sport are from the vague bits and bobs that seeped through onto our screens from the States. When it came to the players, in the mid-Eighties only one star had a fame that reached across the Atlantic into this Croydon boy's consciousness, and it wasn't Joe Montana, Dan Marino or even O. J. Simpson. Dan had introduced me to him: the Fridge. I didn't know this guy's real name and I kind of hoped he didn't have one. Was he so-called because of his ice-man temperament? Nope. He was just an utterly massive bloke called William Perry. The archetypal big unit. A glance at the history books shows that the Fridge's reputation was well earned, as he won the Super Bowl in his rookie season with the Chicago Bears, and to this day he remains the heaviest player to ever score a touchdown in the NFL at 335 pounds (152kg). That's an amazing record, which to achieve takes a rare mixture of fitness and fatness. Given modern levels of athleticism it will surely never be surpassed. But back then I didn't know any of that. All I knew about the Fridge was that, as his nickname suggested, he must be cool.

So hard to find was American football in those days that

Dan and I played it more than we watched it. On video games, naturally. To begin with, our choice was sparse, and we had to make do with *Grid Iron* for the Amstrad, a ropey simulator for an even ropier computer. It involved two teams of appallingly animated sprites doing not very much while Dan and I basically picked sides and watched. In those days kids were easily pleased. We loved it. Turning things up a notch, the early Nineties heralded the arrival of the Sega Mega Drive and, like everyone else at school, I had to have one by hook or by crook. By crook proved to be nearer the mark, as getting a Sega turned into a bit of a saga.

I thought I'd done the hard part, raising the cash for it by selling my Nintendo at a good price, to Derren Brown's kid brother, as it happens. (Was it really a good price? Maybe he just made me think it was.) I'd never held so much money in my hands. But just half an hour after we'd been round to the Browns' to make the sale, that wet Saturday afternoon took a turn. Mum had to pop into the local library to run an errand, and this left me and Dad in the car for some valuable father-son time. Fresh from failing at being a publican, Dad used our moment of bonding to persuade me to give him all the cash so he could go drinking. I can't recall the exact words he said, but I do remember he did a proper number on me, even convincing me not to tell Mum. While a thunderstorm drummed on the windscreen, Dad rained on my parade. By the time she was back in the car, I'd been made to feel I'd done a good deed by handing over the notes; by the end of the weekend every single pound had been poured down his throat. Easy come, easy go. It was a dick move. But Dan was there to comfort me.

Dad's daylight robbery put paid to my plans for a while, but not for good. Six months later, Mum managed to recoup my losses by cajoling him into selling the old gun cabinet he'd had for his clay pigeon shooting, which by that point was empty because he'd already sold all his guns. Finally reimbursed, I was ready for my first ever trip to Toys R Us and – feeling a faint and unwarranted sense of guilt that I'd deprived Dad of his precious cabinet – I was free to buy the games console of my dreams.

Once the Mega Drive was proudly installed at home, Dan and I had a portal into a whole new world of competitive fun, and in the early Nineties the ultimate sports game to try was an American football title called *John Madden Football*. It might not look like much now, but compared to *Grid Iron* this was like jumping from the Lascaux cave paintings to *The Matrix*. In one particularly stunning technological advance, *John Madden* allowed us to *move* the players. We felt like gods. As with any sport, we both had to choose a favourite team to stoke our sibling rivalry. I liked dolphins, so plumped for Miami. Dan had once inexplicably been given a Washington shirt for his birthday, so he went with the Redskins. Fast forward twenty-five years and, by dint of another small quirk of fate, I wasn't just heading back to Wembley: I was off to support Dan's team all over again.

Sacrilegious though this might sound, the 'home of football' was even more abuzz for the NFL that day in October than it had been for the Cup Final in May. The fans were more chatty, the age and gender mix was wider, the vibe more rollicking, the food naughtier and nicer. Outside the ground a mammoth pop-up merchandising store was attracting thick crowds, on either side of which a pair of monstrous speakers boomed out electro-swing music. Americans call this sea of entertainment a Tailgate Party, and it was magnificent. There was even a fair amount of fancy dress, which I'd have associated more with a boozy day at the cricket than a wet Sunday at Wembley. One bloke walked past me decked out as a surgeon in blood-spattered scrubs, presumably because he had a Halloween party to go to later and was looking forward to a big night. Or he'd come straight from work and had already had one. I'd been to all kinds of sports fixtures in my time, but I wasn't used to this kind of zeal before I'd even got through the turnstiles. In bringing a touch of Stateside razzle-dazzle to the October grey-ness the NFL had raised the bar. I learned from a programme seller that today's match was the seventeenth in an ongoing London Series, which had been bringing regular season games to the UK for the last ten years. I was a latecomer to the party, but it was still in full swing.

Before I could head to my seat I had to pay homage at Dan's stone. But today this was easier said than done. The heaving crowds made the little memorial harder to find: several rows of identical slabs radiated out from Wembley's walls, engraved with all manner of messages to the living and the departed: 'To Our Special Ellie', 'Happy 50th, Neil', 'Geoff, Rugby League Fan', 'Simon, who could of played here [sic]'. And then I found it. 'Special Friend Daniel Harvey'. I crouched down and stared. This time I felt it more keenly: this small artefact; the huge hole it represented. I didn't stay long. Right now Wembley needed to be a brazier to relight my brother's embers, not a cemetery. As if this needed confirming, suddenly something whistled over my head. And then back again. I looked up to see a souvenir American football that two wannabe quarterbacks were throw-ing to each other, using Dan's row of stones as their halfway line. Well, he did love being close to the action. I wanted to pick up the phone and let him know. The scene was a snapshot of the reality I needed to come to terms with. However I chose to go about marking Dan's memory, beyond my inner torment life was going to carry on turning.

It was game time. I touched the stone, muttered 'Miss you, bro', and headed to the gate.

I reached my seat just in time for the opening pyrotechnics. In one corner of the arena, two rows of flamethrowers unleashed a corridor of fire, out of which trooped first Washington and then the Bengals. Replete with helmets and body protectors, they looked more like armoured brigades than sports teams. At once it deepened my appreciation of rugby: the men and women who play either code of our home-grown oval ball game have only the thickness of a cotton jersey between them and the next bone-crunching collision.

Every fan knows the final minutes before a big match kicks off aren't all drama, apprehension and thrills. There are the national anthems to be got through first. When it comes to the British one, we've all heard it so many times and the melody is so deathly dull, it barely feels like music any more. It's a dirge to be endured, not enjoyed. Goodness knows what the Windsors really think of it. The rendition that afternoon, however, performed by a brass quartet with exquisite harmonies, was unlike any other I'd previously heard: it sounded really good.

My seat was way up in the top tier and side-on to the pitch, so that while the players looked like ants on a table mat, I had a fantastic view of the action. Some sports are best experienced as close up as you can get – sitting courtside at the NBA Finals must be a hell of a sight – but here, being further away let me drink in the full panorama. No wonder that in the States, grid iron is played in colossal mega-stadia even at college level. It's a sport that exudes bigness. The new Wembley, an Americanised bowl light years away from the creaking epic of its prior incarnation or the vibrant intimacy of old haunts like Selhurst Park, and like a hundred similar superdomes around the world, certainly fitted the bill. Indeed, having had the chance to make a comparison within the space of a few months, I got the distinct impression that Wembley Mk II suits American football more than it does 'proper' football. (It took the Lionesses' Euros Final six years later, for which I was lucky enough to have a ticket, to disavow me of that.)

At 1:35 p.m., Cincinnati kicked off the game and with it the official start of my grand tour. It was a dream start for Washington. They put together an opening drive of fifteen consecutive plays, culminating in a touchdown for an undrafted running back making his first ever NFL start. His name was Rob Kelley, although he was better known by his teammates as 'Fat Rob', as he'd battled his way into the pro game after struggling with academia and weight problems. The comparison with Dan wasn't lost on me. Debuts didn't get much more fairy-tale than Rob's. Were we witnessing the birth of a cult hero? A new, slightly more portable Fridge?

Stung by their early concession of seven points, the Bengals returned fire with a touchdown of their own, based on a huge 66-yard kick-return by Alex Erickson. (He couldn't quite match my marauding end-to-end run on *John Madden Football*, but then he's only human.) A field goal squeaked Washington ahead again, and they went into the break 10–7 up. The game was brewing up nicely. It called for a cuppa.

Given the tenor of the occasion, I was expecting an elaborate, acrobatic half-time show, but nothing like that materialised. Knowing how fantastic such a thing can be from watching Olympic basketball in 2012, it was a bit disappointing. But I needn't have worried. In its place we were treated to something else that Dan would have found far more entertaining. Down at pitch side the stadium MC had lined up a set of interviews with star guests, beginning with a two-time Super Bowl winner who waxed lyrical about the Wembley atmosphere. With so many fans of so many teams in the house, he said, today was as close to the Super Bowl as you could get without being at the Super Bowl itself. That meant a lot. It validated my feeling that I'd stumbled on something fabulous here; that this was a worthy start to my voyage.

But it was the MC's next guests who provided the real fun. They were a pair of French footballers well known to British crowds, Paul Pogba and Thierry Henry. Pogba was greeted with friendly applause. Henry, it's fair to say, wasn't. Maybe it was because the 84,488-strong crowd remembered his utterly filthy handball against the Republic of Ireland, which enabled teammate William Gallas to score and stopped the Emerald Isle from reaching the 2010 World Cup. Maybe it was because he played for Arsenal. Maybe it was for his 'Va-Va-Voom' Renault adverts. Whatever the reason, the entire stadium ba-ba-booed the great striker. So cacophonous was the noise that the interviewer couldn't get through a single question. I almost felt sorry for Thierry. Almost. It was good-natured sledging, and all around me the boos were followed by guffaws of laughter. Dan would have been slapping his thighs in hysterics at this spontaneous outbreak of pantomime comedy. Flashing a wry smile, Henry took his casting as the villain in good humour. For that, you had to hand it to him. Just as he'd done to Gallas.

Into the second half, Cincinnati made swift work of reversing Washington's dominance, opening up a 20–10 lead before the Redskins replied to pull back in front at 24–20. In the process they scored London's 100th NFL touchdown, rousing a loud bonus cheer from the crowd. That just pushed the Bengals to even higher heights, with wide receiver A. J. Green taking a spectacular 40-yard catch to set up another touchdown and wrest back the lead at 27–24. It was a classic. With just one minute left on the clock, fans all around me were picking up their belongings, ready to dart to the exits and beat the queues home. But Washington weren't done yet, and kicker Justin Hopkins converted a field goal to tie the scores at 27 apiece. For the first time in ten years of fixtures, a London NFL match was heading into overtime.

This led to some frantic Googling on my part, as I had no idea what overtime entailed. (Answer: the match is extended by an extra 15-minute period, and once each team has had the chance to take possession the first score wins, a bit like the short-lived golden goal rule in football. If the teams are still tied after overtime, the game ends as a draw.) With the last scoring opportunity of the day, Hopkins had a shot at another field goal to win the game for Washington, and he duly slotted the ball through the posts. But in the middle of his run-up the wily Bengals called a timeout, which annulled the goal. I didn't know you could even do that, but it meant that poor ol' Hopkins had to take his kick again. Which he did, shanking his second effort left of the uprights. The Bengals' 'home' crowd erupted; the Washington players stood with hands on heads, as they watched victory sailing away from the kicking tee and out of reach. The match ended as a 27–27 tie, no good for either team's Super Bowl hopes but a just conclusion to an awesome spectacle. Reporters hailed it as the best NFL game London had ever seen. Unlike that final field goal, I was converted.

Of course there were moments that day when the sadness took hold. When I felt Dan's absence. I couldn't outrun the shadow, but for the first time in a long time I wasn't trying to. Instead I embraced the chill, holding out hope that enough warmth might thaw the ice just a bit. During one break in play, the PA system played Cincinnati's old-time theme song, 'The Bengals' Growl', a ditty that's as pleasingly old-fashioned as the kind of music that crackles over football tannoys on Saturdays across Britain, and there was a comfort to it that tugged at my heart-strings. As I tucked into a surprisingly delicious portion of Wembley fish and chips, I wished more than anything that Dan was here to share the fun, the chips, the whole expedition that I'd begun today.

Then I almost choked on my cod. Another song was starting up on the stadium speakers. 'Glad All Over.' The Palace song. Dan's song. I shook my head and smiled. I knew it was nothing more than coincidence, but it sealed the deal. While so much in life still felt so wrong, being here felt right. Today I'd begun my adventure for Dan. And in a small way it was with him too.

8

Watching a World Championship Die

If you ever decide to take off on any kind of odyssey, brace yourself. It's going to send you venturing beyond the frontiers of normal life and into stranger, more exotic climes. This is part and parcel of life for the itinerant hero: Marty McFly drove into the past, Dorothy took the Yellow Brick Road to come face-to-face with an enigmatic impresario, while Odysseus himself descended to the Underworld. I never imagined I'd face any of those experiences. But then I took a trip to the World Darts Championship.

Sunday, 8 January 2017: Darts

It was noon, and Frimley Green Station was being gently coated in a wintry, shiver-your-tits-off mizzle, as I stepped off the train flanked by my good friend Will. A fellow long-suffering Spurs fan, Will is one of the two remaining musketeers (along with James) who regularly saddle up to join me on sporting adventures, and this morning we'd committed heresy. Would we head across London to the familiar turf of White Hart Lane for the icy treat of an FA Cup third round tie? Tempting, but no. Outrageous though it would sound to the thousands of Tottenham die-hards who'd soon be packing those creaking stands and fogging the air with hot, breathy roars, the promise of a home game against Aston Villa had to be spurned. For us today, football itself had been relegated, forced to play second fiddle to another January tradition in the sporting calendar. One that was indoors and, blissfully, centrally heated. It was the subject Will and I had bonded over when we'd met as first-year university students at the end of the Nineties. And now, finally, it was calling us south. For Shakespeare the undiscovered country was death. For *Star Trek* it was the future. For us it was the Lakeside Country Club, home of the BDO World Darts Championship. Today was my first pilgrimage in Dan's honour to one of the iconic sporting venues I'd never set foot in before. A lifetime itch was about to be scratched.

Soon enough we were able to swap the cold for the welcoming stench of a local taxi. This was a trip I'd spent decades envisioning, and each signpost to the venue we passed was more tantalising than the last. It was the same sensation I'd felt in Greece on that dusty Peloponnesian road that leads to ancient Olympia. Except more so. This time I was about to be a tourist in my own childhood. I felt fortified with a Ready Brek glow. At last the cab turned into the car park. Had we truly made it to the World Darts Championship? Could it really look this ... shit? Immediately I sensed that my first time at the Lakeside might be my last. There was something rotten in the state of darts. And I'd stepped right into it.

This dilapidated sprawl of buildings might rank as the least glamorous venue for a World Championship on the planet. The only sporting Mecca more downtrodden than your local Mecca Bingo. Still, ordinarily this wouldn't be a problem. The barebones sight before us was 'very darts', befitting a sport that enjoys calling itself 'Arrers' and wears its working-class roots on its tattoo-embellished sleeve. But there was something else going on here. A strong, sad sense of decay prevailed, encapsulated by a rusting and bashed-in Transit van parked on the cratered tarmac. 'British Darts Organisation', you could just about pick out on the bodywork beneath the dirt, above the barely legible slogan: 'The Future of Darts'.

Will and I joined a queue a couple of dozen strong, all of us hoping that, as battered as this sporting cauldron looked on the outside, it retained some magic within. A set of matching Day-glo orange T-shirts announced that eight fans in front of us must be from that other European hotbed of darts and beer, the Netherlands; the memo to wear outsized stripy clogs appeared to have been missed by three of them. What had happened to this proud tournament? I pondered, clutching my soggy print-out ticket. The answer was the same thing that had inspired me to come here in the first place. Television. On the battlefield of broadcasting a war had been raging across three decades for the soul of darts. The endgame was now in full swing and one side was heading for categorical, catastrophic defeat. The BDO side. Our side.

For a British armchair sports fan, the World Darts Championship is the first major event of the calendar year, after the curtain has been raised by that other staple for the oversized athlete, *World's Strongest Man*. Throughout our childhood Dan and I used to love getting our annual fix of darts on the BBC, as a succession of fantastic champions were crowned in the boozy bonhomie of the Lakeside, a comforting echo of the Christmas just gone. The husky brogue of Tony Green, the diminutive Lancastrian commentator (of ITV's *Bullseye* fame), was so famous in our household that it received the prestigious accolade of being one of Dan's impressions. Forget the BAFTAs: this is when you've really made it. I can't recreate in words the wonder of Dan's mimicry, but suffice to say what he lacked in accuracy he more than made up for in enthusiasm. As time rolled by, champions and eras came and went at the Lakeside: Eric 'the Crafty Cockney' Bristow, Richie 'the Prince of Wales' Burnett, Steve 'the Bronzed Adonis' Beaton, Les 'Looks a bit like Sloth from *The Goonies*' Wallace . . . The turnover of talent was conspicuously rapid: no sooner had a player climbed the darting Everest than they seemed to vanish. What the hell was going on?

Behind the sequined razzmatazz lies a sad tale. Back in 1992, sixteen top players, including every world champion still playing, realised there was more money to be wrung out of the sport through sponsorship and television coverage than the fusty old British Darts Organisation (BDO) had been managing. Unthinkably, the gang of sixteen, led by Bristow and Phil 'the Power' Taylor, opted for a no-deal Darxit and walked away, forming their own rival organisation and signing a contract with the nascent Sky TV to broadcast a batch of fresh tournaments. An affronted BDO, who'd been used to ruling the roost, deemed the new circuit illegitimate and banned the rebel players from competing at its showpiece event, the sacred World Championship – the one the BBC beamed into millions of living rooms every January, including ours. The outlaws retaliated by starting their own. From 1994, darts found itself with two world champions. The sport with possibly the warmest atmosphere of all had snapped in two and slipped into its very own cold war. The Iron Curtain had barely collapsed when a tungsten one arrived to replace it.

Year after year the new rebel grouping, now named the Professional Darts Corporation (PDC), skimmed off the cream of the world's darting talent from the old and more established BDO. Once a player left, they never came back. For an innocent pub game to be so strictly segregated – a system of *Adartheid* – was nothing short of farcical. The BBC and Sky commentators responded by indulging in a bizarre *omertà*, neither deigning to acknowledge that the other championship or its players even existed. For me and Dan watching this play out on TV, it became a joke. For a Canadian player called John Part, it must have been preposterous. He'd won the BDO in 1994 and promptly switched to the PDC (which he later also won), while at the same time striking up a sideline commentating on the BDO champs for the BBC. But he must have been told by his producers not to make reference on air to the Sky Sports trophy he'd just been competing for, against players who just twelve months earlier the Beeb would have been lauding to the skies. This might explain why the sport's most garlanded player of all time, Phil Taylor, took so long to become a household name in the UK: all the time he was smashing records and racking up sixteen world titles in the PDC, millions of viewers – who didn't have cable or satellite – had seen neither hide nor hair of him. Who'd have thought the oche could get so icky?

More astonishing is that for so many years it didn't seem to matter. As fast as top players kept hotfooting it to Sky, terrestrial viewers like Dan and I got to see new talents like Jelle Klaasen, Simon Whitlock and Dave Chisnall come up through the stellar nursery of the BDO, which lost its lucrative tobacco sponsorship but retained the old venue, the old trophy and somehow the old splendour. Crucially, the BBC stayed loyal too, keeping the Lakeside firmly in fans' imaginations, and for roughly two decades a fragile balance endured. But eventually something had to give, and the BDO began to suffer death by a thousand cuts. There are only so many stars any sport can stand to lose, and by the 2010s, when the absentee list counted not only the previous year's champion but also the bloke who called out the scores, you could tell there was trouble.

The canary in the coal mine was the career of Martin 'Wolfie' Adams, a highly beloved player and cult hero but a serial failure on the Lakeside stage. That is until the mid-Noughties, by which time a critical mass of adversaries who'd previously vanquished him had jumped ship to the PDC and so no longer stood in his way. Now Adams was facing rivals of a different calibre, most notoriously an Australian gentleman named Anthony 'Fleety' Fleet. During their first round encounter in 2010, Fleety dropped his darts several times after succumbing to nerves (and to my eyes possibly some excess Dutch courage). He failed to win a single leg, and nearly failed to stand on two. Thanks to results like this, by 2011 Wolfie had snaffled three BDO world titles, and there's never been a more popular winner. Pleased for him though I was, I couldn't help speculating how many championships Jimmy White and Tim Henman would have won in their sports too, had Stephen Hendry and Pete Sampras done the decent thing and sodded off to another circuit.

As the years ticked by, a new generation of fans weaned on subscription sport knew all too well that the 'real' darts was on Sky. Not only did they have the best players but they also found the ideal venue, with Alexandra Palace providing a raucous energy and competitive quality the poor old Lakeside couldn't match. Of course, the men and women filling the executive roles at BBC Sport had grown up in this new reality too. Results from the enemy PDC began to percolate into BBC News reports, and occasionally a new competition even popped up on terrestrial telly which, through some contractual gymnastics, managed to cross-pollinate players from both codes. Nonetheless, every January Dan and I stuck with the BBC's offering, and there were still good reasons to do so. It was certainly the more progressive option, playing host to a women's event in parallel to the men's and dispensing with the outmoded draping of 'walk-on girls' over the arms of male contestants as they entered the arena. (Sky belatedly followed suit in 2018.) More than anything, though, it was tradition! To us that mattered. It really mattered. But the tide couldn't be held back forever. Dan didn't live to see the coup de grace: in 2016 the BBC did the unimaginable. It pulled the plug.

So had Will and I left it too late for the Lakeside? First impressions had made us fear the worst, but there was a chink of light: a TV outside broadcast van sat in the car park. For any travelling sports fan that tends to be a sign you've arrived at something noteworthy. It belonged to Channel 4, who'd gamely stepped into the breach vacated by the Beeb. Maybe this was the best possible news, and they would do to darts what they'd done with cricket in the Noughties, reinvigorating it on free-to-air TV for a new generation and playing host to some of the finest action in the sport's history? But then we reached the front of the queue and stepped inside.

In my experience security at public events is more an art than a science. Consistently inconsistent, it covers the whole gamut from nonchalant to borderline molestation, and my bag check at the darts was particularly special. It wasn't so much complacent as just resigned. There seemed to be a tacit acceptance by the guard that no terrorist was going to target this place, for the simple reason there was no guarantee it would make the news if they did. Once admitted to the foyer, we were confronted by the merchandise stand, if you can call it that. The small spread of goodies included a shirt as worn by the bookies' fifth favourite, Scott 'Scotty Dog' Mitchell, a mere snip at £45. I say 'as worn' advisedly – it was hard to tell whether this was a replica or if Scott was trying to make a few quid by flogging his actual kit. Next to that was a pair of Martin Adams wolf masks for a fiver each, which looked more likely to be destined for a Surrey dogging site. As the vendor noticed us, a glint in his eye, we hastened away.

Then, on the opposite side of the room, I spotted something I recognised from the decades of TV coverage. Every inch of wall space was covered in framed photographs of entertainers who'd graced the Lakeside stage: Freddie Starr, Frank Carson, Bobby Davro, Jimmy Cricket, Wayne Dobson, Jasper Carrott, Roger De Courcey, Keith Harris and Orville, Hale and Pace . . . Hundreds of once-famous faces regarded us from every direction, almost universally male, with the notable exceptions of Tammy Wynette and a luxuriantly coiffed beauty it took me two glances to realise was David Essex. Once upon a time they'd all been household names; now their stars were as faded as their pictures.

These weren't just any pics, though. Almost every shot was astonishingly bad, so unflattering to its subject that the mind struggles to visualise the frames the photographer must have discarded. The world of stale British celebrity is a rich vein for comedy, and this place was a treasure trove. The entire aura is preserved in my memory by a single line from Tony Green's commentary when the BBC cameras once picked out a couple of celebrity fans in the crowd: Graham Cole (aka PC Tony Stamp from *The Bill*) and the bloke who used to play Charlie the cabbie in *Eastenders*. 'They're all in!' screamed Tony in astoundment at the star power on display. 'They're all in!' Three small words, one giant subtext, summing up precisely what this tournament had become.

But these dated publicity shots on the Wall of 'Fame' also made me think of my brother, and smile. Dan was never bothered about being on trend. He just liked what he liked. He was impervious to fashion, which in our consumerist society amounted to an unlikely but charming superpower. Nostalgia ran through his soul as through a stick of rock, and he transmitted it to me to the extent that, not for the first time, I felt I was seeing with his eyes as well as mine. If Dan had been standing alongside me now, this gallery of old-time greats would have been a visual pick-'n'-mix. His gaze would have darted to and fro as he merrily recalled TV hits from the Seventies, Eighties and Nineties and cackled at the kaleidoscope of memories. He'd have thrown in some terrible impressions for good measure (Tommy Cooper invariably topping the bill), and I'd have had to beg him to stop. The inherent crapness of the place was overwhelming, but it was also marvellous. This démodé wall of joy symbolised a more innocent time in our lives, and a brand of entertainment that brought Dan copious joy throughout a difficult childhood. Suddenly the setting for this decaying old darts competition seemed perfect for where I was emotionally: there was an intangible, latent warmth here I wanted to wrap myself in. I'd already got my £55-worth and we'd yet to see a single dart thrown.

Now it was time for the action. The Lakeside. A cavernous banqueting hall, a cathedral to revelry and alcohol. Above us six enormous chandeliers floated like a bloom of blinged-up jellyfish. The scene somehow blended stag party, hen do, cheesy wedding reception and bingo night into a peculiarly British cocktail, fruity but on the turn. Darts crowds are famous for fancy dress, but here their efforts seemed decidedly under-cooked: I spied Captain America, one Power Ranger, a pair of flirty nuns and the Pope. The Avengers had not assembled. Be that as it may, there was a good crowd in. At the back, a beige canteen was selling even beiger food, which would soon be testing everyone's personal dividing line between being hungry and *not that hungry.*

We arrived just in time for the Parade of Players, a nice touch in which all the competitors – male and female – took to the stage together to salute and warm up the crowd, effectively per-forming a reverse curtain call. We scoured the programme for the draw and one first-round tie the following day immediately stood out: Jimmy Hendricks versus David Cameron. The com-mentators would have a field day with that. *A tragic figure who loved to wield his axe until he suffered a premature end caused by a self-induced catastrophe . . . versus Jimmy Hendricks.* Then at last it was down to business with our opening match of the day: the one Will and I had been salivating over. We were about to watch Wolfie . . .

Lights flashed. Music pumped. Dry ice billowed. And out stepped Martin Adams, to the strains of Duran Duran's 'Hun-gry like the Wolf' and high-pitched howls from his adoring fans. Gone, I noticed straight away, was the pristine white England darts top and the jet-black mane of his pomp, replaced by a new-look red shirt and a more silvery hirsuteness that betrayed his age and befitted his lupine styling. What hadn't changed a jot was the jewellery that adorned his left hand. Sandwiching a chunky gold bracelet on his wrist was a chunky gold watch and a chunky gold ring on each chunky finger. Were Martin to bequeath his bounty to the nation, he could replen-ish the UK gold reserves sold off by Gordon Brown and still keep the watch. Will and I whooped at the sight of a cherished childhood memory made flesh. Might we be about to witness the first step on Wolfie's march to a fourth world title? Or had

Old Father Time stolen the powers from his arrers? Standing between him and a place in round two was a fellow Englishman, 'Relentless' Ryan Joyce. We'd never heard of him, but that was part of the fun. He could be the next darts superstar in the making, or the next Anthony Fleet. With the BDO you just never knew. As the master of ceremonies bellowed 'Game on!' it was time to find out.

Despite all the troubles, we still saw some spectacular action. Because darts is brilliant. It blends the tension and precision of snooker with the blow-for-blow rumble of heavyweight boxing. In no other sport is the microscopic margin between winning and losing less forgiving, or the elasticated waistline of the players' trousers more forgiving. And there's a gigantic inverse proportion between the smallness of the action and the volume of the reaction it engenders. TV gets around this by its cunning split-screen coverage, which allows simultaneous close-ups of the board and the thrower, transmitting in glorious detail the agonies and ecstasies of a millimetre's difference as each dart spears into the board with a satisfying, bassy thump. (Whether or not this delectable sound comes from the dart itself or a kick drum sample added by the production company is, as I write this, a controversy that continues to rage.) Compared to the telly coverage, being in the thick of it to watch this cosy pub game played out in a cavernous hall has a faintly comical edge. For a deafening noise worthy of the Kop to greet the sight of a distant figure tossing a glorified needle into a minuscule sector of cork is patently a bit mad. But it just – works. Superbly. And that Sunday afternoon Wolfie and Ryan served up a classic.

The two girthsome gladiators traded the opening two sets. Whenever either player hit a three-dart maximum, fans all around us would greet it by brandishing '180' signs, forming a canopy layer of beer-soaked card above our heads. After Wolfie fired in a tricky 115 checkout to pull slightly ahead in the third set, it seemed as though the match might peter out into a procession. But then, as in so many sports on the grandest stage, the front-runner started to falter. Adams squandered three gilt-edged chances to win the fourth set. Now my allegiance was split. Did I want this last surviving titan of a fading golden age to win through and fly the flag for his generation? Or would it be more redolent of the BDO's heyday for him to suffer a Wolfie wobble and tumble out of the tournament? The match seesawed, as though waiting for me to make up my mind.

It was Ryan who had the first chance to close out the match, earning a shot at double 18 to claim Wolfie's scalp and the most significant win of his career. Hearts in mouths, we watched as Ryan's dart fluttered wide of the mark, before Adams conjured another heroic 115 finish to save his bacon. The battle went all the way to a tumultuous sudden-death leg, testing the mettle of the now sixty-year-old wolfman. It was a classic dust-up between youth and experience. A final punishing 180 by Adams was decisive, and he landed the killer blow by thudding a dart into double 9. Ryan was left contemplating what could have been, while Martin spun around to receive the adulation of the crowd. He'd beaten back the sporting grim reaper, for now at least, and that was a mighty achievement. My mind was made up. Wolfie took a bow and I howled in appreciation. The whole hall howled.

There was something else going on that Dan would have treasured. He always loved an underdog. And here the biggest underdog was the tournament itself. Once again I could feel my brother's thought processes inhabiting my own. My mind now swelled with a connection from the past I felt only we could have made. For the two of us, the shenanigans that had cleft the darts world in twain and left the Lakeside championship in tatters rang a loud bell. We'd been girded for precisely this eventuality by another of our formative shared TV experiences: wrestling. Not the Greco-Roman Olympic kind, but the stupidly fun pantomime kind. Here I was, at the darts, thinking Dan's thoughts about the silliest 'sport' of all.

*

In *mano a mano* showdowns, audience atmosphere and nick-names, darts and wrestling could be said to be cousins. An extra joy of wrestling springs from the fact that it involves about as much common sense as it does clothing. (Thankfully skimpy Lycra is one trait not shared by darts players.) My first hazy memories of wrestling come from the fag-end days of ITV's *World of Sport* in the mid-Eighties, when Dan would entice me to spend Saturday teatimes watching a procession of heroes and villains strut their flabby stuff. There was masked mysterioso Kendo Nagasaki; human gout mountains like Big Daddy and Giant Haystacks; Dan's favourite, Rollerball Rocco, whose walk-on music introduced this six-year-old's ears to Bizet's *March of the Toreadors*. (Don't let anyone tell you TV isn't educational.) And there was also that childhood rite of passage when you real-ise that, just like Santa, wrestling isn't real. I had Dad to steer me through this: back in the Seventies, he explained, it used to be less clear whether the antics of these weird warriors were spon-taneous or choreographed. Then one week a wrestler managed to perform an Irish Whip – making his opponent take a somer-saulting crash to the canvas – using only the power of his mind. From that point on, Dad said, they stopped pretending it wasn't pretend. Even so, it was fun to watch. But not long after I'd got into it, ITV cancelled the show for being, well, a bit rubbish.

It's what happened next that had made wrestling spring to the front of my mind now. A few years after *World of Sport* dis-appeared from our screens, taking British wrestling with it, a replacement emerged from across the Atlantic. Like they were to do later with darts and football, Sky signed up the rights to broadcast the World Wrestling Federation (WWF), just as its main protagonists, Hulk Hogan, the Ultimate Warrior, the Undertaker et al. were becoming global superstars. Soon I'd be hearing their names from friends at school and seeing their faces on lunch boxes and in video games. They became ines-capable. But, lacking satellite television as we Harveys did, I never got to watch them.

What could an eleven-year-old kid do in 1991 when they didn't have money but wanted a wrestling fix? All was not lost, thanks to Dan and a recent chain reaction in his life. After doing well at primary school and often being top of the class, Dan struggled at secondary level and did poorly in his exams. What caused his trouble? I remember some of it I put down to his innate Dan-ness. A lot of it I put down to Dad. And to be fair, some of it I put down to me: the arrival when he was nine of some new siblings – first me, and then Lucy, appearing within the space of a year less four days – might not have helped either. With an underwhelm-ing set of 'A' Level results, his plan of studying History at Royal Holloway morphed through the clearing system into Informa-tion Systems at Brighton Polytechnic. He hated it and quit the course after a year, moving back home and working nights at a local petrol station. Not a glamorous start to life in your twenties, and as his kid brother I worried about him. My only frame of reference for his job was a scene from *Robocop*, where a student manning the out-of-hours kiosk is victimised by an armed rob-ber who blows up the entire forecourt. I'd watched that film under-age and I was scared. Dan assured me that the environs of the Hamsey Green Jet Garage were safer and sleepier than down-town Delta City. Time proved him wrong on that front, when some years later two men were murdered with shotguns in the car park of the Beefeater restaurant opposite. But Dan seemed surprisingly content working there in the small hours, his happi-ness coming down, I think, to being paid to spend most of his shifts watching the delights of *ITV Night Time*. This was a motley set of programmes, ignored by the vast majority of the popula-tion, that Britain's third channel used to offer its nocturnal viewers. And among the second-rate films, a Viet Nam drama, an extremely annoying student cookery show called *Get Stuffed* and the original American incarnation of *Gladiators*, there was wrestling. World Championship Wrestling.

WCW was ridiculous. Dan discovered it and he knew I'd enjoy it. So he'd watch an episode on his Saturday night shift and tape it onto VHS, to sit through it all over again with me the next day. It was a window into a surreal stateside Spandex soap opera, the bastard child of Mr Universe and *Dallas*. There were fantastic characters of all shapes and sizes, from the tall (7-foot-2-inch El Gigante) to the wide (Big Van Vader and Abdullah the Butcher) to the insane (Cactus Jack). And there was the hero figure, Sting, who in one memorable show is hospitalised with an injured leg that's stopping him from defending his US Championship title against chief rival 'Ravishing' Rick Rude. Sting is in danger of losing the belt *in absentia*, as Mr Rude's manager (Paul E. Dangerously) emphasises by waving the fight contract at the camera. So Sting limps out of the ward when his nurses aren't looking, steals an ambulance and makes it to the arena just in time. Thanks to the mischief of the scriptwriters, Sting still lost. We weren't happy about that, Dan and me, but the whole thing was great and we gobbled it up.

And it seemed to be our little secret. In early Nineties Britain we never heard a single soul talk about WCW. On our side of the pond it was getting pummelled in a PR rumble against its arch-rival, WWF. But over in America it wasn't clear to begin with which of the two was going to win, just like the animosity in the world of Arrers. In a further parallel, contestants kept hopping between organisations: one minute they were WCW superstars, the next they'd never existed (unless you had a satellite dish). Darts and wrestling: two different disciplines infected by the same madness.

Wrestling being wrestling, there was an extra ludicrous edge to the feud. When competitors moved to the other code they often changed their name too. So WCW's Sid Vicious turned up on WWF as Sid Justice, 'Stunning' Steve Austin became 'Stone Cold' Steve Austin, and when Jake 'the Snake' Roberts respawned on WCW he was billed on-screen as 'the Snake', Jake Roberts. Ingenious. At one point in the States it even looked as though WCW might emerge as the victors, but any advantage was short-lived. By the turn of the millennium it was clothes-lined by financial pressures and then belly-to-belly suplexed by Turner Broadcasting, who canned it. The leftover crumbs were hoovered up by the renamed World Wrestling Entertainment (WWE), who in the meantime had lost their own naming fight with those indomitable warriors at the World Wildlife Fund. And that was that. Dan and I had picked a side, rooted for it, and had seen it comprehensively thrown out of the ring. To me the mouldering state of BDO Darts smelled very familiar.

A quick gulp of fresh air outside, and Will and I headed back into the Lakeside. Once again, gazing out from the Wall of Fame, the smiling ghosts of a thousand TV variety nights mesmerised us. At the front of the banqueting hall, nestled among the mugshots, we noticed what looked like a school photo. The rows of figures weren't kids in uniform, though, but adult males in black tie. On closer inspection we could see that the heads had all been cut out and crudely stuck onto other bodies. 'The Grand Order of the Water Rats', read the caption at the bottom. An old UK entertainers' charity. We tried to make out some of the faces. That guy up there on the left: was that Brian May? The one in the corner – Kenny 'R2D2' Baker? At the bottom, arms outstretched in Chief Rat garb, could that be Melvyn Hayes, aka Gloria from badly-dated colonial sitcom *It Ain't Half Hot, Mum?* Two along from him was Paul Daniels. In my head Tony Green's voice was yelling *'They're all in!'* To be fair, these Water Rats could boast of connections with some of the biggest pop culture icons of our time – *Star Wars*, Queen, the *Carry On* films – *and* they'd known Paul Daniels too. Just then I felt two firm taps on my right shoulder. Had we done something wrong?

A short, old man in a dark, well-tailored suit was standing behind us. With a craggy face and a short crop of silver hair, he looked a bit like a friendly goblin wearing his Sunday best. 'Looking at that?' He gestured at the photo with pride in his voice, holding out his hand to shake mine. 'I'm Bob Potter.'

Bob Potter. The owner of the Lakeside. Were we being thrown out?

The opposite, in fact. Bob couldn't have been more welcoming. He just wanted a chat. And, boy, could he chat. Stories tumbled from his mouth in an avalanche. As far as I remember, it went something like this: 'I'm not allowed to be a Water Rat myself, because I'm an OBE and I'm still earning. Nor can Prince Philip, but he's a Companion instead . . . I used to be in the Bob Potter Band, which made lots of money. We were the only non-strings group to play St Mark's Square in Venice, 'cos I met the Mayor of Venice on the *QE2* and he was impressed . . . As well as the Lakeside I've got a new place now in Aldershot. It's the old Victorian soldiers' mess. We've got the chef from the *QE2*, and one from the *Queen Mary* . . .'

As he regaled us with his anecdote megamix on shuffle mode, it suddenly struck me who Bob Potter was. He wasn't just the owner of the Lakeside. He was quite possibly the inspiration for Brian Potter, the famous fictional club owner in Peter Kay's *Phoenix Nights*. If so, Kay hadn't even bothered to change the surname. Just as I twigged this, Bob confirmed he believed this to be the case. 'Peter used to work for me, you know. Remember the fire that burns down the club in the show? That's based on what happened here.' The man in front of us was a living piece of British variety folklore.

Still his memories kept gushing. 'I'm eighty-eight now, but I look younger because I keep working . . . Denis Thatcher used to come round every fortnight in the Eighties when Maggie was away and invite himself in for a drink. Denis would say he was passing, and I wouldn't want him to go past without coming in . . . Maggie was great, she used to open all my venues . . . Tom Jones owes me one . . . I'm responsible for Brian Conley's career . . . Brian was doing shows for me and I said, "Don't get an agent and go on TV, I'll get you twenty shows a week, I'll get on the phones myself!" . . . Once I played in a band with Screaming Lord Sutch.'

My ears pricked up. 'Oh my god!' I said. 'My dad used to tell me he once played drums for Lord Sutch, and I've always wanted to know more about it.'

But Bob just jumped off again on another digression. 'I was in a band with someone, and he tells me we're both getting a hundred and forty quid a night. But the other guy was keeping the rest. Then one time the bloke who was paying us gave me the envelope instead and I counted it, and there was something like twelve hundred quid in there! So I said to my mate: "Oi! I've done all the driving and I'm the one who filled it up with diesel." The other guy said, "Keep the money, and I'll get you the rest." . . . That guy owes me too. The tall guy. You know, with the other one. On that programme. Where they go through a tube. Bradley Walsh, that's him. He owes me one. I always tell him when I see him and he says, "I know, Bob, I owe you a week." 'Cos he left to go and do TV.'

Forty-five minutes later we were still standing there. Behind Bob's back the next darts match was getting started, but that didn't stop him. Eventually he reached for a copy of his self-published autobiography from a nearby counter, signed it and handed it over to us for free. He looked us straight in the eyes. 'Any time you want to come down here, let me know and I'll sort it out.' He must have made that offer a million times but it didn't matter. There was a charming warmth to Bob that was infectious. He might have summed up why the Lakeside was running out of time, but he also personified what made it tick. Will and I shook hands with Frimley Green's own Wizard of Oz, and headed out into the foyer, exhausted. We didn't need any more darts after that.

We got something better. Standing slap bang in front of us was Wolfie. He'd swapped his red match shirt for a blue one promoting Prostate Cancer Awareness, and he was affably chatting to a few fans. We congratulated him on today's win and said we'd been watching him since we were kids.

'How old does that make me?' the cult hero said in a throaty south London chuckle, and posed for a photo. When we shook his hand his gold jangled. It felt as though we'd taken a safari to a sporting Jurassic Park, and seen the T-Rex up close and personal.

But there was no escaping the conclusion. Starved not just of the stars it had birthed but also of BBC oxygen, the BDO contest was playing at being a World Championship. The echo of its glory days was truly, sadly, fading. The tackier, louder Sky darts had won. As a sporting mirror for the friction I was feeling between warm nostalgia for the past and a fraying, uncertain future it couldn't have been more apt.

Postscript

I can report that my prediction came true. The BDO World Darts Championship is officially no more. Its death throes weren't pretty. The year after our visit, Channel 4 decided it had seen enough. The 2018 edition was shown on an obscure digital channel called Quest, compounding the event's Alan Partridgian quality. In a last throw of the dice the BDO decided to move the tournament away from its spiritual home at the Lakeside. Away from Bob. From 2020, it was announced, the new venue would be the O_2 in London, an appropriate choice for something in dire need of a breath of fresh air. Though not the 20,000-capacity enormodome that Peter Kay sells out, but the little adjacent IndigO2 theatre most visitors don't even know exists.

It made no difference. The organisation was already terminally shot. Its 2019 World Masters event descended into farce when players were told they had to stump up a surprise twenty-quid entry fee, before it was further discovered that there were fake names in the draw. When the 2020 World Champs came around, ticket sales were disastrous. Eighty-five per cent of seats went unsold. Not only had the BDO lost the war with the PDC, but now it had also managed to alienate its own die-hard Lakeside loyalists. With a massive hole in its coffers, the organisers took the drastic step of cutting the prize money. Top players like rising female star Fallon Sherrock responded by pulling out and concentrating on the PDC. Time ticked on to the opening week of 2021, and there was no BDO World Darts Championship. *Game shot, and the match.* The next year saw a rebirth of the ill-starred event under a new umbrella, the World Darts Federation, but it's a shell of its old self, and in this fan's eyes the magic's all gone.

At some point in my life this beloved flagship of British sporting tradition had hit an iceberg, and I'd got there just in time to see its hull disappearing into the big blue. For someone who'd been inspired to visit by my own grief for Dan, a day at the Lakeside had been sad, cathartic and enchanting all at once. At least this time I'd been able to say goodbye.

With Martin Adams, Will and the Wall of Fame.

9

Show of Hands

If you were to get stopped in the street and asked to think of any sport on the spot, the chances are you'd think of something that takes place outside. Which stands to reason, because outside is where sport was originally meant to happen, going all the way back to Olympia. The ideal conditions for most sports, now as then, are moderate warmth and glorious sunshine, and the ancient Greeks would decry us northern Europeans, who are cursed to live in such an inhospitable climate, as crazed masochists for pursuing our fix whatever the weather. But that just goes to show why the Spartans could never have won the English Premier League. They might have been able to show their quality in the heat and dust of Thermopylae, but could they do it on a wet Wednesday night in Stoke?

These days our love of sport can't be held back by a problem as paltry as the changing of the seasons. The winter months are not an obstacle but a blessing, playing host to exotic disciplines that either need to be played indoors, can be endured in the mud and rain, or even depend on snow or ice. Never mind how well known they are to the world at large, each has the potential to thrill. (Just search 'Nick Brett World Bowls Pairs Final' on You-Tube.) And buried in the deepest depths of the 2016/17 sporting timetable was a weatherproof treat perfectly timed to fill the lull after the Christmas season. Better still, it had the power to cast me right back to London 2012. And tickets were cheap as chips. As mouthwatering as all that sounds, I bet there were only a handful of people in Britain who had a clue it was going on at all.

My brother loved a juicy stat, and Rio 2016 had left me with a new and unpleasant one. I could now count the time since Dan's passing in Olympiads as well as years. Here was another: for so long my brother had been one of the few constants in my whole life, and now with each passing day he was an ever smaller fraction of it. It was now January 2017: eighteen months after he'd been torn away. I was haunted by the fear that in the long run my memory of him would slip away. His smile. His voice. His laugh. Stoking the fire of his passion could help keep him in my present. Grief was both weather and climate: there were sharp storms to ride out, but just as hard was its long-lasting chill. A season always overcast, even when the sun was out. The more energy I poured into my pilgrimage, the more insulated I felt.

If there was one hobby, beyond fealty to Crystal Palace, Dan would still be pursuing with every fibre of his being were he alive today, it would be seeking out opportunities to watch Olympic sport of any kind. I wanted to tap into his determination. It meant casting the net far and wide – not many summer Olympic events are played in the depths of winter – and in any case 2012 had taught us that sometimes it's the smaller, more idiosyncratic events that are the most spellbinding. Things like beach volleyball, archery, weightlifting or handball. Especially handball.

What a bizarre invention that is. When Dan and I (separately) saw a match at the London Games we were bowled over by its mix of action, entertainment value and novelty. A quick guide would go something like this:

1. The court is a halfway house between basketball and indoor soccer.
2. The action looks like a game of water polo if you emptied the swimming pool first.
3. That's pretty much it.

If it sounds odd, that's because it is.

Afterwards we did a bit of research and discovered that

handball has its own Champions' League competition. We even toyed with the idea of a brotherly jaunt to Europe to see it – unlikely to become a reality, since Dan was something of a hobbit who only ventured to foreign lands once in his adult life. (For sport, obviously, when he was enticed on a work jolly to watch the horse racing at Longchamps.)

But might there be some handball on now? A quick Google on 6 January revealed there weren't any Champions' League games coming up. That was OK, though, because there was something much better: the men's World Championship, starting the following week, a mere Eurostar away in France. C'est la vie! *On the twelfth day of Christmas my true love gave to me, a handball trip to gay Par-ee.*

Every culture's sporting tastes are different. In the UK, handball is a crime committed by Diego Maradona. As a sport it is so niche that Team GB could barely cobble together a team for our home Olympics. Once I'd been bitten by the handball bug, therefore, I didn't just want to go and see it again. I considered whether I could get in the squad. Could this be my back-door route to becoming an Olympian?

No. Handball professionals tend to be tall, athletic, with pace and stamina to burn. As a 5ft 9in chronic asthmatic, I'd have failed the medical to be the team mascot. But dear old Blighty is a bit of an outlier. Across much of Europe and beyond, the game is a really big deal. As I walked through central Paris, the proof was in the pudding. Giant images of French players adorned billboards and bus shelters, and the national team was such a draw that it had done a deal with Lidl to advertise yoghurt. A different culture indeed.

Friday, 13 January 2017: Handball

My destination was the AccorHotels Arena on the Right Bank of the Seine, for a pair of first round matches featuring – drum roll – Sweden v Bahrain, followed by Argentina v Denmark. A harsh judge might say these weren't the most mouth-watering of clashes, especially as this was only the start of the group stage. But to that judge, Dan would have repeated Pitt the Younger's eloquent riposte to Blackadder: 'Pooh to you with knobs on!' Bro was a master at squirrelling out tickets for random sports events with seats at bargain basement prices. A midweek pre-season fixture between Carshalton Athletic and Crystal Palace for a fiver? In Dan's eyes it was the hottest ticket in town. As a celebration of his love of an unheralded fixture, I couldn't do much better than a handball non-grudge match between Sweden and Bahrain, at only 9 Euros a pop.

I reached the swollen arena queue at least as excited as any of the Swedes or Bahrainis standing around me. Possibly even more so. Because for me this wasn't just a random Group D game, or even just a homage to Dan's love of the weird. It was also a chance to recapture something special. Absurd though it might sound next to the glory of 2012's 'Super Saturday', a night at the handball was for me the standout event of the entire London Olympics. In no small part because it should never have happened at all.

Dusk was falling on the final Friday of the Games, which the two of us had been spending merrily at the Olympic Park with my oldest school friend, James. We were fresh from seeing Great Britain's women's hockey team win their bronze medal play-off match 3–1 against New Zealand, the only time we'd managed to witness any of Team GB's heroes secure a medal. I was cock-a-hoop, but Dan didn't have time for a post-game debrief. He was off, scurrying across East London to watch the Greco-Roman wrestling. Lucky him. For me and James the elation of seeing a home victory soon gave way to a sense of emptiness. Because unlike bro, we'd run out of tickets. Our Games were over.

Wanting to hold off the moment of leaving the park for the

last time and admitting the party'd ended, James and I found a spot to rest on a grassy riverbank near the velodrome that's shaped like a Space Pringle. Above us early evening pinks and yellows were blotting the August sky. Nothing lasts forever and, as we shared a drink in the sunshine, I resigned myself to the fact that the jamboree was petering out. But James had other ideas. He leafed through the schedule of events and noticed that around the corner from us a handball match was about to, if not kick off, then do whatever they do to start a game instead. Dan had already been to a fixture in the women's tournament and had been waxing lyrical about how excellent it was, making us jealous we'd missed out. So James suggested heading over to the handball zone, not under any illusion that we'd get in but rather just to wallow in the vibe. This felt to me a bit like Dan routinely arriving for Palace games hours before kick-off, just to 'soak up the atmosphere' of an empty ground. In other words, pointless. But I didn't have a better plan either, so off a-wallowing we did go. By the arena we found a solitary 'Games Maker' volunteer standing outside a lost property tent and, unburdened by any semblance of hope, I chanced my arm and asked if he had any spare tickets going for that night's game.

'I have got one, actually. There you go.'

Were we dreaming? How could it be that easy? Had Dan and I spent all those hours and pounds on our ticketing masterplan for no reason? Could we have just turned up every day on the off chance, asked for some spares and got in for nothing? The alternative was almost as unlikely. We'd had a large slice of good luck fall into our laps just when we needed it. Don't ask, don't get.

Against the odds we now had a ticket to see tonight's men's semi-final between France and Croatia. But that was no good on its own. Somehow we needed to purloin another one, fast. This called for some serious mooching about, in the slim hope that Lady Luck might choose to ladle another dollop of jammy goodness onto us. Minutes ticked by. Game time drew closer. Fans started marching past us and through the turnstiles, and as the venue steadily filled so our odds of success faded. And then two twenty-something women appeared on the concourse, one of them waving a ticket around teasingly. Were they selling? And if so, what? Normally I wouldn't be so brazen, but this was an emergency, so we went and said hi.

That they seemed to find us giggle-worthy probably should have made us suspicious, but we were too much in a hurry to worry. Hey presto! It was for the next handball match, and they were happy to sell it at face value for £30. Yes, please. We made the deal and thanked them, more times than it was probably cool to do. They just giggled again and walked off into the crowds.

We had no time to lose before 'throw-off'. James fed the Games Maker's ticket into the turnstile, which let out a happy beep and welcomed him in. I had the ticket we'd just bought off our new jovial friends, but the machine didn't like this one at all. It issued a loud, electronic grunt and barred me from entry. I tried again. The same angry bleep. An official came over to see what was the matter. I pleaded ignorance and said I was here to see the game with my friend, whose ticket had just been accepted without a problem. The volunteer inspected my ticket, threw me a quizzical look, then looked at James on the other side of the turnstile, then back at me. 'OK', he said finally, buzzing me in. James and I said a plaintive thank-you and speed-walked into the arena, hoping the inspector wouldn't twig what had happened until we'd melted into the crowd. We'd been scammed. The ticket's real owner must have dropped it somewhere and obtained a replacement, rendering the old one void. Meanwhile our girls had found the original and gone looking for some poor sap to flog it to, whereupon we walked straight into their trap. But the Games were nearly over and one kind official had shown us mercy. Hey, what difference did it make? It was that rarest of things: a victimless crime.

I'll always be grateful to those nefarious touts, because without their skulduggery I'd never have got my first taste of handball. The stadium was full to bursting, and James and I had to sit in separate stands. But since then we've always felt a little extra bond from sneaking an unexpected sample of this terrific game. It wasn't just the action that was riveting; it was the environment too. To the French and Croatian fans who'd packed out the arena, this really mattered: the semi-finals had been moved from the small Copper Box venue into the basketball arena just to fit everyone in. Being surrounded by thousands of supporters in raptures over an unusual ball sport which most people know nothing about, it was as though we were a pair of Muggles who'd stumbled into the World Quidditch Championships. After an epic contest, the eventual gold-medal winners France edged it 25–22. It was a humdinger of a night. Of all Olympic sports, there was an irony about getting such a kick out of this one.

Five years later, I was about to reconnect with that island of happiness. And, boy, did I need it. Missing my brother wasn't the only agony I was battling. My latest attempt at an enduring relationship was in its death throes, leaving my heart feeling doubly stepped on. Both ventricles squished. The promise of some innocent sporting fun, to rekindle the Olympic wonderment and add another building block to my memorial to Dan, was the only positive force in my head that Friday the 13th. As the turnstile let me in, this time without a hitch, my 9-euro ticket felt priceless.

I took my seat behind one of the goals, giddy to be reacquainted with handball. The first of tonight's two matches wasn't, objectively speaking, a big one, but a few of the Bahrainis fitted that description. I didn't know the ideal proportions for a professional handball player, but to this amateur's eye some of their squad looked to be carrying a few pounds above their fighting weight. What their opponents Sweden lacked in bulk they more than made up for in mullets, and from my vantage point they resembled a 1980-era Björn Borg clone army. In other words, it was a mismatch. I got the sense that this feeling was widely shared in the hall and that – more than a close match – a carnival was what mattered, replete with songs, dancing and copious Mexican waves. These ingredients revived the Olympic recipe from that electric night in 2012. I love it when a plan comes together.

Handball is frenetic end-to-end stuff, played by two teams of seven who need a heady blend of footwork, teamwork, speed and power. The archetypal pose is of an attacker leaping forwards with the ball in one hand, seeming to defy gravity as they hang in the air and wait for the perfect millisecond to let fly a throw at goal. Given the relative sizes of the ball and net, the odds of scoring look heavily stacked in their favour. There's only one thing stopping the outcome from resembling a basketball score. And that's the goalies.

It's appropriate that the most joyous aspect of this sport is, just like its name, a polar opposite of football. In soccer, the most exciting players have always been goal scorers: Pelé, Messi, Ronaldo, the other (annoying, Portuguese) Ronaldo, Haaland, Crouch, and so on. You can probably picture each one's trademark celebration. But in handball, goal scorers seldom offer the crowd much in the way of celebration. Imagine an NBA star retreating back to their half after shooting a regulation basket, and you've got the gist. The spotlight falls on the goalkeepers, who should really have no right saving any shot at all. And yet, through a mixture of reflexes, flexibility and courage, they so often do – and will then celebrate like they've just defused a nuclear bomb, gesticulating wildly and geeing up the fans to share in their glee. It's a fantastic sight, which makes it all the more curious that these goaltending heroes come dressed the way they do. Whereas outfield players wear a kit that looks pretty darn similar to a football strip, goalies wear tracksuit bottoms and a cheap-looking sweatshirt (usually green). Most strikingly, in a regulation that recalls footballing shot-stoppers from yesteryear, handball keepers don't even wear gloves. The overall effect is less of elite sportspeople with acrobatic abilities and Jedi reflexes than someone who's forgotten their kit and rushed into Primark on their way to the match.

The incongruity between goalies and forwards is magnified to comic extremes when it comes to penalties. As in most sports, a penalty is a dramatic set-piece. But handball's theatrical version sees the stadium DJ playing a shuffled selection of pop hits and movie soundtracks to hype up the crowd. (The James Bond theme is a favourite.) Once the tension has built to a crescendo, the music cuts out to leave an awed hush. Then comes the duel: an attacker winding up their free throw; a hapless-looking keeper standing just 7 metres away in the line of fire, as though awaiting some medieval punishment. No wonder they go bananas when they make a save. Up in the stands it's hard not to do likewise. In this match there was one particularly glorious penalty, a Swedish forward's ludicrously elaborate pre-throw routine disguising a tricksy, gentle looping shot aimed at the centre of the goal: what the football world calls a 'Panenka'. But the Bahraini keeper wasn't fooled. He just stood his ground, and the slow-thrown ball spooned harmlessly into his arms, to delirium from the spectators. Bahrain might have lost 33–16, but their goalie won the crowd.

I needed to pace myself, though. I'd only had tonight's hors d'oeuvre, and I needed to save room for the main course, featuring two nations famous for meat: the steaks would be high for Argentina if they couldn't save their bacon against Denmark. (Dan wouldn't want me to let those puns slip by.) This one was definitely the main event of the night: a hefty contingent of Danish supporters had invaded Paris and were giving off distinct Barmy Army vibes: all the raucousness of England cricket fans, with none of the violence of England (men's) football fans. Just as it should be. I nipped out of the arena for a quick pre-game bite to eat, and at the nearby Café Chabalier a detachment of drunken Danes were having a whale of a time, chanting songs, climbing on tables and quaffing gallons of beer. It wasn't without mishap – one particularly thirsty fan staggered out to the street only to be poleaxed by some mysterious, invisible force field that bounced him backwards and sent him crashing to the floor. He'd incorrectly calculated that the café's plate glass front door was open. Strange things can happen on Friday 13th.

The second encounter proved to be much closer, as you might expect from two heavyweight sporting nations. It was more bruising, too, and Argentina – surprisingly playing in plain white shirts as opposed to their football and rugby teams' famous light blue stripes – saw their number 8 Pablo Simonet end the game in a neck brace after a collision with the Danish goalie. The standout player by a country mile was Denmark's number 24, Mikkel Hansen, with his long auburn locks and bushy beard. Think Beowulf with a headband. *Mikkel Handsome.* He drove his team to a 33–22 win, and it was no surprise to see him voted Most Valuable Player of the match, but it was only thanks to some post-match Internet research that I discovered quite how good this guy was: at the time of writing, Mikkel is a three-time World Player of the Year, with gold medals at European, World and Olympic level. And he just happens to be the highest paid handballer on the planet, worth an estimated €44 million. He certainly had an aura of greatness about him that night in Paris, which transmitted even to a complete novice like me. And just like 'Fat Rob' in the NFL at Wembley, I found it remarkable to watch a star athlete making sport *their* stage and treating fans to a bravura performance. To behold such a feat was to catch a glittering moment in time, like the flash of a firefly in a woodland dusk.

My rematch with handball had been every bit as fun as I'd hoped. A shot in the arm I was in sore need of. I'd carried a fear into the Paris arena that, compared to the Olympics, this belated revisit would feel ersatz. After the Lord Mayor's show. But it took the fuzzy, latent warmth of 2012 and fizzed into something fresher, more alive. As with the Palace season ticket, I felt I was seeing sport through my brother's eyes as well. It couldn't bring him back, but it did bring him just ever so slightly closer. He was inspiring me to explore new worlds and embrace new hope. As the jubilant Danish fans celebrated, I took a final look inside the stadium. Up on the scoreboard the winning country's name was shining out, spelled out in its own language: 'Danmark'.

At the Accor Arena, Paris, to watch handball

10

Stoop to Conquer

Silence. It's a difficult word for the bereaved. It's the manifestation of loss. The presence of absence.

But it's also sanctuary. Space. Peace. The very thing we sometimes need. It has a weird relationship with sport too. It's certainly not what comes to mind when you imagine enthralling, high-octane action. Indeed, the lack of sound can be so abhorrent to our ears that during the heights of the Covid pandemic, which forced top-flight matches to be played behind closed doors, broadcasters piped in fake crowd noise to hide the hush.

A sporting stillness is only a problem, however, when it can't be broken. In small snatches, silence really is golden. The dramatic pause is an essential ingredient in many a moment of greatness: a snooker player on a 147 break lining up the final black; a golfer arching over a putt to win a major; a tennis star at Wimbledon preparing a serve on championship point; or sprinters on the blocks at an Olympic final. All these are soundtracked by silence and, paradoxically, amplified by it too. The larger the audience the more powerful the sensation when everyone is briefly becalmed. And for sheer scale of numbers, the most powerful silence in sport might belong to rugby.

In either code, league or union, rugby etiquette demands that when a kicker lines up a shot at goal both sets of fans should be quiet. These days a diktat is even spelled out in huge letters on big screens: 'RESPECT THE KICKER.' Given the volume of alcohol sloshing around an international rugby crowd, it's a miracle that this custom is ever observed. Most of the time it still is. To hear the silence at its purest, I'm told you need to get to a game between the Irish club side Munster and New Zealand, the two teams whose fans treat the ritual with the utmost reverence. When they combine to hit the collective mute button, a stadium can flick in an instant from baying Colosseum to quieter than a monk in space.

A silence like that was filling my ears right now.

Saturday, 4 February 2017: Rugby Union

In my hand was the hottest ticket in Europe. Gate B, West Lower, Block L6, Row 27, Seat 266. Behind me sat Martin Johnson, Jason Leonard, Mike Tindall and a cluster of other luminaries. Just a few yards to my right stood England head coach Eddie Jones, looking rattled and muttering instructions into his headset. To my left sat a poshly dressed little old lady conspicuous for *not* being a famous ex-player. And in front of me, France were looking to extend their lead in their opening match of this year's Six Nations. I was at Twickenham, or as the faithful call it, HQ, for possibly the most romantic fixture in the rugby calendar: Le Crunch. Fly-half Camille Lopez was lining up a conversion attempt that would push Les Bleus 16–12 ahead with just twenty minutes left on the clock. After a record-equalling fourteen-match unbeaten run, England were on the ropes. How was I here? Because of one woman's extraordinary generosity. Why was I here? Because of Dan's World Cup that never was.

The announcement that the 2015 Rugby Union World Cup would be held in England was major news for the Harvey brothers. It was the first time in nearly a quarter of a century that the William Webb Ellis Trophy was set to be contested on home soil, and our first chance to see it in the flesh. On top of that, it promised to be the biggest single feast of competitive action in England since the Olympic fortnight three years earlier. In the hunt for ways to replicate the London 2012 high, here was another casement of Class A international sport about to land on our doorstep and, rare for our sporting relationship, rugby was something my older sibling came to through me, rather than the other way round.

I have two older men to thank for introducing me to the oval ball game. First there was Dad, who lured me into the joys of Union via the annual Five Nations (as it then was) on TV. Not long afterwards, the crash, bang, wallop of League were sold to me by the nation's favourite uncle, Des Lynam, in the days when *Grandstand*, the Kellogg's Variety Pack of BBC sport (RIP), used to show the Challenge Cup. At this point rugby wasn't really on Dan's radar, but I lapped it up. I even had a go at playing it, until at the start of Year 7, biology convinced me otherwise. Over the preceding summer, virtually every other sport-playing boy my age seemed to have received a visit from the puberty fairy and metamorphosed into an Incredible Mini-Hulk, while I remained stuck inside the smallest body at school. Generally I didn't mind being a titch, but on the rugby field, unless you're Shane Williams, smallness can be a prescription for pain. So I lost my appetite for playing. It's recently been mooted that kids' teams should be delineated by weight rather than age to avoid adolescent mismatches and the potential for injury: I'd have signed up to that like a shot. My last dainty sidestep was off the pitch and onto the sofa. For me, rugby union was for watching, not playing.

And in 1990 my luck was in. This was an exciting year to start following the England team, as the sport went through a revolution that tore it away from its amateur roots. When I started watching, TV commentators would regale viewers with nuggets of trivia about the players' day jobs, which is how at too young an age I became familiar with the phrase 'chartered surveyor'. I didn't have a clue what that meant. I just knew that

Rob Andrew was one. (When he later ended up running the RFU some fans concluded that's not all he was, but I digress.) By the millennium the top tier of rugby union had transmogrified into a new professional area, and amidst some painful rebirth pangs that continue to this day, for England the Nineties was a tale of two hemispheres. In the Five Nations they were dominant, claiming three grand slams, four championships and six triple crowns as they enjoyed the greatest purple patch in Red Rose history. But the mighty southern hemisphere teams were an altogether tougher nut to crack. Throughout the decade first Australia, then New Zealand and finally South Africa took turns at claiming the prize scalp of the English in successive world cups. The 1995 thrashing by the All Blacks was the most chastening, courtesy of a turbocharged human battering ram named Jonah Lomu who left fans particularly flat – a feeling that Mike Catt knows all about. I'm surprised the former full-back isn't still being peeled off the Cape Town turf. From that utter destruction to Jonny Wilkinson's planet-conquering drop goal in 2003 feels a lot longer apart than just eight years. It was a hell of a ride.

Dan's interest also began in the Nineties, but from a more esoteric source. While looking for some affordable summer holiday entertainment at the local Blockbuster, we'd often spot a Super Nintendo game that was somehow always left available for rent. No other kid in the neighbourhood seemed to want it. So one day we thought we might as well take a punt, to coin a phrase. 'World Class Rugby' was anything but world class in its graphics, and for a Nintendo game it was an unusually glitchy affair: every so often the action froze completely, or you'd have to deal with one of your players turning into a frog. But that was all part of the fun. As a simple and addictive arcade rendering of the oval ball game, it was brilliant. I got Dan hooked on it, found a second-hand copy for a fiver, and all through my teenage years there wasn't another game the two of us played together more. For the rest of his life the merest mention of rugby would have Dan mimicking the game's crappy voice sample of a referee calling 'Scrum'.

For us to go to a real game together took another two decades, enough time for the rugby revolution to spread to the English club game. When we were kids, top tier sides existed only as a series of names you'd hear being read out on TV during *Final Score* on a Saturday afternoon. Some were exciting and exotic (Harlequins, Saracens, Wasps) while others, taken together, sounded like an endearingly crap advert (Leicester, Bath, Sale.) By the end of the Noughties the newly profession-alised sport was marketing itself like football, and some lucky teams saw their fan base explode. By 2012 London's two top teams – Harlequins (home ground, the Stoop, capacity 14,816) and Saracens (home ground, Allianz Park, capacity 10,000) – were able to move their derby fixture to Wembley (capacity 90,000). Dangling the W word in front of my brother had the effect of a hypnotist's watch. Throw in the fact that tickets were just twenty quid, and we had no reason not to go. That 2014 game was to be our final joint visit to the great stadium.

Some of Dan's enthusiasm for the Rugby World Cup can be put down to that Wembley derby (which Quins lost 39–17, despite being egged on by their two newest fans). But more than that, he saw it as a chance to be bitten again by the Olympic bug, and in the run-up to the 2015 tournament he was a man with a plan. By pooling our resources, he reckoned, we could maximise our chances in the ticket ballot while sticking to a modest budget, and so, a whole year before the first ball was kicked, we arranged to meet up one night to decide which games to apply for.

He turned up at Piccadilly Circus looking the same as he always did: supermarket carrier bag in hand, wearing too many clothes for the weather, yet also that winning smile. But his happiness soon evaporated. On our short walk to the pub he kept needing to stop, just like on Wembley Way but more so. He wasn't in a good way, and for the umpteenth time I was left racking my brains about what I could do to help someone so resolute about not wanting to be helped. Right there and then I found myself gripped by a nagging fear about how this might end, though not how – and how soon – it really would. Was he looking after himself? I asked, and pleaded that he should. As ever he repeated his usual refrain of 'I know, I know', batting away my concerns in awkward and unconvincing fashion, like Michael Atherton facing Glenn McGrath.

Once settled into our shared happy place, he relaxed, as we lost ourselves in the lovely levity of sport. We pored over the fixture list and devised a cunning plan of which Baldrick would be proud (i.e. not cunning at all – just picking as many unpopular-looking games as we could afford). Whether through strategy or blind luck, we scooped seats at a good few matches, leading to months of impatient waiting for battle to commence. But Dan would never get to redeem the tickets, or the buzz.

The 2015 World Cup coincided with the Crystal Palace season ticket I'd inherited and, as with football so with rugby, I went in Dan's stead. This turned me into a dedicated follower of Fiji. First I went to Twickenham for the inaugural match to see the Pacific islanders play hosts England, which kept up my record of seeing high-profile opening ceremonies. (It wasn't nearly as cutting-edge as the London Olympics but it did the job: less Danny Boyle, more Susan Boyle.) From there, I travelled north to the glamorous outskirts of Milton Keynes to watch my newly adopted team demolish Uruguay in sheeting rain. And finally I travelled with James to watch my beloved Fijians take on Wales at Cardiff's Principality Stadium.

This ground is a masterpiece of sporting architecture that brings the spectator close to the action in a way that defies logic: nothing so vast should be able to get away with being so intimate, as King Kong found out to his cost with Mae West. And we saw it graced with a fantastic exhibition from two nations who pride themselves on running rugby. Up in the stands, meanwhile, there was plenty of joshing among rival fans. They may be a tiny unheralded country with very limited resources, forced to rely pluckily on hope over expectation, but Wales were actually pretty good. I said this to James and a middle-aged woman in a red replica jersey shot us a sharp look, before smiling and muttering 'Cheeky bastards' in a tuneful Welsh cadence. The game finished 23–13 to Wales, which was bad news for Fiji's chances of getting out of the group (and England's). But it did feature a classic Oceanian 80-metre breakaway try, and there was no denying that Cardiff was a hell of a good place to watch rugby. Even if it was bizarre to be there to watch a World Cup called 'England 2015'.

Dan missed all of this. So I was especially keen to build rugby into my super-season ticket, and the natural target was a Six Nations match. But as any fan will tell you, that's easier said than done. (Unless you count going to Rome for an Italy game. Which you'd be within your rights not to.) There are few more sought-after tickets in British sport than an England international at Twickenham, and online exchanges regularly resell seats for hundreds if not thousands of pounds. This means millions of fans only ever get to see their team through the prism of TV, a long way away from the Sweet Chariot's swing. I feel this frustration keenly because every year these are fixtures I like to organise my life around every November, February and March – to make sure that, like Dan Carter in his pomp, I hardly ever miss a kick. If I couldn't get inside HQ, though, I could get close.

Adjacent to the hulking fortress of Twickenham is the Stoop, like a baby moon trapped in the orbit of its mother planet. It's an enchanting, tiny shed of a ground. Like Selhurst Park, only more so. I went along one Saturday, not with a ticket, just a walk-up trip on a whim. I was itching to plunge into my sporting deep dive, and that day's Premiership fixture list offered an inviting springboard: in their 150th-anniversary season Harlequins were playing a rematch with Saracens. I felt slightly freed by the uncertainty of what Fate had in store for me at the turnstiles, which maybe in itself was a sign of things changing. Of coping. Uncertainty isn't a comfortable emotion for the bereaved. But what is sport if not a celebration of uncertainty, and a reminder that it need not always be feared? I was in luck: I nabbed one of the last seats in the house to their biggest home game of the year.

Club rugby grounds rock. They're so cosy, you can practically let the wingers share your chips. I hadn't been this close to the stars of the game since I was at university and someone told me that the girlfriend of one of the 2003 World Cup-winning England squad fancied me. (The next day she asked me if I wanted to come round for tea in her room and, excessively eager not to get my head kicked in, I declined.) I loved even more how at a rugby match the fans from both teams sit among one another, instead of segregated as at football. Both configurations have their place, but the noise at the Stoop was no less exuberant for being less tribal. In fact, the sound of 14,800 cheering on their team seemed as loud as five times as many. The Stoop was established way back in 1866, but it's totally suited to twenty-first-century sport. At the same time, other parts of the spectator experience harked back to a bygone age, such as the silly multicoloured blazers worn by several fans around me in the North Stand. One directly in front of me felt compelled to stand up during every single play and lambast the referee, excoriating a given penalty decision one minute, denouncing a missed one the next. But even as his curse-laden invective became increasingly apoplectic, he took pains each time to address the ref as 'sir'. Now that's something you don't get at Tottenham.

Something else struck me at the Stoop. On the way to my seat I passed a statue of a rugby player, frozen in time, about to unfurl a spinning pass. The plaque underneath read, *Nick Duncombe, 1982–2003, Harlequins and England. 'Carpe Diem.'* Fixed in bronze, here was an image of another life snatched far too soon. A star denied the chance to shine fully. Sadness flooded back over me. The motto was apt, too, for 'Carpe diem' was how Dan had lived his life, albeit not in the way the Roman poet Horace envisaged. He never prioritised the long term; never let himself be led by the question, 'What should I do for the future?' A more instinctive thought – 'What do I want right now? – commanded him, in an innocent but ultimately lethal way. Throw in the addictiveness of sugar, and it made sense to me why he was someone who'd never walk out of a shop with an apple if a Mars bar was the same price. Carpe diem means 'Seize the day', but the original poem continues in less positive vein: 'Don't put any faith in the next one.' I'd never subscribed to such pessimism, but my brother's death forced me to face a hard question: was I wrong? No, I decided. That wasn't how I could live. I needed it to be possible to take the first part of Horace's credo without abiding by the second. In that sense Dan was a model.

As fun as it was following Quins, it didn't sate me. I returned to the Stoop for a few more games, but that still wasn't enough. Every time I visited, the mammoth concrete shell of Twickenham loomed large on the horizon, taunting me. The desire to see an England match nagged away and evolved into a fear of failure. A splinter in the brain. Without the Six Nations, the odyssey would be incomplete. I knew I'd made a rod for my own back, judging myself by a standard that no one else had set. But this was a taste of how Dan's mind worked. He was a rigid completist. So I looked for solutions. Winter 2016 saw the arrival of a Four Nations rugby league round-robin, and I went along to see England's must-win tie against Australia at the London Stadium. (It was a disappointing outing on and off the field, with the Kangaroos easy winners, 36–18, in front of swathes of empty seats.) Now I'd seen England play rugby, and seen rugby near Twickenham. But it wasn't the same as seeing England play rugby at Twickenham. Days before the 2017 Six Nations was due to start, I was ticketless, clueless and running out of time.

Then a silly thought occurred to me. *Why don't I ask?* So, as dumb as it sounds, I phoned the RFU. I felt foolish as I left a message, and I quickly tried to forget that I'd done it. But then, on Thursday afternoon, with just forty-eight hours to go before the big kick-off, my phone rang at work. It was them. I speed-walked away from my desk, took refuge in the office stationery cupboard and listened. The woman on the other end of the phone, who shall stay nameless to protect her from entrepreneurial copycats, said she was moved by Dan's story and she'd see what she could do. I still didn't dare to dream the gambit might actually work, but the next day I received an email which I had to read twice to believe. Through an act of immense kindness, my rugby angel had conjured up a single ticket to that weekend's game between England and France. It was enough to fulfil any rugby fan's dream. And that's before I found out the location of my seat, in the beating heart of the home of rugby. Lucky me. It had been a while since I'd felt like that.

Camille Lopez bent to tee up the ball, England huddled under the posts to regroup for a counter-attack, and I knew my desperation to be here at Twickenham had been well founded. Brought to silence by the conversion attempt, the packed stands were a patchwork of St George's flags, Tricolores and Barbour jackets, while the headgear was a match for Royal Ascot. To my left one group of English fans had come in matching bowlers, only to be outdone by legions of French supporters who had a menagerie of furry animals bobbing on their heads, from penguins and bears to thousands of blue Gallic roosters. Add in a panoply of berets, from navy blue to shocking pink, and the Hat Wars amounted to a clear away win. *Chapeau, messieurs.* During a break in play I read on the BBC Sport app that the Six Nations now boasted the highest average attendance of any tournament in the world (72,000), beating the NFL and FIFA World Cup into second and third place. I really did have one of the hottest tickets in world sport. Thanks to a phone call.

Lopez's conversion bisected the posts and sailed France into a 16–12 lead with just twenty minutes to play. To my biased eyes there were a couple of fishy, forward-looking passes in the build-up to prop Rabah Slimani's try, but it was the least the French deserved in the face of a cagey England performance marred by inaccuracy and indiscipline. It was going to take some trademark Eddie Jones nous to engineer a turnaround. A rousing chorus of 'Swing Low, Sweet Chariot' swelled in the Twickenham twilight.

In the subsequent wake of the Black Lives Matter movement, awareness has increased of this anthem's questionable origin, and England second-row Maro Itoje has stated he will no longer sing it. I'm not sure if I'd feel comfortable doing so again, but that night I joined in. To be part of a full house at 'HQ' trying its deafening best to 'carry them home' was spine-tingling. I looked around me to relish other fans' enjoyment and saw the posh old lady to my left was deeply, contentedly asleep.

Whether thanks to the singing, swinging chariot, England did eventually manage to pick the French lock. After some heavy bashing by the forward pack made vital yards, a try finally came from a bulldozing run by substitute centre Ben Te'o, a classic post-Lomu three-quarter who somehow combines a heavyweight boxer's size with a sprinter's speed, and who arrived onto a final pass from Owen Farrell like the proverbial freight train (on a non-strike day). With Farrell's conversion, England nudged three points ahead: 19–16. It was a lead, but a gossamer-thin one. Just a single indiscretion could give Lopez's boot the chance to rescue a draw for the visitors; just one missed tackle could gift Les Bleus a match-winning try. France marauded forwards, hammering away at the white-shirted wall as the clock ticked past eighty minutes. At last, after a French transgression at a ruck, the referee's whistle cut through the tumult with three final blasts. The English players raised their arms aloft and roared in triumph; Twickenham thundered with relief; the French dropped to their haunches, broken. It wasn't a vintage performance from Eddie's men, but it was England's fifteenth win on the trot – a new national record, secured against a fierce old enemy for extra satisfaction. I watched as a French fan in front of me (navy beret: classic) bared his teeth in exasperation. For the visitors, this was one that got away.

Fulfilled by a fantastic game, most of the 82,000 fans were filtering out of the stadium, ready to head home into the Hounslow night. I looked at the emptying stands with sadness and disbelief. Had they not got the memo? The day's action was far from over, because a whole extra course of the rugby banquet was about to be laid on. In a rarity for the Six Nations, the organisers had arranged for the equivalent fixture in the women's championship to be played here at Twickenham too, straight after the men's match. What a good idea! I couldn't get my head around why double-headers aren't scheduled more often, or why so many other fans didn't want to hang around to watch. Sure, it was a cold evening, but this was international sport, being offered for free. Dan would never have entertained the idea of leaving, and I felt the same. The dogged fans who had chosen to stay for a second helping were allowed to find a better seat. Thanks to my good fortune I didn't need to.

Even before kick-off, as the two squads lined up for the national anthems, it seemed to me that England's women would be a cut above their opponents. They looked stronger, quicker and fitter. Of course, in sport just like anywhere else, appearances can be deceptive, and after just three minutes a stray pass from fly-half Katy McLean was intercepted by Shannon Izar, who ran the length of the field to score an electric early try for the French. England looked flustered, and on the half-hour Les Bleus conjured up an unstoppable rolling maul that rumbled over the line, with Gaëlle Mignot grounding the ball for a 13–0 lead. Um. Maybe I'd called this one wrong.

Half-time couldn't arrive soon enough for the Red Roses,

and whether they were given the 'hairdryer treatment' by their coaching staff or had just used the time to regroup, in the second half they were a side transformed. The women in white scored 26 unanswered points that befitted their status as trophy favourites, turning the match on its head and finishing with a flourish, courtesy of Amy Wilson-Hardy's graceful seventy-seventh-minute try. The match was just as much a privilege to witness inside Twickenham as the men's, and proved women's sport can thrive when it's given the media exposure enjoyed by their male counterparts. After the footballing success of the Lionesses at the Euros, will the 2025 Women's Rugby World Cup – to be hosted in England – be a lightning rod to steepen the upward curve? The fans are hungry. If they build it, we will come.

During the game a man came and took the vacant seat to my right, a chatty fellow called Neil who hailed from nearby Whitton and was a true rugby aficionado, keen to reel off his many loyalties. He regularly went to watch London Scottish play in Richmond, as well as Rosslyn Park and Harlequins. 'Ah, me too', I said on hearing the last name.

'Really?' Neil asked. Was I there at last night's Anglo-Welsh Cup Match to see Quins lose to Sale?

No, I replied sheepishly, reminded that, whatever you're into, there's always someone out there who's into it way more. (Although possibly not in Neil's case.) We shared our stories and Neil revealed that he acted as a carer for his wheelchair-bound dad. They liked to come to rugby games together, and in the past had had front row accessible seats for Test matches, but for today they couldn't get hold of a disabled ticket: neither in the local ballot nor in the disabled ballot nor via his rugby club. Not a sausage. It was just by browsing the RFU website two nights ago that Neil had found a single (able-bodied) returned ticket on sale, enabling him to come alone. I commiserated and explained how Dan's story had led me here, as well as the journey I still had ahead.

'That'll be cathartic', Neil said. 'Enjoy it, as much as you can.'

Here was a fellow rugby lover welcoming me in when he didn't have to. A small thing, but it mattered. Circumstance had flung us together: two solo sports fans, on their own when they should be with their loved one, bolstered by a bit of company.

I bade farewell to Neil by the stadium gates and halted for an instant while I pondered: wait or walk? Twickenham is one of those sports grounds that's a travel nightmare. If you don't time your exit well you can find yourself kettled into suburban nothingness for well over an hour. There is an escape route, but it means a half-hour-plus stroll to Richmond Station. Just then a group of four revellers wandered past me, one of whom was legendary Welsh prop forward Adam Jones, unmistakable with his leonine mane and beard, not to mention his sheer size. He might weigh more than Dan had, but he was an international sportsman with a *slightly* different level of fitness. The reminder of my brother's trouble with walking near the end of his life jolted me into gratitude that I even had the option. So I equipped myself with a cup of tea and began the trek to Richmond. It was so cold that, no matter how far or fast I walked alongside the dual carriageway, I never warmed up. The February night cut through clothes, right to the bones.

Across the Thames the route continued along a main road, to the left of which lay an expanse of muddy grassland, at this time of night nothing but a big, blank void. Then, out of the corner of my eye, a movement in the gloom stopped me in my tracks. A pause, and it came a few steps closer, until it became tinged pale pink under the nearby street lamp. A heron. Just a few metres away. Had he been fishing in the river? Whatever he was up to, he wasn't doing it alone. By his side appeared another. Then another. And another. Four of them – a siege – almost in touching distance, all looking at me while I gawped at them. We stayed there for a full minute, the five of us transfixed. I'd never seen anything like it. If I wanted to feel spiritual, I thought to myself, what might this augury mean? Was there a connection to Kayla the eagle? Deep down I knew what it really meant: herons in Richmond are quite tame.

It was a relief to find that reason still ruled my head. Grief makes us so vulnerable, it's not always easy to hang onto our marbles. But at that moment a peculiar sensation suddenly descended. I didn't know what was going on but it was overwhelming. My head was swimming: relationship troubles, bruised family memories, the generosity of the RFU, the thrill of the rugby, no more Dan. And the loneliness. I felt sick with loneliness. It probably hadn't helped that I'd downed my cup of tea in double-quick time to try and fight the freezing cold. Right now my body had had enough. By the side of the road I retched.

The four herons watched. They probably just thought I was drunk.

Silence.

The England men's rugby union team line up at Twickenham

11

Prawn Sandwich Section

If silence can be a difficult word, elite is an odd one. For a kid growing up in the Eighties, Elite meant a smash hit computer game set in space. In sport too, it tends to mean something in the outer realms of most people's imaginations: the highest level of competition possible and the supreme calibre of the athletes who take part. But there's a flip side. Sport should be an egalitarian activity, whether you're watching or playing it. It's where we get the idea of a level playing field, after all. But far too often it isn't the case. Take cricket. There's an irony that at one of the stuffiest institutions in the sporting world, the MCC at Lord's, the playing field is literally, deliberately, kept off level (in order to preserve the famous slope of the pitch). For other disciplines like equestrianism, your chance to participate can still be barred by your background, family wealth, or the value of your horse.

For that reason, and for its simplicity, football will always be the world's game. *Jumpers for goalposts. Marvellous.* But in my lifetime even soccer has been indelibly stained by a variation of the E-word – elitism – and its commercialisation has ballooned so far it might just have become the guiltiest of all. You need only look at FIFA. Like so many Palace fans who'd been stung by how close their club once came to going out of business, Dan hated what money was doing to his favourite sport. He was someone with a fierce sense of right and wrong, so much so as to boycott the World Cups in Russia and Qatar. (If only he'd found a less extreme way of doing that.) He wasn't bothered about having the best seat in the house, and I loved that about him. He was a true fan. A 'behind-the-goal' die-hard, never a halfway-line Hooray Henry. That's not to say he'd have turned down a Six Nations ticket within earshot of Eddie Jones, but he'd have been just as happy in the dizzy heights of Row ZZ. We knew our place, and it was the cheap seats, two of the many, looking across at what Roy Keane dubbed 'the prawn-sandwich brigade' – a strange but inevitable phenomenon in a modern stadium, into which I was about to make my deepest ever incursion.

26 March 2017: Football, Wembley

It's always handy to have a good boss, especially if they happen to share your love of sport. In 2017 I was working as a producer at Hat Trick Productions, the production company behind such hit series as *Have I Got News For You, Whose Line Is It Anyway?* and *Father Ted.* Shows like these had formed the bedrock of Britain's pop culture tapestry in the Eighties and Nineties, giving many comedy fans a shared lexicon: to my shame (and Dan's pride) we could both quote whole episodes verbatim.

The managing director of Hat Trick is Jimmy Mulville. He's a powerful figure in the TV industry, but in Dan's eyes he was also an 'A' list celebrity, because Jimmy once co-wrote and starred in a little-known sitcom called *Chelmsford 123,* set in Roman Britain. (Largely forgotten though it now is, you have to admire its boldness: not many comedy shows these days would begin with an opening scene performed entirely in Latin.) Jimmy and I were a gulf apart in terms of bank balance, but apart from that we had quite a lot in common. We both worked in comedy. We both loved football. And we were both children of alcoholics. Quite the hat trick. I discovered the role that drink played in his life by listening to his episode of *Desert Island Discs,* which is an unusual way to learn about your boss.

He discovered it about me by a kind of sixth sense that I'll never quite understand.

One day Jimmy called me into his office for an unscheduled chat. Such a summons with a boss can be a good thing, a bad thing, or an ugly one, but this was something else. He invited me to take a seat on his squishy leather sofa, wheeled himself over to me on his bright red office chair, and asked me a direct question I'd never been asked before. 'Is one of your parents an alcoholic?'

Had someone said something to him? What would they have said? Who knew? Who cared? And why was he asking? I didn't know how to respond. Both as a kid and well into my twenties I'd always kept Dad's horrible truth quiet. It began as a coping mechanism, a way for the family to try to hold onto some level of dignity while squashing down the horrors of what was happening behind our front door. Then, eventually, not talking about it stopped being a strategy and just became the normal state of affairs. Growing up in the last years before the internet revolution, as we dealt with our day-to-day pain we felt very alone. Of course, the tragic truth is that millions of people are touched by the social poison that alcohol can be, but it took me decades to work that out. Now, in my thirties, the tale of Dad's drinking was – at last – not something I still made an active effort to keep secret. So sitting here now, wrongfooted by this stark question, I didn't see any reason not to tell the truth. Particularly as my inquisitor already seemed to know. I recounted the potted story of what happened to Dad and Jimmy replied that he wasn't surprised. He said he could tell I'd suffered something like that because of the way I acted. This shook me. I'd always imagined that I'd hidden that side of things pretty well. Was I such a bad actor? Did I present to other people so differently from how I thought I did? That was a trait I'd seen in Dan. Did I have it too?

It was more a case of his antennae being finely tuned, Jimmy reassured me, than my speakers being turned up to eleven.

Alcohol had played a major role in his life too, and he recognised some classic red flags in how I behaved: nervous, compliant, wary.

Just to be told this by someone I respected was a revelation in understanding how I'd lived with my past. (To be told it by a celebrity was even more unexpected.) But Jimmy's motivation wasn't to show off his psychology skills. He wanted to help, and he even bought me a book which he said had helped him, called *Adult Children of Alcoholics* by Janet Woititz. There, staring at me in print, were some of the issues I'd struggled with for my whole life, telling me that the way I was came as a direct result of a childhood trying to cope with the trauma of having an alcoholic parent. I knew it had had a serious impact on me, but I'd never pinpointed how. If it hadn't been for Jimmy I might never have twigged this so clearly. Dan never had that chance.

Could that kind of self-knowledge have helped my brother? Saved him, even? Would he have been equipped to use the information? Did he feel trapped by his situation more than he felt able to express? One thing I know is that he carried a lot of frustration inside him, understandably so. Occasionally his temper could bubble over: as a teenager he once memorably responded to losing at a computer game by throwing his Sinclair Spectrum 48k at the wall, causing it to explode impressively into a hundred pieces. (The next model of Sir Clive Sinclair's unreliable computer, the 48k+, had a far more robust design, so, to be fair to Dan, maybe he wasn't the only one.) I'm sure he'll have known that Dad's alcoholism had been a factor in shaping his character, but I doubt he spent much time considering how it was a problem, or how it might be helped. Compared to him, I think I'd got off remarkably lightly.

After that memorable meeting in Camden, whenever Jimmy called me into his office I had an extra level of apprehension about what might be coming my way. *What else had he worked out about me? Did he know about my obsession with Mario Kart 8?* March 2017 brought one such occasion, but this time he was

playing not psychiatrist but Santa. He'd heard about my odyssey for Dan and wanted to know if I'd be interested in seeing
the England men's football World Cup qualifier against Lithuania. Did I want to see a competitive England match at Wembley
for free? Do bears prefer their toilet facilities to be al fresco,
wooded affairs? I thanked Jimmy and gladly accepted the two
tickets. And that's all I thought I was accepting. But just like on
an aeroplane, at a football match a standard seat and a top dog
seat are two very different things indeed.

The elite experience at Wembley doesn't begin and end with
the ref's whistle. Far from it. It starts when you leave central
London because – and I couldn't quite believe this – premium
'Club Wembley' ticket-holders are offered a complimentary
private train service to ferry them from Marylebone Station to
the stadium. So while thousands of fans squeezed themselves
into the Tube, my brother-in-law David and I had the luxury of
a chartered carriage pretty much to ourselves. This was crazy. A
secret train service out of London that hardly anyone knew
about? It was like picking up the Hogwarts Express from Platform 9¾ at King's Cross, except much better. You can keep your
invisible portals to a wizarding world; getting from central London to Wembley with a guaranteed seat? That's real magic.

Once we'd arrived, David and I paid the mandatory visit to
Dan's stone, but that's where similarities to my other recent
Wembley visits ended. There was to be no circumambulating
the vast perimeter this time, no mad dash to find the correct
one out of the dozens of faceless entry gates that allow access to
the upper tier. Jimmy's tickets sent us straight through the front
door. Foregrounded by the Bobby Moore statue, we were taking the posh way in: an opulent plate-glass aperture guarded by
a pair of doormen in morning suits, each clutching a bunch of
bright red lanyards to bestow VIP access upon the lucky few. It
should be law that nobody should ever be allowed to attend a
football match in a morning suit, no matter whether you're a
king or even the 1996 Liverpool FA Cup Final squad. One of

the two gentlemen seemed to know they stood out; the other's face said, 'I know exactly what I look like, but I don't care. It's a job'. Away from the river of fans streaming up Wembley Way towards the public entrances, we walked past the gatekeepers and stepped into opulence.

For one day only David and I had become members of the One Twenty. If that sounds like a secret cult, it's not far off. It's so named because only 120 members and their guests can join 'the most prestigious club in Wembley's history'. The number of England players ever to lift a trophy here might beg to differ about that, even if the Lionesses have started to redress the balance. The One Twenty are the vanguard of the people you see on TV during Wembley games who populate the exclusive block behind the two dugouts. In fact, they're usually more conspicuous by their absence, when they invariably leave row upon row of empty seats during the first ten minutes of each half. This has always driven me mad, because there are armies of fans who'd give their right arm to watch the whole match. Given how lucrative executive areas like this are, they aren't going away anytime soon. But if it was up to me, I'd at least ensure the posh seats were placed on the same side of the ground as the TV cameras, so the rest of us don't have to have our noses rubbed in it when we're watching at home.

Why wouldn't these lucky fans want to watch the whole game, when they had the best seats in the house? It was a question that had bugged me through all the years I'd been coming to Wembley, with Dan and without him. Now, on this sunny spring Sunday, my bewilderment had an answer. Roy Keane was wrong. There isn't a prawn sandwich section here. It's a five-course sit-down meal with unlimited Laurent Perrier champagne section. For the One Twenty, the opening exchanges between England and Lithuania were always going to be less enticing than another drop of bubbly and a gourmet tiramisu.

Annoyingly, the quality of the football that afternoon bore this philosophy out. But there was a far better reason to be in

our seats before kick-off than football purism (or reverse snob-
bery). Foremost in everyone's mind were the tragic events of
the previous Wednesday, when a terrorist attack on Westmin-
ster Bridge had claimed four lives. After the national anthems
had been sung, a palpably sombre pall fell upon the ground.
The players from both countries, all wearing black armbands,
gathered around the centre circle, where they were met by a
quartet of dignitaries carrying wreaths of remembrance, led by
the Mayor of London, Sadiq Khan. A minute's silence was
observed.

The atrocity cast a significant shadow, but it wasn't the only
source of mourning. There was a footballing dimension too, as
the players and fans next paid respect to former England manager Graham Taylor, who had recently passed away at the age
of seventy-two. Taylor was vilified (and turnipified) during his
turbulent tenure as boss of the national team, but as a club
manager and pundit he was a much-loved figure. His death
brought into focus a puzzle about how, as a society, we choose
to grieve.

Every sports fan will be acquainted with the two main displays of recognition shown to departed greats: shared silence
or applause. That afternoon, given the prevailing mood, the latter wasn't an option. But I wish applause was chosen more
often. The preference of the family affected must be paramount,
but for me it's symbolic of one of the chief lessons of bereavement: the importance, even above mourning the death that has
come, of cherishing the *life* that has gone.

There was a third way in which the fragility of existence was
laid bare at Wembley. Accompanying the veteran England
striker Jermain Defoe onto the field had been the tiny figure of
six-year-old Sunderland fan Bradley Lowery, suffering with
neuroblastoma, who had struck up a famous friendship with
Defoe. Bradley's life chances were by this point very slim, and
it was heart-tugging to see this little boy walking out onto the
pitch; miraculous to see what vivaciousness and spark could be

crammed into so few years. *Carpe diem:* that mantra I'd seen inscribed on Nick Duncombe's statue at the Stoop – it was there in front of me that day. Bradley died later that summer, after a short life that had raised a tremendous amount of awareness for the condition that had claimed him. Soon afterwards, at a friendly match between Bury and his beloved Sunderland, Bradley was honoured – with a minute's applause.

On the Wembley pitch, then, were three faces of grief. All different from mine, all awful to bear. Some deaths are avoidable, others inevitable. Some can be braced for, others are sudden. Most come too early, a few come too late. But all lives need remembering. And if possible, celebrating too. Up in the caviar sandwich section, I looked around me. How many other people were being gripped by existential thoughts in the midst of their swanky corporate freebie? Possibly more than you'd think.

The game was a subdued affair, unsurprising given the circumstances surrounding the match and the general nature of tournament qualifiers. England were stodgy in the face of brave but limited opponents, until a goal from the evergreen Defoe took them into the lead, before a poacher's finish by a substitute added to another striker's tally: it's . . . Jamie Vardy's account. Two goals, a clean sheet, and now 34 qualifying wins in a row: it had all gone completely with the form book, and there was a sense that the England men's team might be at the start of building something. This was Gareth Southgate's first home game since being named permanent manager, and after decades of yo-yoing between glamour coaches (Erikssen, Capello), homegrown disasters (Keegan, McLaren, Hodgson), and self-saboteurs (Venables, Hoddle, Allardyce), the national side finally seemed to have settled on the right fit: someone hungry and proud but who'd hardly won anything. Just like his country. As the man whose sudden-death penalty miss had dumped England out of Euro 96 when they seemed destined to win, his story looked like individual as well as national redemption.

And for me there was a personal dimension to Southgate's appointment: as a Palace player he'd been well known to me and Dan since the early Nineties, and you couldn't wish to see a nicer bloke rise to take the Three Lions' throne. Little did we know then how far his team would go in 2018 and 2021. Or how far over the bar Harry Kane's penalty would go in 2022.

If England heading in the right direction was an unusual feeling, watching from the opulence of the One Twenty super-sized it. I wouldn't be human if I'd gone through the afternoon without thinking, 'I could get used to this', even though I knew I never would. The unreality of the day was at its sharpest as David and I made the short walk back to the railway station. We were assimilated into a host of fans being slowly funnelled into columns separated by steel fences. Queues A and B for London, C and D for destinations to the north. We were about to join the first line and take the 'A' train when we noticed an extra signpost at the far end of the concourse: 'Queue E'. And it was ours. Because Club Wembley members don't just get a private train *to* the ground; they get one back home again too. This added benefit was so ridiculous it made a mockery of the word 'queue', as David and I breezed past the thousands of fans who'd come armed with only an Oyster card, and got waved straight through by stewards along an empty, cordoned-off VIP path. With the opposite platform chock-full of waiting fans, we boarded an emptyish chartered service and took our final taste of the red-carpet treatment. The phrase 'wrong side of the tracks' came to mind, as did the question: which side were we on? What I knew for sure was that in the twenty-first century one thing hasn't changed. Football is still a game of two halves. It's just that the halves are getting less equal all the time.

Watching sport through affluent eyes was by a distance my most unfamiliar day out at Wembley, overtaking its transformation into the home of the Cincinnati Bengals, and the sight of my mum at an FA Cup Final. Astonishing as it was to have infiltrated the sacred order of the One Twenty, though, over the course of that weekend international football was merely the support act. Just the night before I'd been to a bigger staging post in my emotional journey, at a place where the words 'elite' and 'elitism' couldn't have been further out of mind. This was a sport that used to be a regular fixture at the old incarnation of Wembley, but had noticeably been expunged from the rebuilt amphitheatre. Now our local venue was about to be removed from the landscape as well. The date would have been etched in Daniel Harvey's diary for months in advance, and he'd have made sure it was kept clear in mine too. Because it was now or never. The Last Night of the Wimbledon Greyhound Stadium.

Saturday, 25 March 2017: Greyhound Racing

Wimbledon Greyhound Stadium. Even the name is loaded, because 'stadium' is putting it strongly. This ramshackle old rust bucket is so trashy, it's a wonder the Wombles hadn't already shown up and ransacked it. It was Dan's favourite place to spend his birthday: within our budgets and offering the chance to have a sit-down meal and watch sport at the same time. We could even place bets without leaving the table. It ticked every box. This landmark of our lives, a fixture in south London since 1928, was about to be razed to the ground after one final night of action. It was a sell-out, and I had to be there.

As a family we'd been coming to this place on and off since the mid-Eighties, and even then its glory days had long since passed. Had it ever looked brand new? It was hard to fathom the idea that even on its construction this wasn't a dog-eared dog track. So rickety and entrenched in decay, one kick at its corrugated iron walls looked liable to collapse the whole thing like a house of cards. As much as I wanted to reconnect with memories of my brother, on seeing this crumbling wreck again I had to accept that it was due its date with the diggers. Soon it would be replaced by a modern complex mixing retail, housing and a new ground for AFC Wimbledon, returning the club back to its spiritual home on Plough Lane. It was nice to know the developers wanted the area to retain an association with sport – so why ruin it by giving it to the Dons? (Dan would certainly have opined.) This unfashionable relic of Dan's life had outlived him by nearly two years, and to have such a physical symbol of the past stubbed out was adding a new dimension to grief. Time was stamping on a memory.

Most racegoers, us included, don't tend to call it greyhound racing. They call it going to the dogs. And in the course of my lifetime that's exactly where this sport has gone. It's a hell of a turnaround from 1946 when, according to Wikipedia (and who am I to quibble?), attendances peaked at around 70 million for the year, with as many as 250 tracks across Britain, and the Tote betting service turning over (a surprisingly specific) £196,431,430. Wimbledon was arguably the most elite venue of all, and since 1985 had hosted the annual Greyhound Derby, the sport's biggest race. Of course, any comparison between this event and its equine Epsom equivalent ended with the name, and the only king or queen you'd see here were of the pearly variety. When I was a kid, the dogs were an established fixture in the sporting firmament, but in the last few decades this form of recreation has eroded away to almost nothing. In London alone, tracks have disappeared from Hackney Wick, Catford, Wembley, Harringay and Walthamstow (the latter memorialised in the cover art for Blur's album, *Parklife*) and at the time of writing only 19 registered tracks remain in existence, with none in Wales or Northern Ireland. Is it a coincidence that this industry has declined in an era that's seen a marked growth in concerns for animal welfare? Surely they're not unconnected. I wanted to believe that the canine stars of the show were well looked after – I think Dan convinced himself that they were – but it was hard to be certain. Perhaps the number one reason why greyhound racing was never banned is

because there's no need. With countless more glamorous entertainment options on offer these days, and the prize money for
some races tonight being just a few hundred quid, the once-
famous tracks are being snuffed out by market forces. And
their loss is broadly unlamented. It's a sport that's quietly being
brushed under the carpet.

That fateful Saturday Wimbledon harked back one last time
to its pomp. Over 3,000 willing punters turned up on a whim,
with hundreds refused entry owing to fears of overcrowding.
Here was a curious and eternal aspect of human (and canine)
behaviour: all it takes is being told you can't do something to
immediately create the urge to do precisely that. Pretty much
every one of my dozen or so previous visits had been to celebrate Dan's birthday, and in his stead, tonight I was joined by
Tom and James, to celebrate the latter turning thirty-eight. The
three of us have a long tradition of trying to choose unusual
gifts for each other, and James's treat this year was a night out
at the dogs. Fearing that this was a bit of a measly present, Tom
and I pulled out all the stops and threw in a Nick Clegg novelty
face mask for good measure. As a symbol of something controversial fading into irrelevance, it seemed to suit the occasion.

Twilight was falling as we arrived, the queue to get in already
hundreds deep. Our advance tickets – a princely £7 each –
allowed us to bypass the long line of waiting punters and head
straight through the turnstiles. Who needs the One Twenty
Club? But believe it or not, it wasn't all glamour. With its shabby
car park and hand-painted signs, this was a place that made the
Lakeside Country Club look smart. The grandstand – 'grand'
being a euphemism for 'only' – was a small concrete terrace
running the length of the home straight, dotted with independent bookmakers, all called John or Ron and togged up in thick
coats and peaked caps, fingering bundles of cash. They were a
salutary reminder before we placed any bets that, just as with
any gambling, the house tends to win.

Above the stand was the restaurant, insulated from the cold

by a giant wall of glass, affording top-priced ticket holders a perfect view while they wined and dined the night away. Dad used to tell me this was where the nouveaux riches of south London liked spending their cash, and as evidence claimed he'd spotted Vinnie Jones there a couple of times and once stood next to Frankie Howerd in a lift. ('They're all in!') On our more recent visits you couldn't fail to sense a place in decline: the restaurant fare gradually came to resemble a school canteen and more than once we were served by Maureen, an elderly Irish waitress with hair as grey as the meat, who'd tend to have her thumb resting in the gravy as she brought the main course. The saving grace was always the puddings, a selection of unreconstructed 1980s classics starring Black Forest gateau and ice cream sundaes large enough to make an American blush. Even into his forties this simple pleasure still made Dan smile. The feast wasn't just the food but also the nostalgia.

Tonight I could only gaze up at the restaurant for those memories. We'd booked too late to get a table, and our tickets allowed access only to the lower indoor level. It might have been just a flight of stairs further down, but the gap was a chasm. If Dante was looking to add a mezzanine to his first circle this long, beige, dimly lit hall would more than do the trick. It contained a couple of betting kiosks, some fruit machines and a takeaway joint called 'Food to Go', which was an honest appraisal of what their meals would make you need to do soon after. By far the saddest element was over in the far corner, where seven retired greyhounds were sprawled on a pile of filthy tartan blankets, for racegoers to give these veteran heroes a friendly pat and, ideally, a few quid for some biscuits. All were asleep bar one, who was staring at the neon-lit ceiling with a weary expression that seemed to ask, '*Why?*' #Sadnessinhiseyes.

The room did at least offer some much-needed respite from the cold (another similarity with Hell), but we did our best to stay outside on the terracing because that's where the action was, and the atmosphere too. The stand was packed with racegoers chatting, drinking and gambling their way through tonight's twelve-race card. The build-up to each chase would begin with a cheesy fanfare bawling out of the tinny PA system, heralding a parade of the six runners. Each dog would be led past us by a steward dressed in a white coat, giving them the unfortunate look of butchers collecting ingredients for tomorrow night's Sausage Surprise.

Once the contenders were installed in their starting traps – a battered metal contraption that, with Alan Partridge levels of naffness, was sponsored by the 'Tiger Loans Company' (for people who Shere Khan't pay their bills?) – a bell would ring and the restaurant lights would flash off and on. The stadium announcer would call, *'Here comes the bunny!'* and on cue an electrified fake rodent would begin zooming around the far wall. As soon as it passed the traps, a slam of rising gates would unleash the pack.

Greyhounds are astonishing animals: slender, sleek and single-minded. Hare-seeking torpedoes. Most of the races were flat-out sprints, but dotted through the card were a few hurdles contests, enabling us to see not just these athletes' speed but also how they could spring and glide through the air. It was a beautiful sight, and I could only hope they were enjoying it as much as it seemed. My friends certainly were. James studied the form guide in a way to make Dan proud, as if it bore any relevance as to what was going to happen, carefully calculating which canine to put his precious £2 on. In the headline result, hot favourite and track record holder Razldazl Raidio was beaten by outsider Kakantu at odds of 10–1, an enormous price in greyhound racing, earning a £2,000 prize pot for his owners. And twenty quid for James, his only win of the night. (A feeling he describes as being up there with the birth of his son.)

The final race ever to be staged at Wimbledon was played out to rambunctious encouragement from the capacity crowd, with first place taken by the appropriately named Glitzy King, whose reign as a Wimbledon winner would never be usurped.

Once the action was over, some fans climbed over the barriers and wandered onto the track – not an ecstatic pitch invasion like Headingley '81 or Silverstone '92, more a slightly drunken meander in a spirit of, 'Sod it. Might as well.' One lamenting spectator tied a bunch of flowers to a post in respect for what this stadium had provided over the last 89 years. And not just for the greyhound industry. The arena held a small place in British rock music lore as the location for the video to Queen's song 'Bicycle Race', and for decades it had been home to speedway and stock car racing, two other lesser-loved sports that used to feature in the odd clip on TV here and there (usually in blooper compilation shows) but which have all but vanished from visibility, save for the odd wreck of a banger you see being towed down the motorway on its way from (or, more worryingly, to) a race.

Just like in January, when I'd witnessed the dying embers of the BDO World Darts Championship, on this spring night I found myself passing through the final spluttering of a once-cherished occasion as time, tastes and the tyranny of choice conspired to wash it all away. I was seven months into my voyage through sport, and I hadn't expected it to involve so much cultural archaeology, or to resonate so much with the loss I was still struggling to stomach. Dan wouldn't have missed this night for the world. He'd have loved every race, every last soggy chip, and patted the stadium wall on our way out. (Which might have sent the whole thing keeling over.) He'd have shed a tear that they'd tear down this old shed.

In the course of putting into words the strange death of this mainstay of my brother's life, recently I turned to YouTube for a reminder of the stadium in its last days, and clicked on an interview filmed in 2016 with a retired greyhound owner named Bob. Standing by the Wimbledon track and clutching a race programme, a morose Bob gives the camera his top greyhound gambling tip: 'It's always best to back a dog that's named after a family member, somebody you know.' He scans through a brochure: 'Race Five, "King Dan". Well, everybody knows a Dan.' On hearing that my jaw dropped. For my part, I hope Bob's right.

For most people Wimbledon means tennis, but for me and Dan it had always been just as synonymous with dogs, and with the demolition has gone a small but significant part of my sporting life. Even though a few tracks still survive around the country, that Saturday night would always be my last night at the greyhounds. It was farewell to a pastime whose time was past.

That one weekend in March had sent me on a roller coaster, up into surreal levels of luxury and then down to the dingy death throes of a sport that put the 'Heel!' into down-at-heel. Two extremes of the sporting spectrum. And if it came to a choice, mad as it sounds, I'd pick the dogs. Dan's stone lay outside Wembley, but a bit of his soul was woven into Wimbledon Stadium. No wrecking ball could demolish that.

Just a week later, there was to be an intriguing coda to my brush with the elite end of sport and its opposite, as the sporting calendar wheeled around to a famous old fixture that mixed both.

Sunday, 2 April 2017: Rowing

Mirror, mirror, on the wall. Which sporting event is simultaneously the most exclusive and the most inclusive of them all? The answer is something that's free to watch, ticketless, and yet is the purest embodiment of how, even in the twenty-first century, the class system influences British sport. It's the Oxford and Cambridge University Boat Race.

There's a raw simplicity to the Boat Race. Two slim craft gliding over the Thames, cutting clean lines through the water as they charge from Putney to Mortlake; a quarter of a million spectators lining the river banks; sixteen ultra-fit humans straining every sinew to propel themselves to the finish line first. For me, one of the most powerful images in world sport occurs when, after seventeen lung-busting minutes of extreme exertion, the two crews crumple over in sheer exhaustion as they float gently under Chiswick Bridge at the end of the race. Everyone looks so distraught from the pain that for an instant it's hard to tell the winners from the losers.

The best contests in sport are often binary battles like this. For the competitors it's all or nothing; for fans, pick a side. But notwithstanding the chemistry of an ancient rivalry, this annual April duel for Oxbridge bragging rights is an odd one. Nothing else with quite such a high profile reeks so much of class. Sure, in terms of undiluted aristocratic action the Badminton Horse Trials or polo at the Hurlingham Club might take the luxury biscuit, but neither of those gets a primetime slot on BBC One. Nor have either of them been disrupted by a protester invading the course to protest against 'elitism', as happened at the Boat Race in 2012. (This was a complaint that lost some of its power when the intruder, named Trenton Oldfield, was revealed to have spelled out his credo in a rambling blog that encouraged cleaners to deprive right-wing professors of toilet paper.)

Here was the E word raising its head again, and nearly getting decapitated by an oar in the process. But despite that, the Boat Race is also a people's race. That's certainly how Dan felt about it. He had no personal varsity connection, and he didn't see himself as an Oxford (aka Dark Blue) fan just because his little brother was lucky enough to study there. As if I needed any proof of where his allegiance lay, back in 2005 he opted not to come to my graduation day because it clashed with Palace playing Manchester United at Selhurst Park. (The game turned out to be a goalless snoozefest, by the way, but he'd still picked the more entertaining way to spend a Saturday afternoon.) The Boat Race was different. For Dan, it was top-level sport and that was all that mattered. The 2014 edition became one of the last events we ever went to together.

That year the race was staged on one of those freezing April afternoons when the British winter rudely gatecrashes spring. This suited Dan, who was the kind of Englishman who'd probably wear a puffer jacket to a tropical beach. But for me there was an emotional coldness in the air too, which no amount of clothes could combat. I'd been living only a matter of yards away from the Boat Race course, renting a small flat with my then-girlfriend of thirteen years, Sarah. The property sat in an unusual spot, sandwiched neatly between the beauty of Chiswick Eyot and the carcinogenic hellscape of the A4. But in a matter of weeks it would no longer be home. We'd recently decided to go our separate ways and were in the painful process of what Gwyneth Paltrow would call a conscious uncoupling. It was the only serious relationship I'd ever had, and for it to end was casting a shawl of sadness I wasn't used to. A different kind of grief. In those difficult days, Dan and his unquenchable love of sport kept me afloat more than anything. It was his idea to take advantage of where I was living and join the hordes of tourists and gilet-clad graduates on Boat Race day. He knew that going along could give me a boost, and his infectious enthusiasm swept away the fug of heartache. Wherever there was sport, Dan saw fun.

And there was plenty to be had that day on the Thames. The Boat Race is one of the silliest events you could ever hope to attend. The course is so long (at 4 miles and 374 yards), not even the prawn sandwich brigade can hope to see the start *and* the finish, unless they charter a chopper. So virtually everyone's viewpoint is likely to catch only a small portion of the race. In some long events like a five-day Test match or a golf tournament, a partial experience makes sense. But for a short race it's just barmy. The only logical way around this is to watch the rest of the action on a phone – a literal live stream – so that's what Dan and I did. But even doing that doesn't guarantee that you'll see any drama, because beyond deciding varsity bragging rights, each year's renewal brings with it a second binary question: will it be a decent contest? And often the answer is no. With just two teams navigating the meanders of the river, if one crew can establish more than a length's advantage they can hold the racing line and force their opponents to row through the turbulent water of their wake. If you concede a big lead in the Boat Race, it's almost certainly game over. There's no harder job in sports broadcasting than commentating on the Boat Race when the result is obvious after the first thirty seconds. Fortunately, since the turn of the millennium the number of close finishes has increased, including an astonishing epic in 2003 when Oxford squeaked home by only a foot.

2014, when I went with Dan, was not one of those years. This time the Dark Blues won by a massive eleven lengths, after a clash of oars damaged the Light Blue boat. It was the widest gap between the crews since 1973, if you don't include the 1978 race when Cambridge sank. (And Dan totally would include that, because it's funny.) So, depending on how you see it, either we'd watched one of Oxford's greatest victories, or one of the dullest ever races. Well, we'd watched a bit of the middle of it.

Three years on from that record-breaking day, I returned to the same spot by Chiswick Eyot on the north bank, close to my old flat, and a fair few flat memories to boot. But those were subsumed by joy. *Dan's* joy. The weather obliged and, far from the chill of last time, all around me people were in shirtsleeves beneath a Constable-like cloudscape of greys, whites and blues. The local pubs were doing a roaring trade in pints, Pimm's and pies, and had laid on exclusive outdoor seating areas for the deep-pocketed visitor (prawn sandwich, anyone?). I looked out on the becalmed water and imagined the people it must have transported down the centuries: Romans and Normans, kings and queens, Shakespeare and Cromwell, Churchill and Beckham . . .

One thing that hadn't changed since my visit with Dan was the make-up of the crowd thronging the towpath: plenty of sports fans, but many more who were just tourists here for the carnival spirit. 'How many boats are there?' the woman standing next to me politely asked her friend. That might sound naive to aficionados, but her question got right to the nub of the event, and in more ways than one. For a start it pointed at the ludicrously archaic nature of the rivalry. Dan used to love quoting the 1980s comedian Richard Digance on his confusion at Oxford and Cambridge always getting to the final. In the twenty-first century you might think such a closed duel between two ancient educational institutions bears as much relevance to the nation as the Eton versus Harrow cricket match. But the two universities themselves seem to have cottoned on to this, and over recent decades the nature of the contest has subtly shifted: nowadays the personnel in each boat combines promising undergraduates destined for future Team GB Olympic crews with a sprinkling of international talents, whose academic pursuits may or may not be a sideshow to their primary goal of winning a seat in a Blue boat. The event has morphed from a heroic battle between two crews of amateurs into a pseudo-professional target in a top rower's career. That would explain James Cracknell's decision to row for Cambridge at the grand old age of forty-six (though I'm sure he'd have been happy spending a year reading for a master's in Philosophy if he hadn't been selected). Is the Boat Race elitist? Probably. Is it elite? Definitely.

How many boats? For decades the media coverage gave the lie that no female students from either university have ever held an oar in anger. But the truth is very different. The women's Boat Race was founded back in 1927, when it took place on the River Isis in Oxford, not to universal approval. According to a report in *The Times*, 'large and hostile crowds gathered on the towpath' as men voiced their objection to women rowing. An annual female Oxbridge race was only held from 1964 (sooner at least than the Olympics, which took until Montreal 1976 to admit women) and it was as late as 2015 that the female event was moved to the same stretch of the Thames and the same day as the men's. The year after my last visit with Dan. It's incredible that parity took so long. It's dismal that Dan never got to see the event as it is now, and as it always should have been known: the Boat *Races*.

So the answer to that woman's highly pertinent question was *eight*: four head-to-head races, featuring the main and reserve boats for both sexes. It was another example of history moving on after my brother's death; of news he'd never get to hear; of sport he'd never get to see. I computed this and swallowed hard: the metaphor had been staring me in the face all afternoon. Water under the bridge.

When the races did finally come past us at Chiswick Eyot, I realised that even eight was a serious understatement. During each contest, as the pair of yellow slivers slid past us they were pursued by a flotilla of motorised support craft, churning the water behind them into angry white froth. Leading the chase would be the umpire's boat, from which the official would issue megaphone blasts towards any crew guilty of aggressive steer-ing; this sounded particularly odd when he had to warn Oxford's reserve boat, causing him to scream '*Isis!*' at the top of his lungs. In the men's race, refereed by the great Matthew Pin-sent, Oxford edged a close contest by 1¼ lengths, but after a disastrous start their Dark Blue female counterparts were left for dead by Cambridge, who sped away to record another mammoth 11-length whipping. With the reserve boat spoils being shared, the overall result was a 2–2 draw, something that only three years earlier would have been an impossible result, and worth celebrating for that fact alone. Of course, I only found this out by looking at my phone. This will always be a peculiar sporting event for the fact that the closer you get, the less you end up watching. But you get to see a lot more too.

The Wembley top table, Wimbledon greyhounds and the Boat Races. Three events that within a week had sent me criss-crossing the capital more than a mayoral candidate in an election campaign. Separated by only a few miles and days, and yet worlds apart. All of them spoke to a piece of Dan's passion, and together they were giving me good practice. In sport, the more you do something the better you get, and so it was proving with grief. I was learning all the time about the balance between mourning and celebration. It was just as well, because coming up next was one of the biggest challenges of all.

The entrance to Wimbledon Greyhound Stadium, on its last ever race night

12

National Treasure

In many walks of life, there's a single point in the year that dominates the calendar. One weekend that eclipses all others. For festivalgoers it's Glastonbury at the end of June. For the showbiz world it's Oscars time in February or March. But if you're a sports fan, in the plural sense of loving lots of different sports, there's a good chance that your magic moment comes around in the second weekend of April.

Let's look at the menu. To begin with you've got some traditional classics: the Masters golf at Augusta and the FA Cup semi-finals, occasionally joined by the Boat Races too (if they haven't already taken place the week before). Then there are the specials, a slew of unfixed options which will happen to fall at this time: in 2017 these included another rugby union clash at Wembley between Harlequins and Saracens, and the Artistic Gymnastics World Cup. (Artistic gymnastics is the insanely difficult one with the beam and the pommel horse and Simone Biles; as opposed to rhythmic gymnastics, which is the insanely difficult one with the ribbons.) As if all that wasn't enough, there was a near-full Premier League programme too, with Spurs playing Watford at home. It's enough to make Radio 5 Live explode like Mr Creosote, showering the airwaves in engorged lumps of sport. Even if the gymnasts are *wafer*-thin.

There's no particular reason why so many huge events collide in this single weekend of wonderment, but mid-April is one of sport's sweet spots. And for millions of people in Britain and around the world, the Grand National tops the lot. This epic 4-mile-3-furlong marathon around Aintree's famous course is often dubbed the ultimate test for horse and rider, and one need only look at the career of Sir Tony ('AP') McCoy for proof. Twenty times a champion jockey he may be, but it was only by winning the National in 2010 – at his fifteenth attempt – aboard Don't Push It that he was catapulted to the coveted status of BBC Sports Personality of the Year. It's the one annual occasion which for Daniel Harvey meant everything else in life stopped. Nothing could trump it; not even a Palace home game.

It's the World's Greatest Steeplechase, the People's Race, and one of the oldest sporting contests in the world, dating back to 1839. And it completes the jigsaw puzzle of what made Dan tick. Crystal Palace was his long-term constant obsession; the Olympics were a quadrennial fortnight of fireworks; this was his annual spectacular. Palace. The Olympics. The National. The three legs to Dan's stool. Even more than his birthday or Christmas, Grand National Day was the date in the diary when Dan was at his happiest. Negotiating it without him promised to be the hardest single obstacle to be cleared. My own Becher's Brook.

As with the mighty sixth fence itself, there was no way around it. But that was OK. To my surprise I found myself not dreading the arrival of the big day. Dan had piled far too much love into this occasion for that to be possible. In fact, I was eager for it. Once I'd started out on creating an all-sports season ticket, a trip to the Grand National was the first thing on my shopping list. Horse racing was the only sport other than football Dan ever left London to see. Now its showpiece was rolling over the horizon and, for the first time in a long time, I felt the warmth of wanting a day to come around. This was going to be special. It needed to be. And as with the FA Cup Final the previous May, there was only one person to take with me on the ride: Mum. Together we set out to retrace one of Dan's most treasured journeys, from one unlovely English suburb to another: South Croydon to Aintree.

Saturday, 8 April 2017: Horse Racing

The train took three hours of chugging to reach Liverpool but, in a rarity for the West Coast Mainline, it felt quicker. Because there was business to be done. We'd begun the day exactly how Dan would have done, by marching straight to a newsagent and arming ourselves with half a dozen newspapers spanning tabloids, broadsheets and the *Racing Post*. This was a practical step for me and Mum, as we hadn't yet chosen any horses to back and could spend the rail trip rooting through the sports sections for the runners and riders. Dan, on the other hand, would have picked his favourites long before National day and already put money on them to take advantage of their longer pre-race odds. (On race day he'd then place more money on them, at shorter odds, which is something I'll never understand.) As ever, he lived by his own logic, and he'd want to pore over every piece of Grand National punditry he could get his hands on. Whichever horse anyone in our family plumped for, Dan would be able to spit out random gobbets of trivia he'd soaked up in the previous few weeks. Was it a mare? Was it twelve years old? Harshly treated in the weights by the handicapper? He'd have known. This time we were on our own.

Not everyone on our train was feeling so studious. A stag party was on its way to Aintree too, and we could hear the groom-to-be and his mates chanting from two carriages away. The guard checking our tickets shook his head at the noise and, in a melodic Scouse twang, said, 'They're already onto their second pack of Peroni and it's only half-nine. I don't know what all the fuss is about,' he added. 'It's just a couple of horses going over a couple of fences.'

Not to us. Mum and I had a duty to do and horses to pick. Most newspapers title their Grand National pull-outs 'A Pinsticker's Guide', and with good reason: whatever any expert tipster advises you, life has told me there's no science to it whatsoever. As if to make the point, the first ever winner back in 1839 was called Lottery. My bespoke method involved four factors: the horse's name, the jockey on board, the colours of the owners' silks and, following Dan's lore, to think about 'what the story' might be. ('Remember' – every year without fail he'd turn to me, saying with the same gnomic look and eyebrows raised – 'there's always a story, bro.') What he meant was that there's often a fairytale aspect to the victor: it could be that the jockey was a last-minute replacement for a colleague who'd broken a collarbone in a heavy fall the day before, or the horse was a grey, or it was owned by a madcap comedian (as Miinnehoma was by Freddie Starr in 1994), or it was won by an amateur jockey in his last ever race, as Sam Waley-Cohen did in 2022. Anything. With all that in mind, the first challenger I alighted on this year was Wonderful Charm, ridden by Katie Walsh, because I had a hunch that a female jockey would soon win the race; then I chose One For Arthur, just because I liked the name and – in an arcane fact Dan had drummed into me – a Scottish-trained horse had won the National only once: Rubstic in 1979 – so maybe it was time again. Satisfied with this randomness, I ringed both names in Biro.

But my job was only half done. Now I had to work out which runners Dan would have chosen, so I could put a bet on in his honour. This was a breeze. Without a shadow of a doubt he'd have first plumped for Pleasant Company, helmed by Katie Walsh's champion brother Ruby, who'd conjured up two National winners for Dan in the past (Papillon in 2000 and Hedgehunter in 2005), leading bro to back him every year without fail. Then he'd have also picked Highland Lodge, whose colours of pink silks topped by a purple cross matched those of Dan's favourite ever horse, a giant called Party Politics who conquered Aintree in 1992. It wasn't lost on me that right now, two years on from his death, Dan's precise thoughts were living on in my head through the milieu of a horse race. It was a strangely wonderful charm: to feel my brother's flame flickering the brightest yet since he'd gone.

This famous old landmark in the National Hunt calendar would never have been a key day for our family if it hadn't been for Dan. He didn't just love the race. He lived and breathed it, and throughout his life he mounted a concerted campaign to cram every crumb of trivia he could find about it into his little brother's head. Seeing as I still know the name of every winner during my lifetime right back to 1980, you did your work well, big brother. Very well. And that was just the tip of the iceberg. Random National facts continue to rattle around my head, like Bob Champion battling back from cancer to ride Aldaniti to victory in 1981, or Jenny Pitman becoming the first female trainer to win the race in 1983 with Corbière, or 1996-winning jockey Mick Fitzgerald telling the world on live TV that the experience was 'better than sex' – which became the title of his autobiography. All this and much more.

Most of it is the kind of stuff that's common knowledge among the sport's fans. But what marked Dan out from the crowd is that as well as the usual minutiae he used to spin his own mythology, which he'd then impart to me. Things like 'the Grittar Nod', for instance, were recounted by Dan on an annual basis. For the uninitiated (as in, everyone), this refers to the victorious horse in the 1982 race, Grittar, who – in a clip that occasionally got replayed on *Grandstand* – decided to celebrate his triumph in the winner's enclosure by clonking an unfortunate man on the head with his chin. Dan warped my view of the Grand National so much that, in writing this chapter, I had to search 'Grittar Nod' online to see if it is commonly known history or one of Dan's own factoids. In fact, it's a rare example these days of a Googlewhack – which means an online search reveals that nobody else in the world is on record as ever having written about it. Finding this out was a bit like emerging into the light after decades spent locked in a madman's basement. For me as a kid, the 1982 Grittar Nod was as basic as knowing that the Battle of Hastings was in 1066. My childhood was weird.

Dan was aided and egged on in his indoctrination efforts by the BBC, who played a considerable role in cementing the race in the nation's affections, and whose *Grandstand* programme invariably came live from Aintree on the day itself. Presenter Des Lynam clearly relished this yearly shindig, resplendent in a cream trench coat as he interviewed race-going celebrities and indulged in a sparky annual flirt with Jenny Pitman. But there was more to the Beeb's coverage than Uncle Des. As with so many sports, the action itself was inextricable from the unmistakable timbres of the commentators, and for the National this meant Peter O'Sullevan's iconic plummy holler, supported by his husky, unheralded accomplice John Hanmer. The choice of camera angles was a masterstroke too – always climaxing with an astonishing head-on shot of the field as they charged down to Becher's Brook. Perhaps more than anything, the BBC did what it always did so well with British sport in those formative times: it created the soundtrack.

Whoever chose the music that introduced coverage of sport back then deserves every gong going, because it doesn't matter whether you're into Formula One, cricket, tennis, snooker or skiing, you name it, one of the first things a Brit thinks of is the theme tune. For the Grand National, the Beeb picked three particular pieces and played them throughout race day pretty much on a loop, inflicting on me and Dan the mother of all earworms. One we recognised as the stirring overture from *Robin Hood: Prince of Thieves* (it plays during the opening credits of Kevin Costner's hilariously enjoyable cod-epic, over history-mangling shots of the Bayeux Tapestry). But the other two were a maddening mystery to us and, in an age before the Internet or apps like Shazam, we had to endure decades of being unable to identify them. In desperation we even wrote to the BBC asking them to spill the beans, but they never got back to us. For the sake of completeness, which by now you'll know was *very* Dan, they were the theme tune to *Champions* (a John Hurt-starring biopic of the Aldaniti story) and Ennio Morricone's plaintive

'Gabriel's Oboe', the most elegiac of the three and the piece we chose as the opening music at Dan's funeral. I should add that, after the heresy of the Channel 4 years, ITV recently brought back the old music, as well as the 'correct' angle for Becher's Brook. Dan would have been delighted, although he'd still have mocked them for misspelling the seventh fence, Foinavon, in the middle of the race. Unforgivable.

My first memory of the fraternal propaganda campaign inflicted on me for the National goes back to 1986. We were on a family shopping trip to Sainsbury's, and this six-year-old was innocently browsing the desserts aisle. But my mission of choosing that night's pudding was being thwarted by Dan, who was bombarding me with facts and stats about runners and riders. Which horses had I chosen? He made it seem so crucial that I can still reel off the names: Imperial Black, because he sounded like something out of *Star Wars*, and West Tip, as I liked the name and his blue colours. Dan laughed, because he'd backed the latter the previous year only to see him fall at Becher's on the second circuit. That all meant nothing to me, but as far as Dan was concerned I'd entered into a sacred contract. He must have checked three or four times to see if I'd changed my mind, which would have been fine except we were still in Sainsbury's, and he was putting me off choosing a yoghurt.

When race day came along a week later, Dad put a 50p bet on each horse we'd picked, and Imperial Black ended up being about as useful as the average storm trooper. But in a nail-biting finish West Tip pipped Young Driver to come home in first place. I'd picked the winner at the first time of asking! (Beginner's luck, sadly: my strike rate since then had totalled three out of thirty.) A magnificent £6 now belonged to me, which was more cash than I'd ever owned before. Of course, Dad being Dad, I never saw the money.

The novel element in all this was me. Dan's adoration of the National pre-dated my existence by a long stretch. He'd got bitten by the Aintree bug in the Seventies, being just the right age to get caught up in the fairytale heroics of Red Rum, who won the race an unprecedented three times in 1973, 1974 and 1977. As if that wasn't enough, in each of the intervening two years 'Rummy' finished second too. Many racing experts credit him with single-hoovedly saving the race, which had been suffering from falling attendances, waning public interest and a crumbling venue. Dan's interest in racing started with the great race but went beyond it too, with both the Cheltenham Gold Cup and the Derby also featuring on his radar. He even squirreled out some addictive horse-based computer games which together we spent far too many hours playing. Best of the lot was a simulator called *Sport of Kings*, which – it would be banned today – introduced a nation's Sinclair Spectrum-playing kids to the thrill of gambling. He also found a Grand National arcade game, in which you had to take the role of a jockey trying to navigate the fiendish course. It was almost impossible to play this without causing your horse to crash into a fence or collapse from exhaustion, making it quite possibly the most realistic Spectrum game ever made.

It was typical of Dan that the single event he adored above all others should be the one that has courted perhaps the most controversy in the whole of British sport. It's one of those things that everyone's heard of, but these days it's harder to know if liking it is OK. Like The Smiths. Though Red Rum saved the race in the Seventies, jeopardy has never been far away from the National. In 1993 the race became a laughing stock when Aintree's antiquated starting system caused a series of false starts, leading to a herd of runners tackling the entire course in the mistaken belief that the race was on. First to finish was Esha Ness, whose forty-year-old jockey Jon White was a picture of agony as he peeled the goggles off his mud-spattered face and realised the living nightmare of winning the race that never was. After that self-inflicted pantomime, the National seemed to experience another crisis every four years, as regular as a World Cup. In 1997 the entire meeting was abandoned when an

IRA bomb threat forced an evacuation of the course, with the big race being defiantly held two days later. Then in 2001, faced with mud bath conditions worthy of the trenches (or Glastonbury), a joint-record low of four horses managed to finish. What's more, two of those had already fallen, with their jockeys somehow managing to remount and plough on. (I didn't know that was in the rules.)

Dan's brainwashing programme had a long-lasting effect on me. My computer hard drives and USB sticks are named after National winners, and in 2011, as a Christmas present, I took Dan to Aintree so we could watch the race together for real. It was the only overnight holiday the two of us ever took, a fact that shames me as I write it, but which is emblematic of how complex our family life used to be. What's stayed with me from that trip is how happy Dan was back then; how ablaze his enthusiasm; how unthinkable that he had only four years to live. On the eve of the race we stayed in Chester and went out for dinner – it wasn't exactly posh but it was several league divisions up from the microwaved Rustlers burgers that were too often Dan's standard evening fare. Treating ourselves to a meal in a restaurant, just the two of us, was a rare occasion, so rare I'll always flagellate myself for not making it happen more. We chatted about politics, comedy, and of course sport, and I quizzed him about the secret of his sudden success at picking National winners three times in a row at the start of the Nineties. Was it a complete accident that 1990 coincided with the year he turned eighteen and so could legally go into betting shops on his own? And had he put money on half the field to ensure victory? *Or more than half?* Dan said nothing, but flashed a wide smile that said everything. It's a twinkling of happiness I'll always grab onto: my brother's joie de vivre and cheekiness, frozen in a memory.

He was also fitter back then, even though with Dan that was always a relative statement. Despite being overweight he was energised by Aintree, and more than happy expending shoe leather trekking up and down the course, standing inside the ditch at Becher's Brook and visiting every historical artefact on display, from Red Rum's grave to a glass case containing the winning blue silks worn by Richard Dunwoody when he steered West Tip home in '86. (The finest National of all, obviously.) Then, using all his canniness, Dan somehow wangled us a spot in the front row of the crowd right underneath the winning post, the greatest place in the world to watch the World's Greatest Steeplechase. Neither of us picked the winner that year (Ballabriggs, ridden by Jason Maguire) – me because I'm rubbish at it, and Dan possibly because I could keep an eye on how many horses he was backing – but we could both live with the failure. That sunny Saturday in 2011 had been one of the most enjoyable days we ever spent together. Before it was over Dan was already heading to a bookies, to check the odds for next year.

Six years on, and with my world turned upside down, I was leading Mum to Aintree just as Dan had led me. It was only as we stepped out of the taxi to join the droves flocking towards the main gates that I realised I'd made a silly mistake. Over the last few months, attending sports events had become so regular that I'd become locked on sartorial autopilot. T-shirt and jeans. Here that was a big mistake. To the people of Merseyside, Grand National Day meant a lot and you have to credit them for the kaleidoscopic colours, ostentatious designs and vertigo-inducing heels that were out on display. Mum, in a smart but understated spring jumper, looked at me askance and asked why I hadn't told her in advance there was a dress code. Somehow, despite coming here before, it had totally slipped my mind what being at the National was actually like. At least she still looked presentable. The bigger victim of this oversight was me: in a rush to get dressed, I'd grabbed whatever was at the top of my T-shirt drawer, which was a top featuring a screenshot from the old Spectrum computer game *Jet Set Willy*. What I looked like was something similar, minus the Jet Set.

Before the action got started, Mum and I spent time retracing the steps I'd taken here with Dan four years earlier, including a walk of the course and a visit to Red Rum's last resting place. His grave was furnished with fresh flowers and a horseshoe-shaped wreath, on which a dedication read, *'Forty years on, you're still watching over the winners. The Le Mare Family.'* Grief and remembrance can manifest themselves in all kinds of ways, and one fan had even laid a packet of Polos as an offering to Rummy's ghost. Sugar-free, the spoilsports. This was an especially eerie landmark to return to, given what had transpired in the years in between. I'd never expected to be back here like this.

A further link to the past was the annual parade of former National winners, stretching back fifteen years to the 2002 victor Bindaree. Here were retired athletes as impressive as any I'd been lucky enough to see in the flesh, and among them two of Dan's favourite superstars, Hedgehunter and Don't Push It. Both of them had brought him oodles of glee, and a modest amount of cash into the bargain. This caravan of victorious horses offered an equine Rolodex to my life: thanks to my brother, for any year I can remember what I was doing on Grand National Day. Amid the turbulence of bereavements, illnesses, break-ups, family crises and more, this race and these animals have provided something of a comfort blanket. An increasingly uncomfortable one, it must be said, given the hazardous nature of the race and how childhood innocence has given way to conflicted emotions about it. I couldn't avoid noticing, for instance, that the 2015 winner Many Clouds was missing from the parade: he'd died in January, collapsing from a pulmonary haemorrhage immediately after winning another race. Whisper it, but my brother's wasn't the only death that hung in the Aintree air.

Mum and I wove our way through the Tattersalls enclosure and wiggled our way through the crowds until we were able to situate ourselves at the same spot beneath the winning post where I'd watched the big race last time with Dan. Hours still to go. But worth it to get prime position. There we watched the undercard races before Laura Wright, still Britain's top-seeded soprano, kicked off the pre-National festivities with a rendition of 'God Save the Queen'.

'She's got a good job, ain't she?' a Scouse racegoer behind me muttered to a friend. 'Three lines of a nursery rhyme and she's off.'

Speaking of off, I figured that before the full pageantry of the occasion got underway was a good opportunity to nip away for a comfort break, and I was on my way back to the enclosure when a pair of besuited women stopped me. 'Ticket, please.'

I produced my crumpled printout.

'That doesn't allow you access, sir,' proclaimed one of the stewards as they closed a barrier and locked me out of the area where Mum was waiting.

I tried to explain: I'd only just been in that section!

'Well, you shouldn't have been, sir.'

The truth dawned on me. Mum and I (just like Dan and I six years earlier) had got into our plum position by accidentally overreaching our status, sneaking in early before the security officials segregated the viewing areas to ensure only the more expensive ticket holders got the best views. The good news was it meant the Harvey family had cheated the system twice; the bad news was I'd come a cropper in the final furlong.

I pleaded with them that my poor Mum was now stuck on her own, with no phone reception and no doubt starting to worry what had happened to me. That cut no ice. Had I come this far to have the day ruined by my needy bladder and a pair of stewards?

There was only one card left to play. I told them about Dan and why I was here. Maybe the two women saw the sincerity in my face; in any case, their intransigence melted. One of them even accompanied me back to Mum, which I was grateful for, although she was probably just checking I wasn't trying to grift her: having reunited us and seen I was telling the truth, she looked as relieved as we were.

No sooner had my heart rate returned to normal than a band of buglers sent it soaring again, heralding the arrival of the runners and riders for the pre-race parade. From our prime vantage point we got to see every one of the contenders trotting past us, and as we peered at the beauty of the beasts, the odd one seemed to look back. Horses radiate intelligence, and I wondered how much they comprehend about the sport in which they are the unbridled – yet bridled – stars.

They certainly had a right to be peeved with how the humans were going about matters, as the race was delayed by not one but two false starts, to groans from the crowd. Were we about to witness a repeat of the 1993 disaster? Eventually, at the third time of asking, and to colossal approval, the 2017 National was away.

There's a visceral edge to this event unparalleled by any other sight or sound in mainstream sport: a cavalry charge of forty riders on horseback, with a rainbow of heraldic symbols emblazoned on their chests, tearing across the Liverpool turf. It's a spectacle redolent of epic battles from a heroic age: of Agincourt from the Middle Ages, or the Ride of the Rohirrim from Middle Earth. We saw them off as they headed out 'into the country' on the first lap, and then followed the action on a giant screen until, about four minutes later, the pack began approaching again from the far end of the home straight. By the time they swept past us to begin the second circuit, the field had inevitably shrunk. Near us, for instance, jockey Donagh Meyler's hopes ended at the Chair – at 5 ft 3 in the tallest of the fences – when he was ejected out of the saddle by his horse, the appropriately named MeasureOfMyDreams. Still, an impressive thirty-one runners had completed the first lap, and it was still almost anyone's race as they headed out to tackle the remainder.

Pleasant Company, carrying Ruby Walsh and Dan's posthumous support on his back, was having a terrific run until a mistake at Valentine's Brook checked his momentum. As for my picks, they were nowhere to be seen, and had gone unmentioned by the commentator ... until, with just two fences to jump, One For Arthur and Wonderful Charm both spurted to the front. At the final fence, they were disputing a five-way tussle for the lead. That was as good as it got for Katie Walsh, as Wonderful Charm's magic wore off and sent her backwards through the field for a valiant but last-place finish. Meanwhile, One For Arthur touched down from the last flight in the lead and made a dash for the line, exhorted by 70,000 fans. (Especially those with money on him.)

This was a very uncommon feeling for me: I was in with a shout of a win. However, as any seasoned Grand National watcher knows, it was far too early to be cracking open the bubbly. Aintree's notoriety doesn't end with its final fence but with a stamina-sapping run-in, known as the Elbow: 474 yards of track featuring an acute right-hand chicane. This is where hundreds of brave runners and riders have seen victory snatched away from them, most notably the Queen Mother's horse Devon Loch, who in 1956 inexplicably tripped when out on his own and with the finish line at his mercy. It's one of the most astonishing incidents in all racing, and it denied the royal family a famous win, although it didn't do jockey Dick Francis's publishing career any harm. (The title of almost every book he went on to write seemed to rue his fate: *Dead Cert, Nerve, Odds Against, Forfeit, Knockdown, Reflex, Come to Grief*, to name just a few.) Right now, the risk of throwing it away was One For Arthur's, as he was chased to the winning post by Cause of Causes, another prophetic name. With a place in history beckoning, young jockey Derek Fox strained his sinews with every gallop, body coiled and head arched downwards almost in prayer as he coaxed his mount to switch on the afterburners for one last push. The effort was enough to keep his challenger at bay, and we watched Fox and horse gallop past us with plenty of energy left in the tank to win it – just as O'Sullevan described Red Rum in 1977 – *like a fresh horse in great style*. It was a day that would be long remembered: for Scotland, for Lucinda Russell on becoming the fourth woman to train a winner, for twenty-four-year-old Derek, and for me, thanks to the sixty quid I was now richer by. With my predicting skills generally being so rubbish, it was particularly sweet to have picked a winner this of all years.

Racegoers were trickling towards the exits; at least, the ones who still had the motor skills to walk that far. Whatever the weather, National Day is a very thirsty affair. A couple near us had definitely overindulged: the man in a well-cut tartan suit with white bow tie, the woman in a floral summery dress, were leaning on one another as they sat slumped next to the bins. Mum and I knew the trains were going to be hellish, so we stayed for a while. A warm glow still seemed to sit upon Aintree, now bathed in early-evening gold.

Eventually One For Arthur was brought out for a trot on the turf that an hour or so ago he'd made his own. He was dressed in a winner's jacket and led by a stable hand on one side and jockey Derek on the other, with the owners following behind. Mum and I stepped onto the track and at an opportune juncture had a chance to congratulate Derek, who kindly posed with me for a photo. Being this close to Grand National glory, something Dan had cared so much about, had been unfathomable to me until now. In one sense it was just a couple of horses going over a couple of fences. In another it was just a lottery. But it was also sporting heroism.

The final word must go to the owners of One For Arthur, Deborah Thompson and Belinda McClung. They called themselves the Two Golf Widows partnership, having taken up racehorse owning as a reaction to their husbands' obsession, and in a little over nine minutes it had just seen them pocket £561,300: probably a touch more lucrative than their partners' golfing was ever likely to be. Mum and I watched them walk the course with their horse and jockey, enjoying their literal moment in the sun, and we caught one of them saying to the other, 'We've had a rather good day.'

Postscript

Five years after Dan's death, there was another hiatus in the long story of the Grand National, to be filed alongside wars and the false start fiasco of 1993. As with pretty much all top-level sport in the year 2020, it experienced a fall of its own due to the Covid-19 pandemic. But uniquely for a major event, there was some replacement action to watch in the meantime. ITV took the spirited decision to broadcast a 'virtual' Grand National instead, with advanced computer graphics creating an animation similar to the real thing and a sophisticated algorithm simulating the race itself. Bookies even took bets on it. The National is as random now as it was in 1839, so who knows if the computer got it right with its version of events, in which 18–1 shot Potters Corner romped home to victory? What I do know is that Dan would have counted the Virtual National in his own history books, and that he'd have been pretty much as keyed up for that lockdown approximation as he always was about the race proper. That raises a question in itself. Would it be better if the National was just simulated all the time?

It's a live question because the fact is, when it comes to the World's Greatest Steeplechase, there's an elephant in the room. Or should that be an elephant lying on the course covered in tarpaulin? A unique and unavoidable truth about this crown jewel of British sport is that a small number of its participants die. Nobody wants this to happen. The National isn't bull-fighting, and Aintree has taken multiple steps to improve the safety of the course for horse and rider while maintaining the formidable nature of the test. These are much-loved animals, and no owner wants to see a meet turn their horse into meat. And if you don't buy the welfare argument, cold market forces are at play too. A racehorse is worth a lot of money, and not even a millionaire wishes for six-figure sums of their cash to get carted off to the glue factory. But even so, barring the Isle of Man TT, the great race more than anything else in the British sporting calendar remains steeped in risk. When during the 2013 renewal the on-course commentator announced that every runner had cleared Becher's Brook, an immense hurrah rose from the stands. It was a sound that spoke to the fact that equine welfare is a concern in racegoers' minds, and yet it was an expression of relief that we all surely wish we didn't need to hear.

The racing industry doesn't make itself easy to love, either. In February 2021 a scandalous photo was made public of leading trainer Gordon Elliott sitting on top of a dead horse and making a 'peace' sign. It was a sickening, unimaginable sight that you might think would spell the end of a career in the sport. But what was his punishment? A fine of 50,000 euros and a ban so lenient he was able to field seven runners in the 2022 National. (If it was up to me I'd let him keep the 50,000, but only if the seven horses were allowed to sit on him, all at once, and pose for a photo.) This was the guy who only a couple of years earlier had been the toast of the racing world, having trained the incredible Tiger Roll to back-to-back victories in the National, the first horse to achieve the feat since Red Rum. But the horrific image of Elliott and the historic controversies around the Grand National combine to make me question whether, had it not been for Dan, I would ever have appreciated it. Or would I have recoiled from it as an increasing number of people do? I'll never know the answer. I don't begrudge anyone who feels no love for the race. For me, it's no longer the unalloyed fun I was introduced to as a kid. I even undertook a (highly unscientific) poll on my Twitter account and asked what people think of it. Here were the results:

A) I love it – 14 per cent
B) I don't mind it – 18 per cent
C) It's cruel – 39 per cent
D) Not bothered – 29 per cent

(112 votes)

While a simulation would be safer, at the same time there are some things a computer can never recreate. The virtual Grand National was a single race based upon real horses who would have taken part that year, forecasting how they'd fare on a real course. It wasn't a fictional set of animated characters on a fictional track like you see on TVs in betting shops, or the crude blocky sprites that Dan and I used to cheer on while playing Sport of Kings on the ZX Spectrum. No CGI company can match the sight and sound of forty thoroughbred chasers thundering over the Melling Road. And the Virtual National wasn't trying to be anything other than a stop-gap. A bit of lockdown escapism, when we all needed some of that. Without the real race, the world of sport wouldn't have been able to celebrate the stunning achievement of Rachael Blackmore, who became the first woman jockey to win the race in 2021, aboard Minella Times (fortunately, as with Katie Walsh in 2017, I put my money where my mouth was and backed her to do it). Most of all, I can't wholly extract myself from the beacon of joy that the Grand National was to my brother. It lit his happiness in a way few things in life ever did. He wanted nothing other than everyone to come back safe, horse and rider, and to win a few quid in the process, and he saw something unique about the Sport of Kings' biggest day. I can't begrudge him that either. There might be a darkness to its magic, but in the way it touched Dan it contained magic nonetheless.

Whatever I felt about the Grand National going forwards – and my sense of conflict isn't going away – on my return to Aintree, for one day at least I won a victory over myself. I loved big brother's favourite race.

13

Going to Pot?

Wembley. Twickenham. Aintree. By now I'd hopscotched my way through some of the biggest spectator venues in the land: Britain's answer to the Colosseum and our Circus Maximus. Now it was time for something completely different. I was standing outside one of the smallest stages for any major international tournament on the planet: the Crucible Theatre. Spring was building up to its apex over the May Day long weekend, when millions of Britons turn their attention to the prospect of a free day off. On the sporting calendar it means more than a mere bank holiday break: it means century breaks galore. Because it's time for the World Snooker Championship, and I'd ventured north from Croydon to Sheffield for my first real-life taste of it.

I was glad of the change of scene, as just twenty-four hours earlier I'd been witnessing Tottenham take a Wembley walloping (4–2) from Chelsea in the FA Cup semi-finals. Another year, another sniff of Spurs silverware gone for an early bath. Losing stung, like it always stings, but right now that agony, and the much deeper one, were being supplanted by the new sight before my eyes. I'd waited over thirty years for this.

Monday, 24 April 2017: Snooker

The piazza in front of the theatre glistened after a morning rinse of Yorkshire rain. Standing by the doorway was the topiarised figure of a snooker player arched over a hedgerow table. From the good watering it had enjoyed before midday I decided it must be a tribute to Alex Higgins, the game's original maverick and most notorious drunk. Rising high above it was a brutalist concrete bulk fronted with the famous Crucible name in shouty capitals. From sky to stone was a backdrop of overwhelming British greyness, but that didn't matter. It was still as spine-tingling a sight as any I'd yet encountered on my travels. I'd arrived at another of the Wonders of the Sporting World. The tiniest and cosiest one of the lot.

I love snooker. In many social circles, saying so somehow feels like a confession as much as a proclamation, what with the sport's staid image and the ever-lingering doubts posed in some quarters as to whether (like darts) it even counts as a sport at all. To the unenlightened, this fusty mutation from billiards might look like nothing more than a glorified board game: *Hungry, Hungry Hippos* without the fun, or the hippos. But for me it's one of the most endlessly fascinating sports ever devised, whether to watch or to play. Quite how such banal ingredients as balls, cues and pockets combine to such a satisfying effect is a mystery, but the battles of will and flourishes of skill that they engender make for mesmerising drama. A snooker table is a canvas on which can be painted infinite possibilities. (Maybe that's why Damien Hirst loves it?) To succeed on it requires everything from superhuman levels of concentration, extraordinary deftness of touch and laser-like precision to a mastery of tactics and a liquid-nitrogen temperament. Professional snooker players have the ability to bend Newtonian physics to their will. They're Jedi in tuxedos, with sabres made of ash instead of light.

At the same time, a curious quirk of this genteel sport is that for large parts of a game even the best player in the world is likely to be forced to do nothing but sit meekly in the corner of the arena. There they can't pass the time scrolling their phones or binge-watching box sets, but must simply stew over the mistake that has let their opponent in, while a TV audience of millions looks on. No other sport inflicts upon its stars such exquisite, personalised psychological torment as a matter of routine. Throw into a blender the brain power of chess, the ball skills of golf, the suspense of Hitchcock and the edginess of *Antiques Roadshow*, and that's snooker.

As for the Crucible, it might be small but in the nation's sporting landscape it looms massive. Every year the BBC pumps out hour upon hour of blessed free-to-air coverage of it, and in terms of minutes watched, snooker must be right up at the top in the graph of my sporting life. To be here now felt like a dream. I'd always assumed tickets were so hard to come by that I'd never even bothered to try. Only Dan's passion had given me the impetus; to connect with another cherished part of my past. As with the Grand National, the full list of Crucible winners is imprinted on my brain. It's the kind of trivia that can be pub quiz heaven, and dating poison. But the subject wasn't always so niche or uncool. Not so long ago this unexceptional-looking block of a theatre was nothing short of a celebrity factory, and it played host to one of the most watched events not just in sport but in UK television history.

The snooker volcano had been quietly smouldering in Sheffield since the late Seventies, but in 1985 it full-on erupted. That was the year two greats of the game – Steve 'Interesting' Davis and Dennis 'That Bloke with the Funny Glasses' Taylor – fought out the famous Black Ball Final, a fifteen-hour marathon that culminated in the most hair-raising of all denouements: the trophy and winner's cheque would go to whoever could hold their bottle and pot the tournament's last remaining ball. Only 980 lucky ticket holders were inside the Crucible for that totemic finale, but a third of the country's entire population (18.5 million viewers) tuned in to watch, a staggering figure that's still a record for a British broadcast after midnight. My family were five of them, and the climax of that match is my first memory of watching live sport.

From that point on, Dan and I were entranced by snooker. And we weren't the only ones. That nail-biting showdown captivated a generation, and catapulted the game from smoky pubs and working men's clubs into the big time. Throughout the Eighties and into the Nineties, top players routinely became A-list celebrities and could be seen recording pop singles, releasing themed aftershaves, appearing in pantomimes and invading mainstream TV, ending up with their own long-running game show, *Big Break*. In 1988 Steve Davis even won BBC Sports Personality of the Year, the only time a snooker player has claimed the accolade. When I was growing up, sporting hearts were ablaze with baize, and at the centre of it all was the red-hot Crucible.

Times have changed since then, and over are the halcyon days when a teenage girl would adorn her bedroom wall with posters of Bolton heart-throb Tony Knowles. Has the snooker world gone to pot? Not a bit of it. All it took was to walk into the theatre for the 2017 championship to see the game still knew how to pull a crowd. The foyer was swarming with fans and I had to squeeze my way through the throng for an all-important pre-match coffee. A serene middle-aged woman was sitting at the bar, knitting, while behind her a big screen TV beamed out an episode of Michael Portillo's *Great Railway Journeys*. How many other world championship sporting venues could claim that double whammy? But don't let that tweeness fool you: in sheer numbers snooker is bigger than ever. Since the Noughties the game has spread across the globe, especially in China. Just a year before my visit, Chinese star Ding Junhui's run to the 2016 final had been watched by 210 million people in his home country, a figure that knocked the Black Ball Final into a cocked corner pocket. But as we all waited to be admitted into the auditorium, I couldn't help speculating if somehow the game was still living in the afterglow of its golden years. *If only I could have been there to see Steve and Dennis.* Would the awe still be there today? Was I just hankering to turn the clock back to a time that Dan loved?

One ingredient from the past certainly has gone missing, which in our formative years made the game particularly exciting to watch. Even though snooker is generally a contest between individuals rather than a team sport, back then, Dan and I felt, there was a tribal element to it. The best players seemed to belong to two distinct breeds, and you had to pick a side. On the one hand there were the crowd-pleasing cavaliers, epitomised by Alex 'Hurricane' Higgins and Jimmy 'Whirlwind' White. Off the table they were never out of the tabloids: Jimmy once even took his dead brother's corpse out on a pub crawl. (We all have our ways of toasting our bro.) On the table they offered swashbuckling flair and outrageous potting skills, but Jimmy always seemed to be one shot away from missing a black off its spot; Alex one shot away from being off his face. Then on the other hand there were the machines. First off the conveyor belt came the aforementioned Steve Davis, a ginger android among humans who bestrode the sport in the Eighties and took it to new levels of mental fortitude and tactical cunning. Then, inspired by his example, there spawned an upgraded model. The T:1000, Stephen Hendry, made of liquid metal, whose cool Caledonian ruthlessness laid the template for the twenty-first century player. Dan and I were always squarely in the cavaliers' corner. To us the alternative just seemed unconscionable. The only Stephen Hendry fan I've known personally was my teenage girlfriend, Helen. She was smart, funny, into the Beatles, *Star Wars*, football and ancient Greek, and she looked a bit like Claire Danes, with a slight Norwich accent. My dream woman. Then I discovered her dirty snooker secret and, well, young love is a fleeting thing.

If it was victory my brother and I were after, then as with our football teams we'd chosen poorly. Over a spell of eighteen years, the two metronomic titans Davis and Hendry crushed the humans and hoovered up thirteen world titles between them, building a hegemony only occasionally broken by the odd plucky underdog: a Joe Johnson here, a Dennis there. At the same time Jimmy White, who became the king of the cava-liers, somehow contrived to lose six finals, including five years in a row and four at the hands of his nemesis, Hendry. Jimmy remains by a distance the greatest player never to lift snooker's ultimate prize, and he's had to make do with a different kind of immortality as the People's Champion. A fast-living tragic hero. Second-place merchant supreme. When he finally over-came Hendry in the first round in 1998, recording his first Sheffield win over the Scot in a decade, I let out a guttural yell at my bedroom TV, as if this one success exorcised all the pain of the near misses gone by. Of course it didn't. Beloved by mil-lions as he still is, would Jimmy exchange all the fondness with which he's held for just one Crucible crown? Into the 2020s he's still playing on the pro circuit and clinging onto his dream, as it slips ever further from him. Tantalus in a dress shirt.

Might it be more than coincidence that the zenith of snook-er's popularity in the UK coincided with English football's spell in the hooligan-riddled doldrums? This was a time when the public were looking for sportspeople to root for and, in a much less crowded field than today, it delivered in spades. Players boozed and smoked their way through matches, some becom-ing sex symbols and others national treasures. John Virgo even did impressions of his fellow professionals, so quirky and rec-ognisable were the stars. At its height the game was coated in a tobacco-sponsored, nicotine-stained spirit of derring-do. But it couldn't last. By the turn of the millennium snooker's image was going through a necessary overhaul to make it cleaner and more marketable. Yet the change also signified the end of a breathtaking battle of the baize, in which the cue-wielding Cavaliers had been trounced by the robotic Roundheads.

Today's top players go about their business with a poker-faced professionalism, which is understandable given the standards required and the jumbo prize money on offer. (Even Belgium's hard-living Luca Brecel, who won the 2023 world title with a high-wire attacking game, looks tame next to the exploits of the Hurricane and the Whirlwind.) But extinguishing so much of the cheekiness from snooker has had a knock-on effect: most of the game's stars in the 2020s are little known outside their own bubble. Do modern professionals lark about less because panto spots aren't up for grabs? Or are there no panto spots for them because they don't lark about? (Either way, we're unlikely to be seeing Judd Trump's *Mother Goose* anytime soon.) Perhaps in trying too hard to counterbalance its strait-laced profile, snooker has gradually grasped the mantle of being the sport with the silliest nicknames in the world. NFL stars like the Fridge can't hold a candle to Dave 'the Angry Farmer' Gilbert, Midlander Anthony Hamilton aka 'the Sheriff of Pottingham', or Ricky 'Stamina Man' Walden. The only time I watched the Stamina Man play he got thrashed 6–0 in less than an hour.

Walden's hammering was dished out by the one player who has bucked the trend and over the last three decades reshaped the whole game. He's the last of the cavaliers, and the reason why many of the people surrounding me were crowding the Crucible foyer, despite the fact he wouldn't even be playing today. He's the Rocket, Ronnie O'Sullivan. In all my sport-loving days, I've never seen anyone like Ronnie. He's often introduced as the most gifted player to ever lift a cue, but that barely scratches the surface of his talent. This enigma of a man has taken the bravura of Alex Higgins and Jimmy White and somehow combined it with the iron will of Davis and Hendry. In so doing he's achieved the same superlative feat as Roger Federer in tennis, which is to overturn the moral that sport so often used to teach me and Dan: that you can't play with style *and* win. Tottenham Hotspur FC, please take note.

O'Sullivan's astonishing achievements are manifold. In 1997 he scored a maximum 147 break at the World Championship in a record-shattering 5 minutes and 20 seconds. One of his fierce rivals, Mark Selby, has been known to take that long over a single shot. He can score a century using either hand, much to the chagrin of his opponents: when he first showed off his left-handed

ability at the Crucible in 1996 against Alain Robidoux, the journeyman Canadian lodged a complaint and at the end of the
match refused to shake hands. The Rocket replied that he could
play better with his left hand than Robidoux could with his right,
and he was almost certainly correct. Unlike Davis or Hendry,
Ronnie hasn't packed his brilliance into a short reign of dominance, which makes it all the more impressive. His seven Crucible
wins (so far) have been spread over an unprecedented twenty-
one-year span, belying any notion that snooker has become a
young man's game. He can be erratic like Jimmy and irascible like
Alex Higgins, frequently seeming to disrespect the game that has
made his fortune. But, without excusing his missteps, as with so
many of sport's truly towering talents his complexity has only
added to his legend. Most astonishingly of all, he has spent his
whole career teetering on a tightrope of jacking it all in, and after
winning the world title in 2012 it looked as though he'd finally
followed through with his threat. Ronnie spent the next twelve
months choosing not to play a single competitive match, before a
late change of heart led him to show up at the Crucible to defend
the trophy, rusty and ill-prepared. He won it again anyway. That's
an outrageous feat which I'll wager nobody will ever replicate in
any sport. In fact, I doubt anyone would even try.

While O'Sullivan wasn't on today's bill, I'd had the privilege
of seeing him at close quarters a couple of times. In 1999 the
snooker circus rolled into Croydon for a new (and short-lived)
tournament called the Champions' Cup, and a whole brigade
of players had chosen to stay at the hotel opposite our house,
where my sister Lucy was working a holiday job. She tipped us
off that they were having a late-night drink and snuck me and
Dan into the bar for a lock-in, where we tried not to look too
starstruck as Ronnie called out at 2 a.m. to anyone and everyone, 'I'm starvin' – who wants to go for a Chinese?' At that time
of night in Selsdon, satisfying a craving for crispy duck was
going to be harder than a maximum break, but you wouldn't
put it past him. Much more recently, I'd watched Ronnie

contest the 2017 Masters Final at Alexandra Palace against 'the Gentleman' Joe Perry. It was a keenly fought match, but eventually Ronnie's thoroughbred class shone through, with a mixture of precocious potting and Houdiniesque escapology. Victory brought the Essex Exocet his seventh Masters win, breaking yet another of Stephen Hendry's amazing records. Given all that, when he sank the final ball you might think instinct would kick in and he'd . . . celebrate. I certainly did, but he just dropped his head to his chin in relief and then bit the tip off his cue in disgust at how it had not been up to scratch. Mortal minds could only boggle at what Ronnie's up-to-scratch level would look like. While I and every other viewer had been marvelling at a display of sporting artistry of the highest order, Ronnie had been preoccupied with imperfections only he could see. The word genius is overused in sport, as is the sentence, 'The word genius is overused in sport.' But he's a genius.

I'd been dwelling on these memories when a bell rang and the doors to the auditorium swung open. And then I was inside the Crucible. So often had I heard how minuscule the venue is that in reality it was bigger than I'd imagined, with seats rising up in a generous rake to create the 'bowl', or even cockpit, that gives so many iconic world venues their aura. Down on the arena floor, cameramen and producers bustled around two smart-casual figures calmly waiting to film a piece of punditry. One was the 1997 champion, Ken 'the Darling of Dublin' Doherty, and beside him was the Nugget himself, Steve Davis. Once upon a time they'd both been king of this place, but now they looked entirely at home savouring their snooker afterlife among the pantheon of former champions in the commentary box. Any minute now a dividing curtain would descend between the two tables to bisect the arena, creating the extra level of intimacy – and intensity – that makes the World Championship unique. And soon it was time, in the inimitable words of MC Rob Walker, 'to get the boys on the baize'.

My side of the theatre was about to see the conclusion of a

second-round match between reigning champion Selby and upcoming Chinese talent Xiao Guodong, resuming with the score at 10 frames to 6 in favour of the Englishman. Saluting the crowd's applause, each tuxedoed player descended the stairs to their own signature tune; the mood was half boxing match, half *The Price Is Right,* and utterly British. All around me spectators were fixing a small electronic receiver onto their ear – an increasingly common look at a major sports event – to listen to the live BBC commentary. It's no different from the old days of taking a transistor radio to the cricket for *Test Match Special,* but at the snooker it's led to a strange new phenomenon. Should a commentator say something funny it can trigger a collective belly-laugh among the audience, leaving the players nonplussed. Yet another thing for their ironclad concentration to have to withstand. It's definitely not a sport for the paranoid.

Part of the pleasure of watching snooker at home is that certain matches can lull you into a blissful, sofa-slumped snooze. I was far too overcome by the occasion here to succumb to a nap, but within minutes an angry, porcine snore could be heard emanating from a man a couple of rows away, provoking hushed giggles around him, until eventually it was left to one of his neighbours to gently give him a prod. When he came to his senses, Mr Sleepyhead was in for a bit of a shock: the match was already over. Selby had wasted no time polishing off the three frames he needed, putting the bow on an emphatic victory with an impressive 101 break, giving me my first sight of a Crucible century. All well and good for the champion, but it left a question mark hanging over the capacity crowd.

What now? Not long after Selby and Guodong had left the arena the theatre curtain rose again, to reveal that the other fixture, between Graeme Dott and Joe Perry, had concluded early too. Was that it? A few disappointed spectators began to climb the stairs out into the Sheffield spring. But those who left missed out on something unexpected. Something delightful. Something very Dan.

Snooker being such a close-knit sport, there was a will among the organisers not to leave this Crucible crowd short-changed, and it was announced that to fill the rest of the session we'd be served up a best-of-three exhibition contest between two former world champions; a just-for-kicks bonus that's often known as a beer match. The mystery was which members of the BBC commentary team would be stepping out to entertain us. It was pot luck, so to speak. First to appear was the 2002 champion Peter Ebdon, looking dapper in grey tartan and clearly chuffed by the unexpected chance to perform again on this special stage. And his opponent? I couldn't believe my luck. Wearing a white shirt, stripy monochrome tie, and a smile as wide as the Irish Sea, it was Dennis. For the icing on the cake, joining the two legends was maestro John Virgo to give us an irreverent commentary of proceedings. A frisson went through the audience. The next hour promised to be a time warp. I sat forwards to the edge of my seat, beaming, eyes brimming. If only Dan could see this.

There was something uncommonly true to the spirit of snooker about watching two world champions of yesteryear strutting their stuff and letting their hair down (figuratively if not follically). With no trophy or prize money on the line, the gentility and theatre of this remarkable game were given a chance to shine, and the way that this makeshift Ebdon and Taylor Show played to the crowd recaptured the buccaneering flamboyance Dan and I had lapped up in days gone by. Virgo, slipping smoothly back into *Big Break* mode, was in his element. 'That's the CD player!' he declared as Ebdon potted a long yellow. Although a long way from his best, Dennis still pulled out some spectacular banana shots, and even re-enacted his famous finger-wagging, cue-shaking celebration from 1985 when he succeeded in winning a frame. Laughter flowed more freely than the break-building. The game finished 2–1 to the more recently retired Ebdon. 'I'm glad I don't do this for a living any more,' Dennis told the audience.

'So are we,' a good-natured heckler shot back.

There was still a bit of time left, so Dennis used it to wow us with some of his favourite trick shots, building up to his climactic 'machine-gun' party piece, which involved knocking the cue ball gently towards a corner pocket and then firing all six colours into it before the white arrived. Into his seventies he might be, but the old entertainer still had it. He also pulled out some of the repartee he must take around the country on exhibition nights. Of the modern TV graphics that show viewers the predicted path of a player's next shot, Dennis said it was a good job they didn't have those white lines in the Eighties or they'd have been gone in an instant. He's often asked, he went on, if snooker players used to take drugs in those days, and he said he never saw it, 'although one time somebody sneezed and we all felt fantastic'.

Thanks to the double-quick efficiency of Mark Selby and Joe Perry, I'd caught sight of an old swashbuckler enjoying a last dance. Snooker's Obi-Wan Kenobi rolling back the years. To watch Dennis Taylor at the Crucible was to see a true legend in action on the stage of not just his greatest triumph but one of the summits of British sport: the springboard for me and Dan to a lifetime's worship of this marvellous tabletop game. I was a tourist through my own past and through sporting history. How powerful nostalgia can be. Today had truly conjured up the spirit of my brother, and I didn't want the sensation to end. I knew that there was no getting away from the impermanence. Of this afternoon's fun. Of life. Of love. But just for a short while, Dennis had helped hold back the tide.

On the way back to my hotel, hunger crept over me as I was passing a McDonald's. Outside its glowing window I found myself torn. I hadn't eaten at the Golden Arches in well over a decade. But quarter-pounders and Big Macs were Dan's undisputed favourite food. If ever I was going to break my vow of celiburgacy, it was now.

Watching Dennis Taylor bend a cue ball had been a trip back

in time, but stepping into a McDonald's after ten years was a wormhole into the future. Since when did you have to order your food on plasma screens? Or collect an order number and wait at the appropriate collection zone? Why had McDonald's turned into Argos? One person's progress is another's madness. I tapped in my order for a cheeseburger, while a woman behind the counter poured a terrifying amount of salt into a deep fat fryer and two rowing customers behind me called each other 'Wanker' and 'Cow'. Then my number was up. Would I so easily be able to identify any cow?

Out in the street, I unwrapped the paper and took a hungry, curious bite. The patty was wet and tepid, and bound to cause repurcussions later. SpongeMeat ShitPants. But even after so long my taste buds still remembered that classic mix of sauces, cheese, onion and gherkins. Four toppings as harmonious as the Four Tops. Perfect. To round it off, I toasted Dan with a full-fat Coke. McDonald's really could still serve a happy meal.

Dennis Taylor lines up his 'machine gun' shot at The Crucible

14

What Was. What Is. What's Next

Sunday, 14 May 2017: Football

The 12.32 was lurching and shuddering out of Cambridge. Or that's how it seemed from where I was sitting. But it wasn't the train that was struggling: it was my head and stomach. I was dealing with the queasy aftermath of my friend Pete's stag weekend. The only solace to cling to on the way back to London was that at least I wasn't the only one. Eight of us were dotted about the carriage, each sitting quietly, engaged in his own personal battle with the effects of yesterday's post-modern pentathlon: go-karting, archery, quad bikes, Laser Quest, pub crawl. The only medicine I'd taken to fight the pain was a Frankie & Benny's Unlimited Breakfast, and it was steadily becoming clear that this strategy had been unwise. To make matters worse I was wearing my replica Spurs top, at a moment when a pristine lilywhite shirt could turn out to be the worst possible choice of attire. For the only time in my life I almost wished I was an Arsenal fan, and clad in their 1990s crime-against-fashion pizza kit.

There wasn't only the alcohol to contend with. The sheer novelty of the whole weekend had been head-spinning. For a start, this had been my first time on a stag do – aged 37 it was a bit late to be cutting my teeth – and, having never been much of a drinker, I was paying for my lack of experience. Until recently I'd counted myself lucky that my friends seemed to have a collective aversion to matrimony, as it had enabled me to dodge this masochistic ritual. But two years earlier I'd missed one. It had been for Pete's best man, Hugh, attended by many of the same friends who were now suffering on the train with me. It had coincided with Dan's passing, and I was very much off the radar.

Even now on the train, I could feel the poisonous way in which grief had spread, out of my thoughts and into the world, infiltrating my life like a sheet of ice cracking. As if stealing Dan wasn't enough. But it also prodded me to make sure I appreciated the present, not least events like Pete's stag. I seldom had the chance to see this group of friends, as jobs and families had scattered them across the world from Vancouver to Islamabad. So a happy occasion like this had been a tonic – with lashings of gin – starting with the go-karts and ending with a 2 a.m. lock-in at the Pickerel Inn and a singalong of Seventies hits by local 'character' Johnny. (He gave *Don't Stop Me Now* an ironic edge.) It had been a chance to make new memories with old mates. Was the skin beginning to close over a small part of the wound?

As if the stag weekend wasn't enough to stomach, the afternoon was about to offer a sterner test. That's why I was in my Spurs top. Wearing a replica jersey when you're out and about in everyday life is a display of pride in your club, as shown by millions of people, but it's an urge I generally resist because the price can go way beyond the eye-watering cost of an official shirt, inviting anything from gentle joshing about your team's fortunes to snobbish looks from sport-sceptics, to genuine threats if you stray into the wrong place in the wrong kit. '*Audere est facere*' is the Tottenham Hotspur club motto: to dare is to do. Laudable though that can be on the pitch at times (and laughable at others), on the streets of London I prefer a different strategy: '*Abdere est vivere*.' To hide is to survive. I also wonder if I'm the only sports fan who feels a bit of a fraud when I casually dress in the clothes of a highly skilled professional. After all, I'm about as close to becoming a footballer as to qualifying as a brain surgeon, and I've never felt the urge to don the scrubs of a consultant at Guy's. (Maybe the NHS needs to rectify that with a new merch range?) It's a unique quirk of sport to inspire the spectacle of an overfed body cramming itself inside an XXXL Portugal shirt with 'Ronaldo' printed on the back. I'm all for that, by the way. I just steer away from doing it myself. The only exception is match day, when I can blend into a sea of white and navy blue, join the flock, and feel part of something; feel normal.

Today was different. There was no choice in the matter. I had to wear the shirt and, no matter how anonymous I became, there was no likelihood of feeling normal. My insides were gurgling with apprehension, as well as the Unlimited Breakfast, because in a couple of hours' time I would be coming face-to-face with another landmark memory in my life with Dan, for one last time. I was on my way to bid farewell to a home from home, the old ground at White Hart Lane, at its 2,533rd and final game. After today's fixture against Manchester United, the stadium was scheduled for immediate destruction, to be replaced by a massive new arena befitting the twenty-first century (and arguably a better team than Spurs). I'd already said goodbye to Wimbledon dog track. Now for the second time in as many months a piece of the past I shared with my brother was about to be smashed away.

While the train whisked me towards north London, I tried to imagine how Dan would have felt if Selhurst Park had been demolished. It was impossible to compute. That place was simply synonymous with him, as tied to his soul as a daemon in *His Dark Materials*. It was lucky, then, that Palace had got off lightly compared to the many clubs who'd had their old grounds destroyed in the post-Taylor Report revolution of the Nineties. The only substantial change was the replacement of the old Holmesdale Road terrace – where Dan was a regular – with a modern two-tiered, all-seater stand. Even that was enough for me to see how much a physical place could mean to him. On

8 May 1994 he took me to see the Eagles play Watford and experience the old terrace one last time. In the build-up to kick-off, amid a charged atmosphere thick with balloons, Dan was a soup of emotions: smiling at the carnival vibe, shooting me proud looks for having brought me to witness it, and letting slip a few tears. Logic said it was a day to embrace: gone would be the nasty, uncovered terrace and in its place would be born a lovely new edifice with seats, bars, indoor seating and a roof. But Dan was ruled by his feelings, and this was the spot where back in 1981 he'd fallen in love with Palace. Weeks later he somehow managed to get hold of a small, pebble-dashed chunk of the now demolished Holmesdale, and for the next two decades treasured it as though it was a holy relic. After his death, when my brother-in-law David and I drew up the courage to enter his flat and start the clean-up, this ugly lump of rock was the first thing I saw, and one of the few things we made sure to keep.

Given our playful rivalry about our respective football teams, Dan would have had plenty of fun with the fact that White Hart Lane was on death row and about to have its final meal. But he would have felt strongly about the loss of the ground too, not least because it was he who first took me there twenty-three years earlier.

It was 2 p.m. on 27 December 1994, just a few months after we'd said goodbye to the Holmesdale Terrace. Tottenham High Road looked drab and the streets were being rinsed with winter rain, but my fourteen-year-old eyes were full of wonder, because everything was new. I'd been following Spurs for seven years and seen them play a few times at Selhurst Park, but this was a new level of excitement. For a Christmas present Dan was actually taking me to the Lane. It wasn't an entirely selfless gesture. The football fixture computer had seen fit to throw Palace and Tottenham together for a league match during the festive period, and Dan's reaction would have been instantaneous: that's Jon's present sorted.

Outside the ground, I tried to persuade Dan to use some of his hard-earned night shift cash to buy me a souvenir. An official replica shirt was way out of his price range but he was able to stump up for a cheap, unofficial T-shirt with a picture of Jürgen Klinsmann on the front, and his squad number 18 on the back. Klinsmann had only been at Spurs a few months and was already a club legend, but as soon as I accepted the top I realised I was tempting fate. 'I bet he leaves Spurs now', I muttered.

Dan let out his characteristic *hee-hee*. 'Jürgen's not stupid. He's going to leave anyway.'

Six months and an apoplectic Alan Sugar later, he was proved right.

We squeezed through the narrow turnstiles and climbed up to the top tier of the new North Stand to discover that the family section had yet to be graced by a roof. This wasn't ideal for a wet winter's day, but the club had got the situation covered, if not the actual seats, by offering every fan their own FA Carling Premiership-branded bin-liner. Dan thought this was brilliant: it might explain why the Spurs defence was so leaky.

The game was a nil-nil bore-draw, but you could hardly blame the players. These were the days when the oft-bemoaned 'Christmas fixture pile-up' wasn't an exaggeration, and both teams had played another match just 24 hours earlier. They must have been knackered. Still, for me the result didn't really matter. Thanks to Dan I'd got to see Klinsmann, Sheringham, Anderton, Mabbutt and, er, Dean Austin, roared on by the White Hart Lane faithful. You never forget your first.

The train pulled into Tottenham Hale and, after some weary farewells to the stag group, I gulped some welcome fresh air and set off for the ground, jittery about how I'd feel by the end of the day. At every street corner more and more clusters of fans in Spurs shirts were drawn in, like iron filings in range of a magnet. I was blending in, part of a whole, feeling at home.

Along the High Road all the lamp posts were decked out with navy blue banners resplendent with a golden cockerel and the words 'The Finale'. The match-day walk to any stadium is always laced with anticipation, but today's, each step told me, was special. As I revelled in that thought, I passed a set of lock-up garages on my left and saw a corpulent fan relieving his bladder, watched by his young son. OK: not quite every step.

The cover of the souvenir programme featured two black-and-white photos, contrasting the Lane in the 1960s 'Glory Glory' days with how it looked now and – just as with Wimbledon dog track's – two dates: in this case 1899–2017. Were we commemorating a death? It looked like another obituary. But unlike so many clubs who've been through a stadium transition, Spurs weren't leaving the *site* of their home. Their new arena would eventually stand in the same spot as its predecessor. Each stand had already been rebuilt over the years, as I knew well from my Christmas 1994 soaking with Dan, so to what extent did the old ground still exist anyway? The truth, I realised, was more mundane: the club wanted a clean start so it could hoover up millions more in gate receipts, and one day strike a lucrative deal on naming rights to give the place a hateful corporate ring. But banners bearing the slogan 'Hiatus for Corporate Progress' would have lacked a certain emotional resonance.

Holed up at my usual pre-game caff until it was time to meet fellow Spurs sufferer Will, I had read barely a paragraph of Mauricio Pochettino's programme notes when a voice said, 'How are you feeling?' It took me a second to realise the question was addressed to me. It came from a middle-aged man sitting opposite.

'Nervous,' I replied, not least because I wasn't sure where this was leading.

He introduced himself as Lee; he'd been coming to Spurs since 1970. 'This is big,' he said. 'There'll be a lot of grown men in tears today. Which bit of the ground are you in?'

Our tickets were for the corner of the East Stand, which regulars know as the Shelf Side. Lee beamed: 'You'll get a good atmosphere in there, mate.' That morning he'd been watching a documentary on YouTube about The Lane, he told me, when his young daughter had come up to him and said, 'Daddy, why are you crying?' In Lee's words today was 'like saying goodbye to a friend'.

I asked if he was worried the new venue might end up being called something like the Hewlett Packard Arena or the Qatar Airlines Superdome?

'It doesn't matter what they name it,' shrugged Lee. 'We'll still all call it the Lane.'

'Bloody right!' Another fan had joined the conversation – a cabbie called Dave, who quickly described himself as 'a London icon'. Ordinarily that could be the telltale sign of a bell-end, but Dave turned out to be such a friendly and garrulous bloke he could wear such bravado lightly, and like Lee he just wanted to share his Tottenham memories. He even told us his dad's three rules for life: don't buy cheap shoes; money is for spending; and nice people meet nice people. I'd never known this café so chatty. It took me back to the 2012 Olympics, when for that one crazy month Londoners lost their inhibitions and *talked to each other*. Once again sport was bringing strangers out of their shells. Creating togetherness.

Will arrived, and the two of us walked the final few hundred yards to the ground, passing police horses, memorabilia stands and burger vans wafting out the pleasing smells of fried onions and grease. At last we reached Gangway 31, and one last time we crammed through those ancient turnstiles. Twenty-three years after Dan had brought me here at Christmas, the 'world famous home of the Spurs' was looking cramped and dilapidated. But when I'd first clapped eyes on it I'd been like Russell Crowe's gladiator Maximus and friends craning up at the Colosseum: 'I didn't know men could build such things . . .'

On every seat had been placed a commemorative T-shirt

and a large navy-and-white flag: a step up from the bin-liner. The pitch was bathed in sunlight, and again I felt the tingle that comes from catching that first glimpse of lush, vivid green. But there was an ominous edge to the landscape, as building work was already underway: a large bite was missing from the north-east corner of the ground, revealing the street behind, and above us impatient cranes cast giant shadows. Across from us I could see the spot where Dan and I had sat together that festive afternoon over two decades ago. Like the Holmesdale Terrace, like Dan himself, soon it would be gone. The taller edifice of the new stadium was slowly enveloping and eating the old one, like a monstrous, concrete Pac-Man.

That day was like nothing I'd ever encountered at a football game. Everyone waved their flag so feverishly and sang so spiritedly you might think Spurs had just won the Quadruple. ('Or just something', Dan would have rejoined.) It was a reminder that, however state-of-the-art the new ground might be, it would have to go some to match this claustrophobic cauldron. The team would find it hard to match their results, too: by avoiding defeat today Tottenham would complete their first season unbeaten at home since 1964–5. The scene was set for either a euphoric climax or an embarrassingly damp squib – which, after all the pomp and fanfare, would be archetypally 'Spursy'. For one last time the pre-match video 'We Are Tottenham Hotspur' played on the twin Jumbotron screens, and over a montage of classic clips and epic music the immortal voice of Roger Lloyd-Pack boomed out:

The curve of the ball, the billow of the net,
The beating of the trap and the picking of the lock,
The swiftness of thought, the lightness of touch,
We are the collective gasp, the intake of breath,
The flick, the trick, the thirty-yard free kick,
We are the lob, the chip, the dummy and the volley,
We are the hat-trick, the scissor kick, we are Bill Nick,

We are the outside of the boot, the inside of the net,
And those seconds that last forever,
Glory past, glory future,
What was, what is, what's next.
Daring to try, daring to risk, daring to dream,
To dare is to do.

Then the walk-out music struck up, the teams emerged and referee Jonathan Moss blew his whistle to an eardrum-testing 360-degree din.

Now a nervousness hung in the air. José Mourinho's United had experienced a flaccid season by Ferguson-era standards, but their team still boasted a host of attacking threats who could spoil the day. Luckily Spurs came racing out of the blocks and opened the scoring after six minutes via the unlikely source of Victor Wanyama's head. We could relax, slightly, and I purred to Will that this must be the best Tottenham squad we'd ever had the good fortune to cheer on. Having grown up through the nightmare of the Alan Sugar/Christian Gross days, I've had to pinch myself more than once that Mauricio Pochettino had built such a stylish, attacking team who'd climbed up to second in the league and seemed to love playing together. Apart from securing a little of that continually elusive silverware, Spurs couldn't be leaving home in much better shape. And to think I could have been a Palace fan. Sorry, bro.

Half-time arrived with the lead still narrow, leaving a sense of anxiety hanging, along with some menacing clouds. Could the Lilywhites contrive a way to throw this one away? The fans had been promised a spectacular post-game ceremony with a parade of legendary ex-players, but it would feel a bit hollow off the back of a home record-ruining defeat to Mourinho. Having seen the team piss away much bigger leads, I was leaving my chickens uncounted.

Almost immediately after the break Spurs fans received the cushion of a second goal, courtesy of one Harry Kane. It had to be. From a whipped free-kick by Christian Eriksen, he beat the defence to guide home a near-post finish, to a surge of jubilation from the stands. The singing redoubled with a round of Harry's theme song, 'He's One Of Our Own', followed by an impromptu greatest hits medley of chants for Tottenham legends across the last fifty years: classics like 'Nice One, Cyril', 'We'll Take More Care of You, (Steve) Archibald', 'We've Got Dele Alli', and the peerless 'Oh, Ledley Ledley, He's only got one knee, he's better than John Terry, oh, Ledley, Ledley'. And plenty more besides which are unprintable. Here was a musical manifestation of what every football club is: an evolving story, rolling through the decades and filled with heroes. In my section of the crowd, some fans spotted cup-winning captain Gary Mabbutt in the top tier and serenaded him rapturously. Then, through the window of the Sky Sports studio behind him, the same fans spotted Thierry Henry and sang him a very different song. (Proof that going to an American football match and going to a soccer game aren't always *totally* different.) The Spurs flags were being waved so enthusiastically most fans could barely see the game. But nobody cared. It was a party.

For Wayne Rooney to go and score for United was frankly impolite. He'd ruined Palace's dreams this time last year at Wembley. Was he about to do the same to Spurs at the Lane? As the small pocket of away fans found their voice the mood darkened, and so did the weather. It had turned much colder, and the clouds burst, dousing us in a spring shower. Would it literally rain on our parade? United were looking the more dangerous side, but as injury time approached relief began to spread once more among the home faithful. Then – slap-bang in front of me and Will – Marcus Rashford broke through on goal with only Hugo Lloris to beat. It was a final chance for Mourinho's men to rescue a draw and puncture the day. Somehow this seemed definitive. At this crucial juncture, was it to be a nearly-moment to cap a nearly-season for a nearly-club? Or could we dare to dream? Time froze. I winced. Rashford connected. The ball pinged over the crossbar. And now everyone knew: the win was safe, the home record was intact, and a record points haul had been achieved. Tottenham would be leaving the High Road on a high.

Referee Moss blew the final whistle and a stupendous cheer resounded. Some people were on the pitch, but this lot *knew* it was all over and they wanted to be a part of it. The announcer pleaded with fans to stay in their seats, but the stewards were far more streetwise and made zero attempt to stop the multitude. Weighed down by my overnight bag, I was unable to squeeze out of my row, but Will was more agile and got swept up into the melee and down onto the pitch. He was able to pick a few blades of grass from the turf and ended up planting them at home, where they did surprisingly well at living a second life.

Back in the stands, fans were grabbing any piece of memorabilia that they could lay their hands on. One man held aloft a large sign denoting 'Gangway 43', while next to me two others had brought screwdrivers and were frantically trying to free their plastic seats from their moorings. Another bloke who'd turned up without implements was not to be deterred and simply ripped his seat out with his bare hands. Tottenham had missed a trick here – who needed to spend millions on a wrecking crew when there were 35,000 tanked-up football fans willing to do the job for free? It was all good-natured. These were loyal supporters who wanted their own equivalent of Dan's chunk of the Holmesdale; their own relic to cherish. As we finally all funnelled out, I took one last look at White Hart Lane and the spot where I'd sat on that very first visit, as 'Can't Smile Without You' wafted over the crackly speakers. I was still learning to smile without Dan, but also – so much better – I was remembering to smile because of him.

15

A Tale of Two Champions

'Advantage Nadal.' The umpire's voice echoes around Number One Court with two words that have been said together a thousand times. In many cases they haven't heralded just the latest score. They've summed up a match, a tournament, even the entire tennis world. Not now, though. The indefatigable Rafa is clinging on by his fingernails to his place in the Wimbledon championships. It's the fourth round and he is being taken to the brink of oblivion by his doughty opponent, Luxembourg's Gilles Müller. (Nope, me neither.) Against all predictions it has boiled up into a four-hour epic. Two sets all, *nine* games all. It's a match for the ages. And it's advantage Nadal, on Müller's serve. The Spaniard is one point away from breaking the deadlock and striking what would surely be the killer blow. Müller sets himself. Rafa fidgets, crouches, twitches his nose, fidgets again. The hubbub of the capacity crowd fades to a hush. Everybody waits. The knife-edge drama in the arena couldn't be more thrilling. Suddenly a man brushes past me. 'Excuse me, mate, can I get through to the laptops?'

I am not at Wimbledon. I'm eight miles away from the All England Club, in the middle of an electronics department, watching the action on a 'bargain' £1,599 giant TV. And I'm captivated.

I've also been sidetracked. Ordinarily I'd be home by now, but since summer rolled in I've changed my evening commute. Now, whenever the weather isn't too grisly, I swap the ten-minute Tube hop from Camden to Victoria Station for an hour and a half's walk across London. It started as just a way to get a bit of exercise, but it's become more than that. I used to love the Underground, but it long ago lost the allure it held for me as a child. These days every rush hour ride is risking a trip into Hell (via Bank). When things go wrong and a herd of commuters gets stuck on escalators and platforms it can feel like being in a horror sequel to *Innerspace* or *Inside Out:* we're all blood cells travelling through the body of a sick man, passing through arteries that have become caked with an angina of litter and vomit. Boarding a carriage is often a case of taking a deep breath and merging with the stifling heap of contorted bodies within. Once inside, everyone just tries to survive together until it's all over and the Tube spews them back out onto the street. At its worst, it's the world's slowest, sweatiest teleporter.

Compared to that, the particulate-infested air of twenty-first-century London feels as fresh as an Alpine spring. So I've belatedly embraced slow travel. It means I can see where I'm going, and I can get a better sense of distance, scale and how this tapestry of neighbourhoods is woven together. It's grounding me. My new evening walk takes me through the delicately wrought splendour of Regent's Park, along Savile Row, where I gaze up at the site of the Beatles' rooftop gig, down the gentle slope of Green Park and past Buckingham Palace. What a city.

Slap-bang in the middle of the route lies the fading grandeur of Oxford Street, and for a week or so it's not just the BT Tower that has been looming over my steps. Temptation has stalked me too, beckoning me into John Lewis's mighty flagship branch. This evening I've succumbed and popped in to buy a personal fitness strap. I thought it'd be fun to keep track of the miles I've been racking up. And I want to mark my progress because of how valuable walking has recently become. In a strange irony it's become a crutch. These sultry post-work strolls have been leading me not just through Piccadilly and Mayfair but deeper into the knotted thickets in my head, allowing me to spend time with my thoughts against a backdrop of some of the world's finest landmarks. Am I reacting to the struggles Dan had with walking by becoming obsessed with avoiding the same fate? Is it a singleton's way of filling headspace and time? I'm not sure what, but I'm counting myself lucky for everything I still have, as well as still heartbroken for what I've lost. Even to have the time to think such thoughts feels like a gift, and these daily meditations gird me for the difficult moment each evening when I reach platforms 15 to 19 at Victoria. There by the escalator next to Burger King stands a small steel railing, ignored by every one of the millions of commuters who march past it on their journey home. Except me. It's the last place I ever saw Dan.

It was a Tuesday lunchtime, three weeks before the awful day. Lucy and I had just accompanied him to a medical appointment which we'd all hoped might herald a new start. Dan's weight had always been the most pressing problem, but we'd increasingly considered whether there was an underlying health issue that might hold the key to helping him get better. Dan's mental wellbeing had never been properly checked out, and after months of waiting he had a slot to be evaluated by an NHS psychologist. Finally an expert might be able to help. We harboured a hope that if Dan's condition could get recognised, even at this late stage, it might lead to some treatment and self-knowledge. If he was able to understand his own mind, could that help him better negotiate the struggles of day-to-day life?

If only it were that easy. The psychologist posed Dan a set of questions, mainly of the yes/no variety, but that was pretty much as far as it went. I asked if he thought Dan might have Asperger's and/or OCD, and the answer came back: 'He might do, yes.' That was it, pretty much. I'd been hoping some miraculous safety net was going to scoop us up and help Dan towards a brighter future. Instead, we'd left the clinic basically as confused as when we went in. We were offered one level of assistance which could have potentially helped – regular visits from a social worker – but to this Dan said a categorical no. Which was his right, of course. He was an independent man leading an independent life. None of us could force things on him. But whatever he was suffering from, I retained the nagging fear that Dan's intense need for privacy and his difficulties in looking after his own health were a dangerous mix. If he'd said yes to the visits, might that simple binary choice have helped save him? I'll never know. These thoughts rage in my head every evening as I approach that spot in the station.

But there's a warmer memory too. When we'd got back to Victoria after the appointment, the two of us had gone for lunch in an American diner-style restaurant. As if to show his good intentions, Dan had ordered a salad. As if to hex us, the portion size was suitably American, enough to serve an army, topped with what looked like a whole chicken. We shared a chat and a laugh about the National, the Ashes, the snooker, and of course the football: Palace had just thrashed Sunderland 4–1, while Spurs had suffered a 1–0 home defeat to Villa, and he took glee in reminding me of both. It was the two of us, putting the world to rights, insulated from our troubles by each other's company. As adults we didn't do that enough. Afterwards, what with his discomfort from walking and the stress of the morning appointment, I shouted him the cost of a taxi home. Then we said bye.

And that was the last I ever saw of my brother. Now all I have is that unnoticed railing on the concourse. *Dan's railing.* He'd appreciate that bit of wordplay, by the way. If I could set up a plaque at that very spot, it would read: '*Daniel Harvey's railing . . . at an offside decision.*'

Soon it will be time for my next quiet vigil there, but this evening, just for a while, that can wait. A couple of minutes' retail therapy has turned into a more stimulating diversion, thanks to the tennis and a display of John Lewis TVs. I'd stumbled upon the match with the score at five-all in the final set, and blithely assumed it would be over in no time. So I'd hung around, sure that any moment now Rafa would have Müller cornered. Almost an hour later I'm still here, rooted to the spot. I want to go home, but the game is too damned engrossing. Until one of them wins I can't move. I've had to feign interest in buying a 75-inch 4K home cinema behemoth to justify my loitering, after attracting suspicious looks from a member of staff. But that was twenty minutes ago. Now there's no need for pretence, because I'm no longer the only one watching. A small gaggle has gathered: a mum with two tweeny kids; a sprinkling of tourists; a besuited twenty-something sporting a shirt and braces in July and (I'll wager) a Young Conservatives membership card in his pocket; a pony-tailed man in a floral shirt and open-toed sandals who looks like he's bought *Dark Side of the Moon* on every conceivable format; and the assistant who'd been eyeing me earlier. This isn't a shop any more. It's a fanzone. And Müller has just saved match point. Ten-all. We may be here some time.

Only sport (give or take a cataclysmic news event) can glue people to the spot in this state of shared zombification. And there's something exceptional about Wimbledon. World Cups and Olympics have the same pulling power, but on an annual basis is there anything else quite like it? That summer fortnight is one of the very few periods every year when the focus of the entire sporting world turns to the UK. Yet the great British public's relationship with tennis is a dysfunctional one. For fifty out of every fifty-two weeks the vast majority of people couldn't give a toss (ball, coin or otherwise) about it. The Aussie Open? Indian Wells? Davis Cup? They might as well not exist. Then all of a sudden it's everywhere, splattered across television, radio, online, even mineral water adverts. It takes over the BBC so utterly that for decades, during that fortnight the corporation's initials might as well have stood for Barker, Becker, Castle. (Only from 2023 does that tradition no longer hold true, since Sue Barker's retirement and Boris Becker's post-prison deportation to Germany.)

Even then it seems to take a while to rekindle our affections. When the first service is struck on that Monday morning in July, as a nation we can be fairly accused of taking our own Grand Slam tennis competition slightly for granted. Flick forward a couple of days and millions of us are hooked, watching for four hours straight as two players nobody's ever heard of battle deep into the evening for a place in the next round. Wimbledon must be the event that's adored by the most people who don't taste another crumb of sport for the rest of the year. You can hear the difference in the crowd. It can sound more like the Proms than a tournament.

Every year things unfold the same way. In Sainsbury's the strawberries sell out. On Centre Court the British players crash out. Kick serves, code violations and the sunglasses worn by players' spouses become the subject of water cooler conversation. John McEnroe should be President. A home-grown star carries the hopes of the nation. Then they crash out too. Maybe you even dig out your rusty old racket and hit a ball with friends at the concrete court in the local park. Each year we develop a sudden case of mass tennysteria. Then, just as swiftly, it's gone. Forgotten. Ignored until the calendar grinds around to early July. Right now that time has come again, and here in the electronics department it's the only thing that matters.

Nadal 11–11 Müller. Still the two players are refusing to budge, both knackered yet summoning more energy from God knows where to heave themselves through the next point. Rafa spoons a ball into the net and the mum next to me winces in agony. Müller hits an ace and her kids jump and whoop. It's a happy accident when you find yourself watching sport communally like this. I've cheered on Matthew Pinsent's rowing in the Beijing Olympics from the concourse of a German railway station; seen the England football team thrashed by Germany in a beer tent at Glastonbury. You might know the feeling. Just for an instant, total strangers become trusted soulmates. I love it. Being in a TV department of all places has an extra piquancy.

It reminds me of how things used to be in the Dark Ages – the Nineties – when I'd be out with Dan on a Saturday afternoon mooching about the Croydon shops. Palace would have to be playing away, obviously, or Dan would be at Selhurst Park rather than gracing me with his presence. But if we were together when the clock struck 4.50 p.m. there was only one place to be: outside the local Radio Rentals, peering through the fogged-up glass. It was there, in that Land Before the Internet, that we'd catch the final scores on the TVs in the window, as they beamed out the blocky majesty of Ceefax page 302. We'd be among a small band of fans, all hunting for our team's result and sharing feelings of misery or relief. Dan and I would often get to mock each other for how badly Spurs and/or Palace had done. The technology seems comically primitive now. The memory is so alive it hurts.

Nadal 12–12 Müller. This is getting silly. Thoughts are turning towards the 2010 championships, when John Isner and Nicolas Mahut played out a freakish final set that finished 70–68 to Isner. It was the longest match in tennis history, stretching across three days – longer than many British players' entire Wimbledon careers. Would I be needing to pop downstairs to the sleeping bag department? What's unfolding is gripping enough here in the shop, but for the fans inside that sundrenched Number One Court it must be mind-blowing. And each glorious thwack of the ball is a pang in my heart. I'm craving to be there.

I know what's happening. The odyssey has taken on a momentum of its own. I'm being eaten by my own masterplan. I want to do justice to Dan's memory, and the only way is to go at it full tilt. Now that I've made it so far, if I can't make it to *all* the best sporting events I'll have the sense I failed. Would a Wimbledon-sized hole in the jigsaw be too big to fill? I'm overloaded with the same urge that drove me and Dan to see so much of the London Olympics, to fill up our Italia '90 Panini sticker album, and to forge those plans for the Rugby World

Cup that we never had the chance to realise. The thing is, until now Wimbledon wasn't really on the radar. Not because I didn't rate it or didn't want to see it, but because getting in is so much easier said than done. I just hadn't imagined it would be possible to conjure up a ticket. Now I've become a prisoner of my own completism, I need to think again. *Could* there be a way?

Nadal 12–13 Müller. I rack my brain. All the obvious routes are closed. (As his latest attempted passing shot is fended away, I bet Rafa feels my pain.) I can't apply for tickets in the arcane ballot system, because I'd already tried that before Christmas and failed. I can't pose as a player, because I'm way too small and cowardly. I can't join the All England Club's paramilitary wing of ball boys and ball girls, because I'm way too old. And I can't do the old-fashioned thing of joining The Queue, because I'm way too lazy. I'm sure you've seen pictures of The Queue on the news. It's the maddest phenomenon of its kind in the world, where people willingly spend days camping in a field outside the gates, living in a weird perma-state of sleep-deprived euphoria. Fans have been known to wait so long, it makes the Queen's lying in state look like Formula One. The hardy ones who make it to the front (and haven't died beforehand from exhaustion or a lack of scones) might get to see a top seed gunning for singles glory, or they might be served up a bit of Seniors Invitational Mixed Doubles. The Queue is a lottery, with a hint of *The Hunger Games* thrown in for good measure.

Nadal 13–13 Müller. OK: I think I speak for the entire crowd both at courtside and in the TV department when I say, 'Someone win this now, please. I need a wee.' Tennis players don't get enough credit for their extraordinary powers of bladder control. Right now mine's being tested to destruction, and Rafa or Gilles will have my sympathies if either of them have to do an emergency pee, or even 'a Paula Radcliffe'. Müller starts his next service game with his dreams still hanging on a precipice. As he bounces the ball and launches into a serve, Wimbledon is now a sun-kissed siren bidding me in. The fear of failure is eating away at me. I think conspiratorial thoughts about the unfairness of it. Among those spectators who've made it, thousands will have got their golden ticket through a back route, whether they know someone who happens to have a spare, or are part of a secret underground network with a telephone hotline for show court access. (I've been told this definitely exists.) A friend of mine once lucked out when a man she'd just met on Tinder had snaffled some corporate freebies and was eager to impress. Unlike Nadal versus Müller, theirs wasn't a match made in heaven, but the tickets ensured they lasted one more date than they would have otherwise. I don't know about you but I get the feeling that an awful lot of the spectators who make it inside Centre and Number One Courts that fortnight aren't there because they'd queued for days on end or won in the ballot. Maybe this is just in my head, but I reckon it's often a case of who you know. Take this one bloke, for instance, who turns up every year. The Duke of Kent. He must know someone.

Nadal 13–14 Müller. Hang on. I'm such a fool. There *is* a way in. A secret way to gain passage inside the leafy fortress. I should know this because, like the sporting Gollum I am, I found it once before. Every day during Wimbledon fortnight, a tiny number of new official tickets are released to be sold online on the official website. They aren't publicised but they're there. Some are for Court Number Three, which means minor matches (although I'd take that at a stroke.) But a few precious places are made available for the show courts, first-come, first-served. Not a lot of people know that. Not even Michael Caine, although I bet he's one of the lucky ones with a fast track to the royal box if he wants one. The problem is, this route hadn't worked for me since 2013 and I'd long ago given up on it. But failure has never stopped a Brit from trying when it comes to Wimbledon. Maybe this could be my year?

Match point to Müller. The Pride of Luxembourg needs to land just one final blow on the gilded Nadal to taste the ambrosia of victory. He crouches at the base line, ready to receive serve, just as I visualise my own game plan for tomorrow morning. To succeed in the online sale there are three things you need: to be at your computer at precisely 9 a.m.; mouse-clicking skills faster than a Goran Ivanisevic ace; and a hefty dollop of luck. I'm so used to these ticketing websites I've become a black belt in mouseial arts, and in my experience Wimbledon is the trickiest of the lot. But needs must. It's got to be worth a go. Tomorrow I'll make sure I get to the office early, so I can abuse my workplace's sturdy Internet connection and test my reflexes against the world. A millisecond could make all the difference. As it is with players, so it is with fans.

Nadal 13–15 Müller. Nadal's forehand floats beyond the baseline. Time seems to stop. Then the line judge yells 'Out!' And so is Rafa. Incredible! His conqueror stands stock-still, Cantona-like, taking in his achievement, not even celebrating. Just accepting the crowd's adulation. He's Müller Ice. The outsider has done it. In John Lewis we even break out into a quiet round of applause, before our congregation starts melting away into the evening, as if it was never here. I'm enthralled by what I've seen. It's the latest instalment in the battle between struggling giant and plucky journeyman. Sport at its best. The afterglow keeps me smiling on the rest of my walk to Victoria, and as I pass Dan's railing a scintilla of hope nags at me. Hope does that. Just like it used to do when the twelve-year-old me would walk home from school on dark December nights, fingers crossed that I'd open the front door to discover Dad had brought some money in and Christmas would be saved. Hope costs nothing, if you can take a let-down in your stride. Even if I can't be there in the flesh this year to honour Dan, as part of my Super Season Ticket, in the last hour I've had a taste of what makes Wimbledon a key thread in our summer tapestry. All I need now are some strawberries.

Wednesday, 12 July 2017: Tennis

It worked. It bloody worked. One ticket to the gentlemen's quarter-finals 2017, to see first Andy Murray and then Roger Federer fight for a place in the semis. I should pinch myself – this kind of good fortune isn't something I enjoyed much of as a kid. Except for the *Count Duckula* video I once won in a Shreddies competition. (I still have that, of course.) But once in a while we all deserve to be a bit flukey, and this week Lady Luck is flashing me a smile.

The ticket barriers slam open and I'm in a mass of people flooding out of Wimbledon Station, through a plastic arch decked out in the tournament's famous green and purple livery, together with the slogan 'In pursuit of greatness'. A volunteer is handing out pedestrian maps to the venue and, with my pristine fitness tracker demanding at least 10,000 steps out of me each and every day, I take one and set off. Under my breath I whisper a little thank you to Dan, just as I'd done when I'd nabbed my seat via the website. Just once in a while it feels like he's willing me on to reach the events that would be on our dream wish list. Or anyone's. For millions of Brits this one would be at the top. Centre Court, here I come.

The quaint parade of Wimbledon Village rings a vague bell from my previous visit four years ago, and I daydream back to the astonishing action I'd witnessed that day. To one moment, especially, when I couldn't help but let my emotions get the better of me. It was arguably the moment that changed British tennis for us all.

Ah yes. 'British tennis'. For all of my childhood in the Eighties and Nineties, that phrase was a mockery. I was born too late for Virginia Wade's success in 1977, and for my generation the idea of a homegrown player winning Wimbledon became as likely as finding proof of intelligent life on Mars or in FIFA. So bad at tennis were we as a nation, it was faintly embarrassing we still hosted a Grand Slam event. The UK's ineptitude was perhaps best summed up in the BBC radio comedy *On the Hour*, where British player Susannah Sharper (portrayed by Doon Mackichan) is appalled at having lost a match to Moniqua Perez d'Esquelia, despite drinking more barley water than Moniqua and having by far the cleaner kit. Her Bolivian opponent, who had had the temerity to win without conceding a point, was three years old. This must ring true for anyone who watched the decades of plucky tragedy endured by Jeremy Bates, Jo Durie, Tim Henman and Greg (ignore the Canadian accent, he's got a big serve) Rusedski. Then along came the Noughties and a young Scot called Andy who changed everything. But it nearly didn't happen. While he'll always be known now as a Wimbledon champion, getting there needed a great escape. And I was there to see it.

Back in 2013 Andy Murray was just the latest in the long line of gallant challengers seeking to end the curse of SW19. He'd got closer than anyone in my lifetime, reaching the final in 2012 before being swatted aside by the majestic Federer. But later that summer he'd avenged that loss by defeating the Swiss to win the Olympic gold medal on the same court, before securing his first grand slam triumph at the US Open the following month. A year on from that, there was renewed hope that he might have what it takes to seize the ultimate crown on grass. I had a ticket to see his quarter-final tie against Fernando Verdasco of Spain, with Murray the red-hot favourite. To put it mildly, the match did not go to plan. Verdasco came out all guns blazing; he was the more precise and the more ruthless, and raced into a surprise two-set lead. Then in the third set the Spaniard moved into a 15–30 lead in Murray's opening service game. Another break of serve would likely be curtains for the Brit. Were home hopes about to smash against the rock of reality yet again? I felt compelled to act.

Like many people I usually despise the idiots who think it's hilarious to shout inanities like 'Come on, Tim!' during a match involving any other British player. The All England Club should fit every seat with an ejector function just to deal with them. But as I watched Murray staring into the abyss, for the first time I couldn't restrain myself. I'd heard on the radio the day before that Andy was an ardent boxing fan. So in the face of what was now unfolding, my mind turned to the Rumble in the Jungle when – in arguably the greatest sporting miracle of the twentieth century – an unfavoured Muhammad Ali soaked up round after round of punishment from the colossal George Foreman before unleashing an unthinkable counter-attack and knocking him out. Andy needed to channel the Greatest. So in that split second between points, when the cheering was dying down but before the players were ready for the next service, I hollered the name given to Ali's crazy strategy: 'Rope-a-Dope him!' I yelled.

Stupid, I know. But *maybe*, I thought, Andy could make himself believe that Verdasco had tired himself out just like Foreman did? *Maybe*, although the match looked dead and buried, it was still there for the taking? As I later discovered from the BBC television coverage, my voice carried across the stadium. That wasn't all. Boris Becker commentated on the swell of the crowd. 'That's exactly what he needs,' he told the global audience.

And Andy did go and dig himself out of the hole and overcome Verdasco, and did go on to claim his historic first Wimbledon title. A Brit *could* do it. A Brit *had* done it. And it was me. I. Won. Wimbledon.

Four years on from all that and now I'm back. Might history repeat itself? I won't have long to find out as Andy is first up on Centre Court, paired with America's big-serving Sam Querrey. A steward's portable machine spits out a ticket. 'Section 502. Row ZE.' Five rows behind Row Z? That sounds pretty high up. Maybe I should have packed fewer snacks and left room for binoculars. And oxygen. Still, any seat is good enough. The tiny square of paper that is granting me admission to the Mount Olympus of tennis is more suited to a parish tombola – a faint breeze could steal it away. In a way that's the essence of sport, where winning or losing can hang on the most wafer-thin margin. I push the ticket deep into my wallet, and I'm in.

The place is heaving with fans who, thanks to the flightiness of the British summer, have come dressed in various shades of optimism, from bikinis to overcoats. In every direction there are manicured courts and matches already in full swing. Some of the higher-numbered 'outside' courts have barely any room for spectators, and exude a quaint intimacy more like a school sports day than the grandest of grand slams. The sweet music of strings striking balls to ripples of applause is a soundtrack that must be practically unchanged since it was first heard here in the summer of 1877. I could happily lie on a grassy bank and let it lilt me into a comforting afternoon snooze.

There's one enormous difference between now and 2013. Since last time I was here Andy Murray had broken the curse, become a two-time Men's Singles champion and been anointed a knight of the realm. With Murray, people don't just hope any more. They expect. For British tennis that's nothing short of the twenty-first century's most overused word: unprecedented. But just because you've climbed Everest twice doesn't mean scaling it again won't be a bloody pain in the crampons.

I weave my way past strawberry stalls, champagne bars and player entrances guarded by military personnel in gleaming ceremonial uniform. No less impeccable are the ball boys and ball girls who scuttle by to their next posting. Opulence is everywhere. The All England Club lies just 2 miles from the ruins of Wimbledon Greyhound Stadium, but their fortunes are a million light years apart. If you could offer Dan the choice between going to one or the other, I'm utterly sure he'd pick the dogs. Which makes me smile. A venue's beauty or luxury didn't matter to him, and he never once went to an event in order 'to be seen'. He just loved sport, and a flutter. That's not to say he wouldn't have enjoyed being here now. He'd have loved every minute. He'd have just wished for less bubbly and more burgers.

I carry thoughts of him as I pick my way through the crowds and underneath a gantry, on which John McEnroe is waxing lyrical to a BBC camera about what today has in store for us.

Festooned with ivy, Centre Court's exterior wall soars lush and verdant like a mammoth Aintree fence. On TV it seems cosy and intimate; in reality it's awesome. Embedded into the greenery, a jumbo screen beams out faces along with their seeding, indicating the likelihood of them winning the trophy. Andy Murray smiles next to the number '1'. Down at ground level is a more lo-fi display made out of immaculately painted wood, advertising today's schedule for play with a separate slat for each player. I scan the listings from Centre Court down. Murray, Federer and Djokovic . . . but down at the very bottom some other names stand out even more. Martina Navratilova. Michael Chang. Tracy Austin. Conchita Martínez. Henri Leconte. A pot-pourri of living legends from Wimbledons past, who've signed up to play some exhibition doubles matches. I think that's wonderful. Former idols being given the platform to perform all over again, just for kicks. It's a shame more sports don't take the idea on. If Silverstone ever invites Nigel Mansell, Jenson Button and Damon Hill to the British Grand Prix to race milk floats around the car park, I'll be there like a shot.

Row 'ZE' is one from the very back, wedged under the famous sloping roof. From TV you'd never know there are fans up here in the rafters, but even this high up the view is superb: I'm in line with the net, perpendicular to the action. It's a novelty to watch tennis like this, as opposed to the head-on angle we all know on the BBC. Looking very dapper in the middle of the oversized Royal Box are Sir Ian McKellen and Dame Maggie Smith, two of Britain's finest fictional wizards (in their respective aliases of Gandalf and Hogwarts' Professor McGonagall.) Ahead of them in the front row sits a practitioner of tennis sorcery, Aussie legend Rod Laver. Two seats along from him, in the best seat in the house, is the Duke of Kent. Of course he is. Back up here in the gods a friendly mood is building among the Row ZE crew. I discover my two neighbours, Fiona and Annie, have also fluked tickets through the flash sale and we bond through our tremendous good fortune. 'At my club I'm told not to play double-handed volleys', says Fiona, 'but I don't see why. It's all right for Martina Hingis!'

From our lofty eyrie we're the first to get a glimpse of Andy Murray and Sam Querrey emerging from the locker room and, as word of their arrival spreads, applause builds around the stadium. The players step onto the grass to a full-throated Centre Court roar. The champion leads the way, followed by his taller and more lumbering opponent, both carrying their gargantuan kit bags in the way that only tennis players ever seem to do. Knocking some balls gently across the net, they both warm up, and with them so does the auditorium as the sun peeks out from behind the clouds to bathe the court in gold. Almost too splendid to be a stage for combat.

Almost, but not quite. Murray isn't mucking about. His opening blitzkrieg breaks Querrey's serve in the first game of the match, and he demolishes the entire set in a mere 28 minutes. It's so engrossing I've barely touched my crisps. The American is getting a taste of shock and awe. It's a mismatch: one man is frozen with nerves; the other on fire. When Murray goes a break up in the second set, people start rummaging in their bags. It feels as though everyone is readying themselves for an early trip to the bar. But Querrey is no mug and he holds firm against the Scottish salvos, counter-punching with venom and unloading some of his booming trademark aces. Hauling himself into the match, he levels proceedings at one set apiece and takes the third to a tie-break. But the champion finds another gear. Murray has an all-court game, and he digs into his bag of tricks: delicate drop shots, laser-guided passes down the line, Inspector Gadget-esque telescopic defence. He devours the tie-break and regains the lead, two sets to one, to palpable relief in the stadium as we head into the fourth set. The ship has been righted. Full speed ahead, Mr Murray.

If only. His great adversary is yet to have a say. And I don't mean Sam Querrey. The next two games go with service, but something's up. Murray's demeanour has changed. The passion and the desire are still there, but even from Row ZE you can tell he's uncomfortable. Not to put too fine a point on it, he looks crocked. In the next point Querrey wrong-foots Murray with a crunching return that leaves the champion leaning on his racket as though it's a walking stick. Annie turns to me, eyebrows raised. The American underdog makes short work of the set (6–1). In the players' box Andy's wife Kim looks concerned. In the Royal Box the two celebrity wizards wince, magical interference apparently off the agenda. Sir Ian and Dame Maggie might have a combined age of 160 but right now I'd back either of them in a foot race against Andy.

A nearby fan is listening to the radio commentary: apparently it's Murray's hip that's the problem. Whatever it is, it's a marvel he's staying out there; many in the same predicament would retire hurt. There's certainly no chance Andy could make the climb to join us up here in Row ZE. *Wow*, I think to myself. *I'm on Centre Court and able to move more easily than the current Wimbledon champion. That's unlikely to happen again.* The final set is slipping away from the Scot, but it's equally clear how much Wimbledon means to him. Murray is not the sort of man to give up his title willingly. Sometimes he connects sweetly and hits a clean winner, but more often he fails to reach the shot he's so desperate to play and another point goes begging. Bereft of their usual power, his serves are clobbered away by his opponent. Andy started the match as a Stealth bomber; now he's in a flat spin, falling out of the sky. Across the net the unfancied Querrey is calmly going about his business. He's taken a leaf out of the Muhammad Ali playbook and absorbed everything Murray could throw at him. Now he's the last man standing.

The home favourite is out. His crown has slipped. Above him the sun retreats, and a stiff breeze chills the air. The crowd is aghast. The fallen champion removes his cap, slings his kit bag over a shoulder (just about) and trudges off Centre Court, the first traces of a bald patch showing on his sweat-glazed pate. But even now, I remain in awe of Sir Andy Murray. This man had propelled himself to one of the toughest summits in any sport to become indisputably the best men's player Britain has ever produced. At the start of this match it was Querrey's serve that was broken, but now it was Murray's body. After so many years of toil it's surprising he hasn't buckled more often. Will the injury prove just a blip, or is it something more serious? Will he win again? Will he even be back again?

After the five-course banquet of that Murray match, I slip out of Centre Court for a punnet of strawberries and cream. At Wimbledon this costs the equivalent of a month's energy bill, but it has to be done. I find a spot on the slope variously known as Murray Mound or Rusedski Ridge but most of all as Henman Hill, from the times when a multitude used to gather here to watch Tiger Tim on the big screen snatch defeat from the jaws of victory. This famous place is only a stone's throw from where Dan and I grew up in Croydon, and yet when we were kids coming here never seemed possible. It was something *other* people did, like seeing snooker at the Crucible or the Grand National at Aintree. For us, such things existed inside the telly, not in real life. How close we lived as a family to the epoch-making exploits of McEnroe, Navratilova, Sampras and Graf, and how far removed from them our own dramas were. Whatever the circumstances of all the different people sprawled up here on Raducanu Rise (TBC), sport is something that binds billions of us together, in a shared narrative of amazing feats, heroic deeds and agonising near-misses. I don't know where I'd be without it.

I brush some loose blades of Henman off my jeans, wash down the strawberries with a glass of Robinson's Barley Water (when in Rome . . .), and start the climb back up to the Centre Court stratosphere. It's time for one of the greatest shows on Earth: Roger Federer is in the house. I take my seat just as he enters the packed court with his Canadian quarter-final opponent, Milos Raonic. Raonic is one of the next generation of top players long tipped to succeed the Roger–Rafa–Novak–Andy axis at the top of the game, but who still live very much in the shadow of the 'big four'. With all due respect to Milos, today he is nothing but the support act. Every pair of eyes is fixed on Federer and his monogrammed whiter-than-whites. More than any other sportsperson in the world, he's the one I would have been gutted never to see play. I wish there was a VCR in my head so I could record the experience and take the pressure off savouring every second.

Even from up here in near-Earth orbit, I'm starstruck by Federer. He ranks as one of the human wonders of the world. He has the aura of the perfect athlete, a hero from Greek myth in tennis form. Whereas Murray willed himself to the top, here is a man who was simply made to play tennis. Like Usain Bolt in sprinting, Shane Warne in spin bowling or Ronnie O'Sullivan in snooker, he's redefined what was thought possible in his sport. As with the Beatles and the Stones, Federer will always be measured against his arch-rival Nadal, but for me there's no debate. Rafa has bludgeoned his way to the top with tenacity, power and a shedload of French Open titles; Federer has done the harder thing of turning grace into a weapon, and in doing so rebirthed the whole men's game. Before Rog came along, the Nineties had fed us a diet of 'Pistol' Pete Sampras, who hoovered up seven Wimbledons with a method that was nigh-unbeatable yet unradical, built upon an Exocet serve. Simultaneous to Stephen Hendry's iron dominance in snooker, Sampras turned men's lawn tennis into the sporting equivalent of a one-party state. Fair play to Pete, he was a class above the rest, and for four years he didn't lose a single match at the Championships. It was Federer who put an end to that run in 2001, as a nineteen-year-old, and the only question was when the precocious Swiss would one day inherit the crown. In the two decades since, his answer has been emphatic. He is the absolute embodiment of winning with style. And with it has come adoration. The Centre Court crowd's fondness for Murray has been a slow-burning affair; a guarded start that gave way over time to a deeper understanding and affection. With Federer it was love at first sight. This is *his* court. Even the Duke of Kent is a mere subject here.

Word spreads around the grounds that Roger's match is getting underway, and the lucky ticket-holders gather back inside the arena like bees returning to the hive. At once Federer cuts an entirely different figure to the wounded Murray. The Swiss is five years Andy's senior but today he's ten times silkier, and he wastes no time slipping into top gear. He fires backhand shots at Raonic that are 20mph faster than Murray's, yet using just a single hand. One cross-court winner draws not just applause and cheers from the 12,000-strong crowd but, a beat later, a second outpouring as the sheer brilliance of the shot registers, which I can only describe as a Mexican Gasp. It's a paradox that a business as brutal as international sport, which just an hour ago had sent Andy Murray hobbling to the treatment table, can also be the thing of beauty Federer is making it now. Raonic is a hulking Goliath who would beat almost anyone else on the planet. Yet this afternoon he is left looking like a middle-aged dad who should be knocking a few balls around after work with Giles from accounts.

The majority of today's Centre Court crowd aren't just willing Roger to win the match: they want him to go on to claim an eighth title, which would overtake Sampras's record and cement him as Wimbledon's undisputed greatest male player. Why does this matter? Because the drama of sport rests to a large extent upon a personal decision for the spectator: each of us gets to pick a side. Take today's match against Raonic in isolation, and I'd have been more than likely to cheer on the unfancied Canadian. After all, he's up against the overwhelming favourite for both the bookies and the crowd. But zoom out and, in a wider context, Federer is a plucky challenger too. To will him to complete his Herculean labour is to share in the thrill.

Raonic swipes a service return into the tramlines and the

crush is complete. He's been steamrollered in straight sets, 6–4, 6–1, 7–6. The Swiss maestro leaps in exultation and punches the air, his joy as unbridled as if it's his first ever win, which is astonishing to see in itself. It's a flash of the hunger that has taken him to new heights and kept him there; a split-second of motion that emblematises an epic story. I catch a frame of it on my camera, freezing it in time, and, as I join the rest of Centre Court in a standing ovation I also feel wistful. In a sense it's a tragedy that such moments in life are so fleeting. Being in the midst of grief sees me grappling with another, more painful, paradox: temporariness is permanent. How many years does Roger have left in the tank? Will I ever see him play again? How long before anyone eclipses him, just as he's done to Sampras? How unfair it is that Dan will never know the answer to any of this. And how tenuous my own future feels. What does Fate hold in store for me, if my brother's life can be so suddenly snuffed out? Even now such questions can break out unpredictably, and in torrents I can't hold back.

It's clear from Federer's response to winning a mere quarter-final that he feels the sense of history upon him and he's comfortable seizing the mantle. This is what separates the admirable players who win Wimbledon once from the legends who make this place their own. And nobody's owned this one like he has. Given how patriotic sports fans are, not least British tennis ones, that's not bad going by a bloke from Basel.

My head's buzzing. Annie, Fiona and I exchange farewells, wide smiles on our faces. I make my way out of Centre Court, surrounded by snatches of chatter from fulfilled fans. What a day. I've seen the reigning men's champion scrap for all he's worth in a doomed bid to retain his crown, and then his glorious predecessor sail serenely on in his buccaneering quest to regain it. But then I spot something that stops me in my tracks. The Wimbledon Honours Boards: column after neatly painted column of the winners for every year since the tournament's inception. The Gentlemen's Singles goes right back to SW

Gore's victory in 1877, while the Ladies' Singles begins with Miss M. Watson in 1884. What a phenomenal collective effort by so many supreme athletes across three centuries.

But it's the last board on the right-hand side that stands out. This one is for the male and female winners of the Wheelchair Tennis category. And it's virtually empty. Wheelchair tennis is a fantastic sport in its own right, and it was showcased to millions of new fans (including me) at the London Paralympics. It's surely as an aftershock from the seismic success of 2012 that the All England Club has incorporated disability tennis into the Championships. And it's clear from the honours board that I've come here just twelve months since this discipline was belatedly brought into the fold, because only last year's winners are on the board: G. Reid and Miss J. Griffioen. As I end my day at Wimbledon it's this that leaves a mark on me. Dan and I were always obsessed with statistics, and I'm still filled with the awful sorrow that my brother will never be able to add any new names to his trivia bank of champions. But the empty honours board with its ocean of blank space, where future heroes will have their names etched, is compelling me to look forwards as well as back. That's a good feeling.

In subsequent years the wheel of fortune has continued to turn for the titans of our era. Days after my visit to SW19, Roger did go on to surpass Sampras and win his record eighth Wimbledon in 2017 (as well as bagging another Australian Open in 2018), before injury struggles blighted the twilight of his playing days and finally tennis had to comprehend the reality of a Federerless circuit. Meanwhile his two fiercest rivals, Nadal and Novak Djokovic, have survived their own battles (with fitness and vaccine phobia respectively) to overhaul Roger's record of twenty grand slam wins. Thus the debate about the greatest men's player of all time continues. As it always will. And as it does in the women's game too. 2022 saw Serena Williams, the undisputed queen of her generation, take her final bow after one valedictory

US Open campaign at Flushing Meadows, leaving her destined to always be mentioned in the same breath as Navratilova, Graf, Evert and King. In her stead a wide field of contenders has been left vying for preeminence, including Bromley's own Emma Raducanu, who came out of nowhere to win the US Open in 2021 and join a very select list of British grand slam winners. Her career will be defined by how often she can recapture that sublimity again. We've come a long way from the Eighties.

As for Andy Murray, after I watched him hobble out of Centre Court he was dogged by injury woes for the next five years but, through perseverance, persistence and pain, he somehow rebuilt himself physically and mentally to stage a return to Wimbledon in 2022. His challenge was snuffed out in the second round (by that other record-breaker John Isner), but simply managing to make it back to the championships looked to me like being the Scot's most tenacious achievement of all. But I was wrong. At the 2023 Australian Open, the thirty-five-year-old veteran engineered two unbelievable fight-backs from the brink that rivalled the 2013 Verdasco epic: his five-set ordeal against Thasani Kokkinakis took five hours and forty-five minutes, ending at 04:05 a.m., the third-latest finish at tour level in tennis history. Murray isn't made of granite. He makes granite look like Play-Doh. Thankfully for the rest of us, just occasionally he can look human. Days after his Melbourne heroics, he tweeted: 'School drop off this morning. My 6 year old: "daddy don't give me a kiss and a cuddle anymore when you drop me . . . just stay in the car." ☹ Tough game. Back to reality!'

At the time of writing, Federer recently hung up his racket and Murray's chances of more silverware are diminishing, before Time hits a final clean winner and sends him surely to the commentary booth. But I'd been lucky enough to catch sight of these two mighty stars with the naked eye, as one began to fade and the other rose towards its final zenith.

Reigning champion Andy Murray on his way to quarter-final
defeat by Sam Querrey

Roger Federer clinches victory against Milos Raonic,
en route to a record eighth Wimbledon title

16

Not All Balls Are Round

'There are known knowns; there are things we know
we know. We also know there are known unknowns;
that is to say, we know there are some things we don't
know. But there are also unknown unknowns – the
ones we don't know we don't know.'

So said American Secretary of Defence Donald Rumsfeld
on 12 February 2002, when he was asked about the existence of Iraqi weapons of mass destruction (that didn't exist).
Rummy's infamous philosophical soundbite might stand as a
worrying summary of a superpower's foreign policy, but in
the here and now of summer 2017 it was applying very well to
my adventure. Some events I'd been to were ones I'd already
had a taste of in the past, like rugby, snooker and tennis, so to
an extent I knew in advance what I was likely to get. There
were other sports which I knew were going to be entirely new
affairs for me, like darts and American football. And then
there was that third category. The possibility of coming upon
something truly exotic: something I not only didn't know I
could watch, but which I didn't even know existed. My very
own unknown unknown. Being a fan of pretty much every
sport going, from the Olympic 100 metres final to sidecar racing, I doubted I was going to stumble upon anything that fell
into this last variable. But then I got a call from my friend
Matt Parker. 'Jon, do you want to go to the World Rubik's Cube
Championships?'

The Rubik's Cube is a strange object. Physically it's unremarkable, nothing more than a small, twistable, six-coloured block. But this humble 3D puzzle is also quite possibly the most recognisable toy in the entire world. Invented by Hungarian professor of architecture Ernő Rubik, it's an Eighties icon as enduring as Tom Cruise. It's inevitable that at some point in your life you'll have played with one; it's highly probable that someone in your family has owned one; and it's just as likely that you've never solved the damn thing. For most of us, the prospect of completing the cube is akin to Tony Blair recovering his reputation or Palace winning the league: it's not going to happen. It's a toy from a more innocent era when, as with early computer games on the Spectrum or the Amstrad, the idea of finishing it was the stuff of a madman's dreams. Back then, just having a go was distraction enough. Did this novelty item really have its own world championships?-

If anyone else had made the suggestion, I'd have assumed it was a joke. But not Matt. His occupation is 'Stand-up Mathematician'. In other words he gets paid for being funny about maths. The guy likes a challenge. Over the last ten years he's carved out an impressive niche, accruing millions of clicks for the ingenious, nay, headache-inducing videos he posts online. Flipping a coin 10,000 times to see how many times it lands on its edge? He's been there. Making a rudimentary computer out of a gigantic domino rally? He's done that. Now his YouTube Channel was sending him across the English Channel to cover the planet's premier Rubik's cube tournament as it came to Paris. Matt knew I was in the midst of my own sporting mission, so he wondered if I wanted to join him for a weekend of competitive 'cubing', as it's known in the trade.

Hmm. Did I want that? I was having a bit of a moment. My relationship with Dan had been lit up by revelling together in the innocence of childhood. It was part of our lifeblood – to wallow in nostalgia. But that word, in the original Greek sense it was suffered by Odysseus, doesn't just denote wistful sentimentality. *Algia* means 'a painful yearning', *nostos* 'for returning home'. That's how I was feeling it. I still needed nostalgia's warmth, its shelter. But now it came with a terrible ache. Grief had crept into all of our old shared passions and buried its roots in the warm memories. It hadn't stolen them. Just battered them. I don't hate things lightly, but I hated that. The Rubik's cube was a tiny totem of that fuzzy, unreachable past: in our family it was Dan who'd owned one. (He never finished it either.) So when Matt first mentioned the famous toy, the past flooded in. Dan still pervaded everything.

Yet by now, slowly, subtly, something was changing. Bereavement breaks and remakes your world, and you with it. When it comes to leaping off the springboard of familiarity into the brisk waters of the unknown, in the old days you'd never have found me at the front of the queue. In that I took after my brother. But since circumstance had flung me into my new normal I'd been forced to think again, and I was saying yes to new things – opening my eyes wider and broadening my horizons – more than I used to find natural. This had helped me begin to realise that change can be a medicine. By trying new experiences I was dulling and diluting the hurt. It was an odd discovery, that looking forwards can help guard your back.

Even so, I didn't expect the World Rubik's Cube Championship. *'Nobody expects the World Rubik's Cube Championship!'* I could almost hear Michael Palin screech. *'Its chief weapons are surprise, ruthless efficiency and an almost fanatical devotion to complex mathematical algorithms.'* What the hell would it be like? Is it even a sport? There was only one way to find out. 'Matt, count me in.'

I won't lie, I was still a bit unconvinced about the whole idea when we met up in a Soho pub one summer's evening to plan our expedition. (The same pub where Dan and I once plotted how we'd get to the Rugby World Cup.) Matt sensed my scepticism, but he took it in his stride. He simply smiled and produced from behind his back a small pouch tied up with string. 'That's for you.' I reached inside the bag. It was my very own Rubik's cube, to celebrate the delights of the adventure to come and, who knows, maybe even convert me. It sat there in front of us, pristine, dwarfed by our two beers and ready to befuddle. I felt inadequate just at the sight of it, and decided to come clean. I was, I confessed, one of those poor saps for whom a Rubik's cube was something you picked up, fiddled with for as long as you could bear, and then tossed away in frustration. Could there really be much more to it than that?

Matt raised his eyebrows, sighed, and picked up the scrambled cube. He proceeded to solve it with unbroken serenity in just under a minute, and placed it back down between our drinks. All six colours aligned. Alchemy. I knew I was a geek, but this guy was a *professional* geek. His feat drew impressed glances from nearby tables. I had been schooled. I felt like a callow Luke Skywalker watching Yoda lift an X-Wing from the depths of a swamp, cool as you like.

'I don't believe it.' I gasped.

'That is why you failed.'

Matt's voice had more of an Aussie lilt to it than a Yodalese croak, but his mastery of his subject seemed to be on a par with Dagobah's finest green little wizard. If Matt had this kind of ability, I wanted to know, did this mean he'd be entering the championships himself?

'No way. I'm nowhere near good enough to take on those guys.'

'How fast can they do it, then?

'Oh, seconds.'

This I had to see.

Just before we get there, take a pause and imagine what you think the World Rubik's Cube Championships might be like. Form a picture in your head.

Nah. It was weirder than that.

Saturday, 15 July 2017: Rubik's Cubing, Paris

'Paris' was stretching it. The taxi had swept north until the Eiffel Tower was not so much as a matchstick on the horizon. By the time we'd crossed the city's ring road I'd started imagining we'd wandered into a sequel to the movie *Taken,* and we were in the process of being kidnapped. Luckily I was soon shuddered to my senses, as the driver slammed on the brakes and turfed us out on the edge of a nondescript industrial estate. After half an hour of hearing about twists, buffers, arcs and algorithms, had the cabbie found our deep-dive Rubik's bantz just too boring? You couldn't blame him. But our phones assured us we were in the right place: Les Docks De Paris. At the far end of the site we found a conference centre converted from an old warehouse, appropriately cubic in design. It had a brutalist frontage softened just a smidge by a recent lick of paint, with two pink stripes fringing a crimson centre and a gold leaf design above the entrance. All in all, it looked less like a Hasbro hobbyist's heaven and more like the setting for the Chinese Communist Party's National Congress.

Even though I'd prepped myself to expect the unexpected, I was still wrong-footed by what confronted us inside. The foyer opened out into a massive deserted antechamber, filled with dozens of large round tables and chairs, all strewn with backpacks, empty drinks cans and the odd completed cube. It resembled the scene of the world's nerdiest wedding reception, and we were witnesses to the aftermath. Or after*Maths,* to be more precise. This, it turned out, was the 'training area', where competitors had been honing their skills for the hot cubing action ahead. The sheer scale of it was staggering. It dawned on me that as much as this event might be an unlikely curio for me, for the people involved it was no joke. This shit was real. But where had everyone gone? We didn't need to wait long for an answer. A round of applause from the next hall told us we needed to get moving. Battle was about to commence.

We were stopped in our tracks by an information board posting the schedule of events. It was huge. As with a golf tournament, the championships were spread across four days from Thursday to Sunday, with the prizes due to be awarded tomorrow on Finals Day – by none other than Professor Rubik himself. And as with a swimming meet, there wasn't just one type of racing but all kinds of different titles up for grabs, with many of the top performers vying for multiple gongs à la Michael Phelps. This was news to me. I'd assumed these world championships would just involve a bunch of people trying to solve the famous toy as quickly as humanly possible. But the competition was divided into a bewildering array of disciplines: small cubes (2x2x2); big cubes (every size up to 7x7x7); a triangular variant called the Pyraminx; a dodecahedronal variant of that variant called the Megaminx; the corner-twisting Skewb; and – an Argos catalogue favourite of yesteryear – the Rubik's Clock. And that's just for starters. There were also separate crowns for doing it using only one hand, doing it while wearing a blindfold – we're still talking about Rubik's Cubes – and even for the person who could solve the Cube fastest using only their feet. Although that one's controversial, Matt told me: apparently feet are looked down upon.

The other revelation from reading the schedule was that we'd turned up at an interesting point in the festivities. Tonight the main championships were taking a break to allow space for a separate event: a knockout competition in which national teams were going to duke it out round by round in a relay race of cube-solving. At the end of the night only one country would be left standing, and they would be crowned winners of the world's very first Rubik's Nations Cup. Ohmigod. This was the Uruguay 1930 of the nerd world, and we'd arrived just in time for kick-off.

The arena was big. Facing the stage a single-tier stand rose Kop-style, with space for 1,500 spectators and barely a spare seat in the house. But the first thing that hit us wasn't the size of the place. It was the noise. All around us was a constant, crazy *clickety-clack*. It befitted an army of angry rattlesnakes, but belonged to the assembled horde of Rubik's lovers – competitors and spectators alike – simultaneously solving cubes in whichever direction you looked. At first this perpetual thrum was disconcerting, even a bit annoying. But it didn't take long to acclimatise, and I quickly came to embrace it as an essential ingredient of the occasion, like the vuvuzelas at South Africa's 2010 World Cup. It was all part of the soup. This was unlike anything I'd come across before. Around me was so much mathematical acrobatics that for the first time in my life you could actually hear the number-crunching.

As impressive as the grandstand was, those were just the cheap seats. Cordoned off in front of Row A was a 'golden circle' area, for the use of teams and (believe it or not) the VIP guests. I shook my head. What is the world coming to when even the wholesome world of Cubing has a prawn sandwich section? If that wasn't bizarre enough, there was even a standing zone for the most raucous contingent of fans. That's right, folks. As crazy as it sounds, the World Rubik's Cube Championship had terracing. Meanwhile up on the stage were two solving tables, both equipped with a hi-tech digital timer and three seats for each trio of players. Everything was set for the cerebral slugfest to come. And on the back wall, just like at every world-class sporting venue, was a giant screen to relay the close-up action for the benefit of us fans. Yup. There was no getting away from it now. I was one of them.

It was then that I received another lesson in the importance of knowing the right people at the right time. Out of the bustle I could hear a name being shouted. 'Matt? Matt Parker?' The voice had a soft German twang and was owned by a young man named Gregor, who had hurried through the crowds to meet us. He was a cheery, bespectacled student mathematician, and a cuber himself. Tied around his neck was an eye mask which, I soon discovered, was the telltale sign of a blindfold solver.

Gregor was piqued to the point of giggliness by spotting Matt, being a fan of StandUpMaths on YouTube. Matt and I were more interested in Gregor's T-shirt, which told us he was one of the official stewards. Could he be our ticket to penetrating Professor Rubik's golden circle? Gregor shrugged. 'Sure.' Through the crowd he led us, into the posh seats, while I grinned at the unlikely power of mathematical celebrity. Right there and then, I knew I'd arrived at the single strangest point on my voyage through the world of sport. All we needed now was some action.

A master of ceremonies in a white linen suit appeared brandishing a microphone. His name was Scheffler. Ian Scheffler. And he was a cuber too. It dawned on me that I was possibly the only person in this mass gathering who wasn't. Here I was, surrounded by hundreds of people, and in with a shout of being the least geeky individual in the room. This was the first and almost certainly the last time that was going to happen. I could tell I was going to enjoy this. Out of Ian's mouth spilled an enthusiastic Californian holler that welcomed us to Paris, and he beckoned up to the stage the two teams drawn to face each other in the opening first-round tie: 'The United States versus Mongolia!' Now there's a fixture you don't see every day. In the grand tradition of cup competitions, were we about to see a giant-killing? And in the world of Rubik, which one was the giant? Either way, cubing had obviously gone global. Not many sports could boast an international reach this wide. In fact, could any? The Americans certainly weren't half-arsed about it. They'd brought no fewer than four teams bidding to conquer the world, and their number-one unit made short work of the plucky Mongolians. We were off and running.

Every match was a miniature drama in itself. Two by two the teams would take to the stage, kitted out in matching white T-shirts bearing their national flag. The only exceptions were America's second team, a good-looking trio all of athletic build who went off-piste and chose to sport sleeveless vests instead, to show off their well-honed biceps. They were an immediate crowd favourite, even if their title hopes soon bit the dust. (In the world of Rubik, brain always beats brawn.) When Canada were drawn against Spain the Canadians were serenaded with vociferous chants of 'Ca-Na-Da! Ca-Na-Da!'; Spain's fans retorted by bellowing the Macarena. Almost all the contestants were scrawny and introverted, but the idolising rowdiness that greeted them was worthy of Wrestlemania. You couldn't fail to get swept up in the euphoria.

There was a knowingness to this bearpit atmosphere. Every-one watching was loving the incongruity of treating cubing as though it was the Super Bowl. For the competitors, though, this was serious business. They were being tested in public against the best in the world, with national pride at stake. And for the first time in Rubik's history it wasn't just an individual pursuit. Now they had team-mates too, whom they mustn't let down. It's this last thought that must have been swimming through the players' heads as they sat ready to do battle. Tonight, in front of a large crowd and on the ultimate stage, another solver's shot at glory could depend entirely on you.

Once a pair of teams were seated at their respective tables, they were effectively on the starting grid. In front of each com-batant an official would place a small cardboard bucket that looked like an upturned Happy Meal. With the blare of an Indy-car announcer Ian would issue the command, 'Prepare for inspection in three, two, one, go!' Hush would descend and all six players would remove their bucket, revealing a freshly scrambled cube which they would pick up and study with alac-rity. That was it. No solving; just looking. This was the calm before the storm, a chance for them to consider their method. After a few seconds Ian would yell, 'Please place your hands on the timers!' The players would put their cube down, still staring at it intently, and rest both hands on a touch-sensitive pressure pad. In athletics terms they were now on their marks. As soon as they moved their hands from the pad, the timer would start. This was it. You could cut the tension with a set square. Even the background cube-clicking would fall silent. 'Ready. Set. Go!'

The first player on each team would grab their cube and start twisting as though their life depended on it. They were so fast, their fingers melted into a furious fleshy blur. Mere seconds later they'd be dropping the solved cube onto the table and slamming their timer, allowing their next team-mate to pick up the baton. Each cube was differently scrambled, so there was no benefit to watching your friends working out their own solution. All you could do was will them on and wait; when it was your go, you were on your own. At last, once player three had completed their cube the aggregate timer would stop, the crowd would cheer and judgement would be served. Whichever team had mopped up all three cubes the quicker would be through to the next round. For the runners-up, it was game over. Goodbye, cruel world. Swotting had never seemed so cut-throat.

The speed of the performers was gobsmacking, faster than Max Verstappen on a dodgy last lap. Almost every team could get through three cubes in under 30 seconds, which was half the time it had taken Matt to impress me by completing one. It all seemed so friendly and good-natured, I was surprised to notice that to one side of each solving table sat an adjudicator, to ensure everything stayed in order. I whispered to Gregor about how that looked like overkill. Without averting his eyes from the stage he muttered, in a very matter-of-fact tone, 'There may be cheating.'

'No!' I exclaimed, probably too loudly. But Gregor had a sad truth to share. Not even the squarest sport on the planet was immune from people trying to cut corners. At a previous championship, someone had apparently pretended to set a new world record in the final of the Rubik's Clock event, but it later emerged that he'd fixed the result. There'd been a brouhaha, said Gregor, and the perpetrator had been kicked out to make an example of him.

'Was he banned from future tournaments?'

'No.'

Where's a statue of Zeus and a hall of shame when you need one?

The skullduggery went further. Gregor explained that over the years judges have been abused, blindfold solvers have been caught peeking under their masks, and one case even involved the police. Who'd have thought the 1980 Toy Of The Year could incite this level of international intrigue? Neither was cheating the only cause of controversy. Some cubers have been in such a rush to finish that, as they drop their completed cube and hit 'stop' on their timer, one coloured layer has ended up not quite aligned with the rest. When this happens the cube must be inspected by the adjudicator and, if they find a layer more than 45 degrees out of sync, the contestant is whacked with a two-second time penalty. That might not sound like much, but to a cuber it feels as long as a geological era, or the experience of watching the movie version of *Cats*. I spent a moment taking in what was on display here. Once again, albeit in the oddest of settings, I was in the presence of heroes treading the magic fault line along which runs the essence of sport, where the chasm between triumph and tragedy can be decided by a nanometre.

The semi-finals featured the wildest incident of the night. The USA trio who'd overpowered Mongolia in the very first match had made it through, with a team of super-solvers that contained the talents of individual 3x3 world champion Max Park as well as Patrick Ponce, who boasted the fastest individual solve of the entire tournament: a ludicrous 5.47 seconds. They'd sailed through to this stage, but now at last they were up against some serious opposition in the shape of Australia, anchored by the cherubic yet lethally quick Feliks Zemdegs.

Throughout the evening both Gregor and Matt had been pointing out Feliks to me as the sport's number one global star, with
records and titles galore under his belt. (Since my visit, Feliks
has got so big he's even had an Oscar-nominated documentary
made about his cubing exploits.)

The two teams matched each other twist for twist, cube for
cube, as the audience's awed hush broke out into *ooohs* and
aaahs at the completion of each solve. Finally, a mere 25.6 seconds after Ian had cried 'Go', both anchor-leg players seemed to
drop their finished cube and slam their timer in unison. Was it
a dead heat?

The Americans looked behind them to the scoreboard and
then jumped for joy. By milliseconds they'd stopped their
clock first. Their supporters cheered. The Australians commiserated with one another. In the stand, fans gave a standing
ovation. Only one person didn't leave their seat: the adjudicator at the USA table. Amid the celebrations I watched as he
craned forwards to look at the first American cube – not
touching anything, but staring intently. A fellow official
noticed his concern and joined him. Now both of them were
stock-still, pointing at the object.

Was something wrong? Within the blink of an eye, they'd
decided that there was. The Americans' first cube had been left
with an overly skewed layer. Team USA had to be served a penalty. Cameras confirmed the problem and relayed it up on the
big screen for all to see. I couldn't believe what I was witnessing: a crucial decision involving VAR. Video Assisted Rubik. It
took a second or two for the reversal to register among the
crowd, and then a new, louder din broke out. The Americans
slunk away in defeat. Feliks smiled with relief. The Aussies were
in the final.

The amount of attention I'd devoted to the Rubik's cube in
the last couple of hours had eclipsed the sum total I'd given it
in my previous thirty-seven years. Now it was everywhere,
overloading my senses. There was the incessant crackling of

countless cubes; the musk of teenage sweat; the sheer scale of nerdery. If anyone harboured any doubt as to how seriously the contestants took it, it would evaporate upon seeing the spectacle of players spending every last second before a match compulsively twisting their own practice cube. It was obsessive. These people were code-crack-addicts.

As silly as it appeared, just as with everything in mathematics this quirk could be explained by cold logic. They did it, Matt revealed, to keep their fingers warm by practising 'perms', which are the algorithmic moves that every solve calls upon. Each perm is named after a letter, denoting the rough shape of the twists they make on the cube: T, J and Y are three of the main ones. Fair enough. That explained it on a practical level. But I sensed there was something more to it. It looked as though it had become ritualistic – an affectation that had been adopted by all players, like bouncing the ball in tennis before a serve. Not necessary, but somehow vital.

It could be down to commercial factors too, added Gregor. All the best players had their favourite brand of cube, he said, and the top-ranked ones even struck sponsorship deals with manufacturers.

'Sponsorship deals?' I sniggered. Now this really was sounding like a modern professional sport. Perhaps it's only a matter of time before the big multinationals get in on the act and Nike designs an *Air Cube* featuring its iconic swoosh, but with the tail extended out into a square root sign. (Michael Jordan, call me. We can go halves.) With multiple makes on the market, the Nations Cup had decided to level the playing field by making everyone use a new, officially sanctioned cube made by a company called Gans. This sounded sensible to me, but apparently there had been rumblings among the players over having to perform with a model they weren't used to. By way of comparison Matt pulled out his own cube to show Gregor. 'This is a Thunderclap,' he said, a note of apology in his voice. 'It's not great, but it's my travel cube.' Gregor examined it and agreed that 'it has been surpassed. But back in the day, this was one of the go-to cubes.' I half thought the two of them were joking, only going into this much detail ironically. But no. They meant every word. It was charming to discover that in this niche world, fanatics could pore over the differences between technical equipment, like the pros and cons of Mercedes and Ferrari engines in Formula One, or cricket bats by Gray Nicholls or Gunn & Moore. There seemed to be no bottom to the Rubik's rabbit hole.

If my weekend can be summed up in a single image, it was when I was confronted by the sight of a man clutching a cube and solving it one-handed while standing adjacent to me – at the urinals. This told me I really had entered a parallel universe. I returned from the loos to find Matt once again being mobbed by fans. He even signed a cube for one teenager, who could barely contain his glee as he emerged from the scrum and scurried past me, declaring to anyone who'd listen that 'my friends are going to flip out!' Also in the throng was a player called Tomas, who introduced himself to me as being the Best Blindfold Solver in Sweden – a Scandinerdian answer to the Fastest Gun in the West. Tomas's party piece was the ability to recite pi to 1,024 decimal places, a feat of concentration I felt I matched by holding back the question that was trying to escape my lips: '*Why?*'

MC Ian's booming voice broke through the hullabaloo to summon us all back. After more than three hours of dexterous drama and seventy teams' hopes having bitten the dust, it was time for the first ever Rubik's Cube World Cup Final. Vying for supremacy were Germany and Australia, England's two greatest sporting nemeses, brought together for a rare showdown. For an English sports fan, it was akin to the tagline of *Alien Versus Predator*: 'Whoever wins, we lose.' Both teams lined up on stage and the players stood to attention for the national anthems, while their fans sang lustily. How adorable that the organisers had chosen to mimic the ceremonials of the World

Cup Final. Then I checked myself. No, this *was* a World Cup Final. I took out my phone and started filming, slowly panning across the faces of each team as their anthem was played. All we needed was Barry Davies in a commentary box.

Perhaps it was because the players thought of the Nations Cup as a bit of a sideshow and so the pressure was off. Or perhaps it was because this particular event had never ever been staged before. Or maybe it was just an inherently brilliant format. Whatever the explanation, being in the hall that Saturday night was intoxicating: a mix of competition and celebration among a cornucopia of nations, fuelled by an infectious and innocent joy. This was Eurovision for boffins. It was *Neurovision*.

How had this magnificently mad jamboree of mental gymnastics come to exist at all? I think there are three reasons. The first, of course, is Professor Rubik himself, who'd given birth to this craze that was now enjoying a golden age. The second is the Internet. A Rubik's World Championship for individual players had in fact been staged as early as 1982, pre-dating the Web, but back then there was no easy way for the international cubing community to connect and grow, or for the idea of a tournament to bed in. So it withered on the vine and disappeared for two decades, until in 2003 another attempt was made. This time it blossomed, since taking place every two years in a different host city, just like the Worlds in Athletics. Each iteration was bigger than the last, and now here in Paris I'd seen it burst into full bloom. The cube's relationship with the Internet is something of a paradox. If it hadn't been for the Web, the cube would never have been celebrated in the amazing way it now is. But with the infinite distractions we're spoiled with in the 2020s and beyond, if Professor Rubik had invented his cube today it's unthinkable that it would be the worldwide success story it became in the Eighties.

And the third explanation? It's the same reason why sport thrives at all. Humans have the capacity to turn pretty much anything into a sport. You name it: hairdressing, shin kicking, toe wrestling, pint-glass filling, marble running, dog food eating, tortoise racing, camel jumping, tea-bag throwing . . . golf. Our appetites are endless. (Unless you're in the dog food game.) It's about the thrill of playing, the dream of glory, and the joy of watching. Sport has the power, even if just for an instant, to transport you out of yourself and into the kind of unbeatable drama that no one could write. (We know some bookmakers have tried. And indeed, have been tried.) There will be some people who wish that greyhound racing and the BDO darts were still in their pomp, and that for them to be overtaken in popularity by the Rubik's cube is everything that's wrong with the world. But while the sports we choose to watch will change, from ancient Greece into the far-off future, sport itself will remain timeless. A never-ending story. Like *EastEnders*, except somebody wins.

I left convinced the Nations Cup would only get bigger, and that it most definitely should. All this circus needed was its own Barry Hearn or Don King as ringmaster. Maybe that could be me? Or you? After all, the TV rights are there for the taking. Speaking of sport on television, while I was in France that sunny July weekend, Roger Federer had been busy sealing his historic eighth Wimbledon, while Lewis Hamilton won the British Grand Prix and England battled to save the Second Test against South Africa. I'd just spent two whole days in a windowless warehouse watching young nerds playing non-stop with toys. And I loved every minute. I don't think Dan would ever have picked this as an event to go to, but wallowing in a blend of competitive fun and Eighties retro culture was very him. My two days in Paris had touched on an essential truth about my brother. He was someone for whom life had been lit up by an obsessive passion. The cubers had taken that same quality and raised it to something extraordinary.

I departed in no doubt that it is indeed a sport. A mindbendingly tricky one at that. Donald Rumsfeld did say that 'unknown' unknowns tend to be the difficult ones, so maybe he had a point after all. More than any other event on my travels, the Rubik's Cube World Championship put the odd into odd-yssey. It had been one of the most eccentric excursions of my life, and also one of the most joyous. I'd had a ball. A very square ball.

Oh, and what was the result of the Rubik's World Cup Final? The Germans won it. Of course they did.

Competitors at the 2017 Rubik's Cube World Championship, Paris

17

Open Secrets

Golf is big. Very big. According to recent estimates, 1,256 square kilometres of land in the United Kingdom is covered in golf courses. That's roughly equivalent to the size of Greater Manchester, and only just less than the entire area of the country that's covered by housing. It's a crazy statistic which speaks to issues of social inequality as much as sporting taste, and something my family could see evidence of right on our doorstep. Selsdon isn't exactly the most salubrious spot in the world, but from Mum's front door there's a choice of no fewer than seven 18-hole courses within walking distance, the nearest one being slap-bang opposite our house. It's cast-iron (or even 7-iron) proof that for a certain swathe of the population golf is an obsession. It's the sport that other sportspeople choose to play on their day off. It's a lifestyle. A social event. A business meeting. A diplomatic summit. An escape. And it's a rare example of a sport about which Dan didn't give a shit.

It's not that he actively hated golf. It was just one of those uncommon outliers that never really featured on his radar. An exception that proved the rule. So he'd have chuckled at the thought that it was thanks to him I'd travelled halfway across the country and was now queuing up to watch a day's tournament play. And not just any tournament. The word 'open' doesn't mean much on its own, but prefix it with the definite article and it becomes a different matter entirely. Say 'The Open' and suddenly you've got one of the biggest occasions in the sporting calendar. Among individual sports (as opposed to team events), it vies with Wimbledon as the most sought-after annual title that can be won on British shores. For four days each July, the best male golfers on the planet converge on a picture-postcard corner of the UK to compete for the famous old Claret Jug, watched by hundreds of thousands of fans on the course and millions more at home. Today was the opening round of the 146th staging, and I'd just arrived at Royal Birkdale on the north-west coast near Liverpool, to pop my Open cherry.

Thursday, 20 July 2017: Golf

Dan would have been most interested in the sands. And I don't mean bunkers. He'd have wanted to head straight to nearby Southport beach, not for its sea views but for its obscure place in sporting legend. It was there, back in the Seventies, that Red Rum used to train for the Grand National by galloping along the shoreline, because he suffered from a bone disease and the sand was thought to be therapeutic for his hooves. But while bro's priorities would have lain away from the course, he'd still have endorsed my trip to Birkdale. Paradoxically, golf being less relevant to him made today all the more meaningful: being here was about honouring Dan's love of completism, that peculiar fire in his bones which made him long for a pre-season friendly as much as an FA Cup Final. The wellspring of his joie de vivre. He'd have known as well as I did that no grand tour of the sporting world could exclude the Open. And as soon as I was through the gates and entering the tented village, I sensed that the organisers would brook no argument about which event had the fairest fairways of them all.

There's a clue to such pomposity in the fact that the grandees who run British golf call themselves the R&A, short for 'Royal and Ancient', a name that would sit well with a Tutankhamun Appreciation Society but for a sports club sounds firmly up its own back nine. Wearing such fustiness on its sleeve is emblematic of distasteful elements in the way the game has historically been administered: only as late as 2016 did the R&A strip Muirfield of its status as an Open championship venue for continuing to not admit female members, a decision that forced Muirfield to end its disgraceful policy the following year. There's a further hint of bombast in the unsubtle effort every year to hammer home the name of the event as just 'the Open', when the rest of the world steadfastly disagrees. For everyone else it's the *British Open*, for the understandable reason of distinguishing it from the dozens of other open championships held around the globe. But of course that makes the original one sound less special, which for the R&A won't do at all. The most twee assertion of its grandiloquence comes at the trophy presentation every year, when a suited man stands on the 18th green behind a wooden desk and proclaims the winner to be 'the champion golfer of the year', as if it's the only golf event that *really* counts. Which even I know is bollocks. The truth is that these days, of the four majors that constitute the sport's grand slam, it's the US Masters that holds the strongest allure. The R&A will never admit this, but deep down it knows. It's an *open* secret. Still, at least it's not the US PGA, which I'm told is very much the Ringo of the group.

As I went through the turnstiles, and beyond the outer rim of Dan's sporting enthusiasm, I was still riddled with guilt. Guilt that I was alive without him. Guilt over whether I'd done enough to help. Guilt about whether I was being true to his spirit. But this morning, more than any point so far in the last two years, competing emotions were starting to recover ground. Celebrating him in new ways, opening my eyes to fresh adventures, and above all saying *yes* – all of it was helping me try to become a better version of me, more equipped to live in the moment and to savour it. With every new event, I was a little bit more like Asterix, feeling the hit from a fresh glug of potion.

Golf courses being massive, on arrival at Birkdale every

spectator was handed a map. I had to hold on tight to stop it flying away in the buffeting wind, and I wasn't the only one. Several others near me were huddling together and trying to find their bearings, with good reason, because a curious quirk of the Open is that being a regular attendee doesn't necessarily help you. Unlike several other great annual events like Wimbledon or the World Snooker Championship, the UK's premier golf competition has no fixed home. It marauds across England, Scotland and Northern Ireland, with hosting duties rotated between a selection of world-renowned courses (and Muirfield). Today was the first time since 2008 that the circus had returned here to Birkdale, and I must have been far from the only one trying it for the first time. To prove the point, a young boy near me was looking up at his father. 'Daddy', he asked, 'where are the batters?' ('Someone on our wavelength', I wanted to tell Dan.)

Still, the majority of the fans flocking past seemed far more comfortable in these surroundings than I was. Among them were clusters of middle-aged, sports-casual men, who'd all be wearing lashings of *Eau de Top Gear* if such a thing existed. I overheard one such gaggle competing with each other about how many courses on the Open roster they'd not just been to but played. 'Have you done Muirfield and Troon?'

'Oh, yah!'

It wasn't the first time in the last twelve months that I'd been a fish out of water, but this felt like a different ocean. Was I one of the few spectators here who didn't play? That's if you don't count crazy golf, which was the one format of the game Dan and I did enjoy a brotherly round of. (As beautiful as Birkdale was, bro would have said the greens could definitely benefit from a few novelty windmills.) This place had the potential to eclipse the Rubik's Cube World Cup as the most alien sporting environment I'd yet explored, and as if in affirmation an augury suddenly appeared: a man marched past me with a humungous bird of prey on his wrist, looking completely blasé (that goes for both man and bird). I knew golfers loved getting eagles but wasn't that a bit drastic?

Mark Twain is said to have quipped that golf is 'a good walk spoiled'. Dan would probably go further and say that a walk is a good rest spoiled, and to spend a whole day roaming across open land would have been close to his idea of hell. In this regard I disagreed with my brother, and never more vehemently than now. I was looking forward to getting through as much shoe leather today as possible, because in the last few weeks I'd become slightly fixated by my fitness tracker. Actually, that's not quite accurate. Totally mesmerised would be nearer the mark. It didn't take a psychiatrist to figure out this was my latest deflection strategy. At least it was a wholesome one, compared to Dad's liquid option. But there was a darker motivation at work: a latent, gnawing fatalism. Dan had lived with obesity and, directly or indirectly, it almost certainly had a say in his death. Dad had been chronically overweight too, and also passed away too young, at fifty-seven. Now I was the only male left in the family. The spectre hovered that one day I might share their premature fate. (Truth be told, it still does.) So two competing forces were driving my Fitbit fetish: a desire for distraction, and fear.

This new addiction to walking had been starting to get a bit silly. A few days before the Open, I'd decided not to take the bus home to Mum's from East Croydon Station but to walk it instead, turning a breezy fifteen-minute ride into a sweaty hour and a half's uphill trek. Twenty-two thousand, six hundred and thirty-two daily steps clocked: a new personal best. In stark contrast, yesterday's eight hours in an office followed by a long train journey up to Liverpool had left me a country mile away from the sacred 10k target. A rational person would think nothing of it, but my rational self and I were having some time apart, and I couldn't let myself go to sleep until I'd jogged up and down the length of my cramped Premier Inn room again and again until I'd made up the deficit, springing on the balls of my feet to keep my steps light and avoid annoying the occupants below. Since I'd bought the tracker I'd never felt fitter, but wearing it had driven me a bit mad, like Frodo and the Ring. (His daily step count was similarly off the charts.) As I lay in bed that night, tripping off the fleeting appearance in my bloodstream of an exercise-induced endorphin, some self-awareness drifted back: grief was still doing odd things to me, and turning a hotel room into a hamster wheel was probably something best not to repeat.

Thankfully, with the wide expanses of Birkdale now opening up in front of me, there was no need to manufacture an excuse for some exercise. I had the best reason in the world for clocking a high step count: a day-long country walk, with world-class sport in every direction I looked. And it was the sport that really mattered. I couldn't claim to be the world's most avid golf fan but, unlike Dan, I've watched bits on TV over the years and kept a weather eye on the game's landmark tournaments: cheering Nick Faldo as he reeled in an imploding Greg Norman at the Masters; wincing as Jean van de Velde threw away an Open victory at Carnoustie's final hole and waded into a lake to play a shot underwater; disbelieving as Europe performed the 'Miracle at Medinah' to capture the 2012 Ryder Cup. The last of those was particularly fun.

Maybe it's the novelty of seeing such a doggedly individual pursuit as golf being turned into a team competition, but there's something magnificent about the Ryder and Solheim Cups. They can inspire even the most ardent Brexiteer to paint their face blue with a ring of gold stars. Better still, they've enabled some of the game's cult figures, who've never won a major, to seize the limelight and secure their legend: in golf the Jimmy Whites can find redemption. During the Nineties that mantle fell upon Colin Montgomerie, after which it passed to Ian Poulter, nicknamed the Postman 'because he always delivers'. At the time of writing Poulter is undefeated in Ryder Cup singles over seventeen years, and it was his five consecutive birdies that infused Medinah with one of sport's most improbable comebacks. I knew enough about Poulter to be a bit of a fan (this was years before he was lured by Saudi cash to play in the rebel LIV league), and a glance at the giant scoreboard in the tented village showed my luck was in. He was on the course right now, in the middle of his first round. More than that, he was the early leader, a shot ahead of the field at 2 under par. I knew where I had to head.

According to the map, my best bet for intercepting the Poulter group was at the 15th tee, so with that as my target I ventured out along the viewing galleries. The environment was captivating, and in more ways than one it felt like the Glaston-bury Festival; like the Eavises' mud-spattered musical piss-ups, the Open sprawled across time and space, covering acre after acre and spanning the best part of a week, with ticket holders spoiled for choice about where to go and what to see. Just like the stages at Glasto, each hole felt like a miniature event in its own right. Having said that, the soundscape of a music festival couldn't be further from a golf major's. For 99 per cent of the time I was at Birkdale, it was so quiet that birdsong and bee-hums were audible. The calm was only punctuated by the occasional swoosh of a club, a pocket of applause to acknow-ledge every shot, and the odd cheer to greet a spectacular putt, chip or bunker escape. Spectators at the Open are quickly schooled that tranquillity is treated with awed reverence, to the extent that before every shot marshals raise a luminous placard proclaiming 'SILENCE'. That's definitely something you'll never see at Glastonbury. More's the pity when Mumford & Sons take to the stage.

Before I could reach Mr Poulter, I stumbled upon another group of players busy tackling the front nine: Shiv Kapur, Mike Lorenzo-Vera and Charles Howell III, the latter displaying that quirk whereby Roman numerals, usually appended to kings, queens and popes, can also apply to American golfers. (And strangely often the third in a dynasty: see also Davis Love III and Harold Varner III.) This trio weren't attracting a large crowd, and as their approach shots plopped onto the tenth green, the hushed serenity of the occasion struck me again. This was surely the closest a top-level championship in any sport feels to just spending a Sunday afternoon having a quick pitch 'n' putt at your local course. As a rabbit's fluffy tail disappeared into a hedgerow, it was easy to admire how, unlike almost all modern professional sports, golf takes place in the midst of nature. That's if you ignore the swathes of wildlife bulldozed to create the course in the first place. To remind spectators that this wasn't just any old rambling route, along the footpaths large signs read, 'Caution, Golfers', a warning that could have been meant for the animal inhabitants as much as for humans.

As brutal as the construction of a golf course can be, there's a beautiful purity to the action that goes beyond its ambience. Can sport get any simpler than trying to move an object from A to B with a big stick in the fewest possible moves? It's so easy to understand that you might expect it to be played by more people. But in England, at least, golf seems to have been fenced off by money in a way few other sports can match. Clubs can be notoriously expensive, whether we're talking the membership kind or just a decent putter. Still, what can often seem like a cordoned-off world – another treat for the elite – is not totally impenetrable. Of the seven courses encircling Mum's house, one used to be cheaply accessible to the public, and as a teenager I occasionally had a go, playing eighteen par-three holes for a smidge over a tenner, including club hire and balls. I wasn't a natural, and the brief hope that golf might be my métier never got off the ground. The ball barely did either. (Lofting a drive is a lot harder than they make it look on TV.) But although it was peripheral to our lives, this was also a game I could actually imagine *playing* with Dan, in another universe, if he'd been well. Where we could exercise our chats, our competitive spirit and our legs, and be not only sports-mad but a little bit sporty too. How would that have felt? What is it like for the brothers and sisters out there who do that? As precious as our friendship had been, there were pleasures we'd never known, and would never know.

I reached the 16th tee and quickly chipped my introspection into the undergrowth, because there I finally found Poulter. He was busy lining up his next drive still from a position of 2 under par, now in a tie for the lead. A monogrammed kit bag lay beside him, and he was dressed in a navy sweater and white trousers, a colour scheme that – rather like his record in majors – could be described as Spursy. (He might not take kindly to the comparison, being an Arsenal fan.) Watching a player's process was immediately fascinating: how he examined the yardage book and consulted his caddie before taking aim at a minuscule hole a quarter of a mile away. Two months earlier I'd been astounded by the microscopic accuracy of snooker stars in Sheffield. Now, on the other side of the Peak District, I was getting the macro equivalent: golf requires precision on a brain-meltingly large scale.

I scooted ahead of the players so I could watch each one making his pitch: first, Scotland's Russell Knox scooped his shot into a nearby bunker; then Swede Alex Noren's ball sounded a delightful *plop* as it hit the green before bouncing off again, to leave a tricky chip back to the pin; finally, Poulter's ball hung in the air for an age before landing more definitively with a satisfying *thunk* just 10 feet from the hole. Poulter acknowledged the fans' applause as he walked towards us with his trademark gait: an unnaturally long stride beneath puffed-out chest and ramrod-straight back, exuding a confidence that bordered on arrogance. It was a peacocking prance that in any other context might look borderline Pythonesque, but which somehow befits a top golfer. The only player who can outdo Poulter in the swaggering stakes is Spain's Miguel Ángel Jiménez, whose walk – to my eyes at least – carries the charisma of a Mafia boss and whom one somehow can't picture without imagining a lit cigar in his hand. (Multiple YouTube videos show him partaking in a very idiosyncratic warm-up routine while puffing away on his favourite Cuban brand – they're well worth a look.) Arrogance is a weird attribute: in everyday life it's usually repulsive, but in sport it does have a place – an important place – adding a theatrical quality every fan craves. It's why I find it odd that certain sportspeople get criticised for showboating. To paraphrase Maximus Decimus Meridius, do we not want to be entertained? You could tell just from the way he carried himself that Ian Poulter knew he was good, and he wanted you to know he knew it. It's part of what made him a star.

Throughout his career, one of Poulter's trademarks has been to wear particularly gaudy clothes, most famously (or infamously) a pair of Union Jack slacks that once made him the Geri Halliwell of the golf world – Birdie Spice. So it was a bit of a surprise to see him in some simple white troos, but maybe the explanation was all around me: several other players and hundreds of spectators had come dressed in all manner of ludicrous attire: purple tartan, grey tartan, red and blue gingham, electric green with golf ball designs . . . Justin Thomas even played his round in a tie and cardigan ensemble designed for him by Ralph Lauren. Perhaps Poulter had decided that if he wanted to stay ahead of the curve, plain was the new demented. Or possibly just that, in the sartorial stakes, his work here was done. Either way, the absurd clothing choices on show brought to mind a sketch from one of Dan's favourite TV shows, *Not the Nine O'Clock News,* in which Rowan Atkinson commentates over footage of championship golf, but the sport is irrelevant to the far greater matter of a Pro-Am 'Silly Trousers Tournament'. 'Here's Dave Stockton', runs the commentary, 'displaying a pair of canary yellow Everpress that even Jimmy Savile wouldn't be seen dead in.' That sketch was written in 1980. *Plus ça change.*

The Poulter group finished its round and enacted one of the iconic scenes in golf, walking up to the 18th green at a major championship to accept the applause of the crowd. To experience this after you've just spent the last few hours constructing a strong round must be exquisite; galling in equal measure if you've had a pig of a day and are dying for the ground to swallow you up. There's a glacial excruciation about a bad round of golf. Noren, Knox and Poulter all escaped that indignity and, after holing their last putts, removed their caps and shook hands, with the Englishman's score of 3 under par putting him in early contention. On past form, Poulter's challenge was likely to fade, but even so it had been a privilege to watch a modern legend literally strutting his stuff.

Whichever way I turned at Birkdale I kept seeing superstars, as if they were a wild species on migration and I'd stumbled upon their breeding ground. One minute I was watching Zach Johnson, in all black and shades and looking every inch the sportsman; the next I was following Masters winner Sergio Garcia, who was all smiles as he teed off having recently broken his major championship duck at the seventy-fourth attempt; the next I'd found Ernie 'the Big Easy' Els, the giant South African and former world number one who these days was more big than easy, and looked to me less like a multi-major champion than a grumpy old man who'd got lost on his way to a garden centre. But a legend all the same. At one point I did an elaborate double-take as I spied Rory McIlroy trudging through some nearby undergrowth with a flustered expression. I didn't know it at the time, but he'd started out with an appalling five bogeys on the first six holes, leading to this reported exhortation from his caddie JP Fitzgerald: 'You're Rory McIlroy. What the fuck are you doing?' It did the trick, and Rory didn't drop a shot for the rest of the day, recovering to finish his round in a creditable 71.

There was so much going on it was impossible to take it all in without help, so I switched on BBC Radio 5 Live to guide me through the day's play. The presenter was John Inverdale, who had just been in the news for being one of the BBC's top-earning stars (pocketing north of £200,000 a year), and the coverage was as you might expect: comprehensive, brilliantly produced, and dripping with the fanboying that often accompanies golf broadcasting. I tuned in just as 'Invers' and his colleagues were expounding how extraordinarily difficult 'links' golf is. Even a casual listener like me knows this is an annual tradition, and a frustrating one at that, because nobody ever bothers to define what links golf actually is. (Apparently it comes from an old English word *hlinc*, meaning rising ground, but these days it refers loosely to rugged courses that lie next to a coast, relying on the weather to offer a challenge to top players. Thanks, Wikipedia.) Repeating this adage on air is also a hostage to fortune, and just days (or even hours) later, when the wind has failed to blow sufficiently and someone's blasted an impressive score, the same pundits invariably hold an inquest about how links courses are too easy for top players in the modern age. To bear this out, two days after my visit, South Africa's Brandon Grace posted a score of 62, breaking the long-standing all-time record for a single round at a men's major championship.

Still, it was worth tuning in to hear the score updates and a fantastic interview, conducted not with a player but with a key figure called Luke Summers: the bloke I'd spotted at the start of the morning brandishing a bird of prey. He revealed that his avian friend was in fact a twelve-year-old peregrine falcon called Jet who was there on business, employed by broadcasters to scare away the local seagulls and stop them from scavenging food scraps all over the course. I hadn't seen a single gull all day, so Jet was earning her salary.

I hadn't known what to expect from Royal Birkdale, but the sporting brilliance on display was overwhelming and invigorating. From thumping drives to delicate putts, every hole bore witness to feats of excellence. By the end of the day golf had done a job on me: I was a convert. I felt a newfound affinity not just with the sport but with the players too, including America's

Matt 'Kooch' Kuchar, whose round I followed as he began to build a campaign that would see him finish runner-up to the eventual winner Jordan Spieth. As for me, I've never been a natural adventurer. It took me until the age of twenty before I stepped foot on a plane. By spending a day traversing the wind-swept countryside of the north-west coast, I'd never been more alone. This was the furthest I'd ever travelled without company to watch sport, for an event I knew little about. Vast. Wild. Isolating. Open. But although I was alone, I didn't feel quite so lonely as recently. Something had reignited within me, and this time it wasn't just my brother's sporting passion. I'd taken a step forward in learning to let go and rediscover myself. Even if it wasn't an Ian Poulter stride, and couldn't be measured by a fitness tracker, it was a start.

Rory McIlroy walks past me through the Royal Birkdale undergrowth

18

One-Day Wonders

Sunday, 23 July 2017: Cricket

In the course of a British summer, an annoying number of days simply aren't made for cricket. Cold, gloomy, leaden. One of the eternal mysteries of that ancient bat-and-ball game is how it was invented in such an inhospitable place to play it. Then again, maybe that helps us to appreciate the action all the more when it does happen. Once again, Beavis and Butthead got it right: you need the bits that suck to make the bits that rock rock harder. A typically caliginous soup was filling the skies of north London this morning, and it was putting the fate of a big match in doubt. I'd reached the penultimate stop on my wanderings, and until now the weather gods had refrained from tearing up any of my plans – a mercy they didn't show Odysseus. If they chose to make their presence felt now, and in their caprice pop the black clouds that were hovering above St John's Wood, it would have been horrible timing, not just for me but for sport in general, because it could deprive the nation of the most important occasion in the history of women's cricket. England were about to play a World Cup Final, against India, in front of a packed house at Lord's.

It was three days since my ramble around Royal Birkdale, and my feet were plotting mutiny. Marathon runners speak about 'the wall', a final test of strength and willpower that they usually encounter at around the 20-mile mark, when they have to dig into their deepest reserves of stamina, ignore the furious impulse to stop and instead carry themselves through to the finish. Was today going to be my wall? I imagined the likelihood of rain washing out the match and pushing me into the warm refuge of a nearby cinema. Tempting, but no. I couldn't falter now, so close to the end. I could hear Dan telling me: that would just be Spursy.

Then, as I approached the famous ground along St John's Wood Road, I noticed something that pulled my querulous body into line. I'd been to the Home of Cricket™ countless times, but today the vibe was peculiar. Or peculiarly unpeculiar. For a start, there seemed to be a distinct lack of MCC members. For those not in the know, the Marylebone Cricket Club, custodian of Lord's, likes to think of itself as the keeper of cricket's sacred flame: gaining entry to its exclusive ranks is a quasi-Masonic exercise that can take decades. Its members are easy to spot when a Test Match is on, because most like to announce themselves through wearing garish clobber in the club's red-and-yellow, 'egg-and-bacon' striped colours. Thousands of them will march (or in some cases stagger) in through their exclusive entrance at the Grace Gate just round the corner from Abbey Road, some looking like rejects from Sergeant Pepper's Lonely Hearts Club Band, thrown out by the sarge for being that little bit *too* lonely. To me the sight was inseparable from any visit to Lord's. But this morning the members had turned up only in dribs and drabs. Had they been put off by the weather? Or had they turned their noses up at today's Final? Either way, they'd made a duff call.

The pre-match entertainment was a minimalist affair: a single acrobat in a silver jumpsuit suspended in mid-air under a balloon, somersaulting her way above the outfield. It wasn't quite the JetPack dude at the 1984 LA Olympics but to this amateur's eyes she put in a flawless performance, until a slightly clumsy landing that put the WG into grace. Still, compared to the annual chaos of the 'Mascot Grand National' at Twenty20 Finals Day this was a night at the Bolshoi. I was happy enough, warming myself up with a classic opening partnership of tea and bacon roll. Over to my left in the pavilion, players from England and India were clustering on their respective balconies, surveying the pitch below and the clouds above, wondering which of the two would prove to be the more fateful. And to my right was an empty seat.

I'd bought two tickets for this, and a couple of friends would probably have jumped at the chance to come along, but I'd held off asking. Not for any specific reason. Just a feeling. That day spent traipsing around the fairways of Royal Birkdale had given me an unusual amount of concentrated time with my own thoughts, and I wasn't quite done yet. This wasn't the raw loneliness of early grief, of those early days replacing Dan at Selhurst Park. (Replace? As if. I mean represent.) It was acquiescence. Now being by myself wasn't only a symbol of loss. It was a small sign of strength too: that maybe I could do this, and plot a way forward. Not selling the ticket was going to cost me twenty quid, but that didn't matter. The spare seat could be Dan's. Not by design, but now it felt right. An offering. And an apology too, for the times in my life when I'd had the chance to take Dan to watch sport and hadn't done. That admission might serrate the clean lines of this story, but there were such occasions. I knew a lot of it was out of his power, but his mental and physical state could make him exhausting company. So although we did so much together, there were times when I actively chose to see live sport without him. Not a crime, but a source of guilt, then and now. Today, that seat next to me could be a reminder that all my fondest memories were with him. And Lord's was a place where this resounded strongly.

Opposite the pavilion at the Nursery End was the Compton Stand, another ugly sporting edifice scheduled for the wrecking ball, but which held sentimental value for me. In fact it was the location for the warmest cricket memory of my life, where in 2000 Dan and I had sat to watch the denouement of an epic Test Match between England and West Indies. It was the hundredth Test to be played at Lord's, and was such an incomparable encounter that it soon became known as the Ultimate Test. With both bowling units running amok and wickets falling like ninepins, this game featured the first instance in cricket history when action from all four innings featured in a single day's play. We had tickets for day three, which turned out to be the climax, as England attempted to brush off a whopping first innings deficit of 133 to reach a victory target of 188. The home team were motoring along serenely enough, reaching a commanding position of 95–1 and looking certain to prevail until, in a depressingly familiar sight for any Nineties cricket fan, the batting order performed a spectacular collapse. In the blink of an eye the likes of Atherton, Vaughan, Hick and Stewart perished – all mere cannon fodder at the hands of the Windies quicks. Reduced to 160–8, England looked set to have found yet another creative avenue for their own demise. But this time, thanks to some doughty lower-order runs from Dominic Cork and Darren Gough, they clung on for a famous win over a foe that had dominated them for decades. It even hinted at more promising times to come.

When Cork hit the winning runs, the jubilation was so immense that it sparked a pitch invasion of the hallowed old ground, and for the only time in our lives Dan and I felt compelled to partake, joining the hordes spilling out of the Compton Stand and over the boundary rope. Unlike the recent trend in football, there was no aggression in this infiltration of Lord's, only glee. As joyous an occasion as it was for English cricket to start clawing its way back from its Nineties abyss, there was also a bittersweet note to the match, because it was the final time two of the game's undisputed greats would play here in a Test. Curtly Ambrose and Courtney Walsh were the last pair in a dynasty of world-conquering West Indian fast bowlers, and for me and Dan they were two of our all-time favourite players. In a surreal moment for us, as we delighted in milling about on the outfield we found ourselves walking alongside these two

literal giants of the game. 'Well played', we said to Curtly, craning our necks to catch his eye. From what seemed like cloud
level he shot us a wry look of, 'Not now, mate.' Fair enough. The
three of us in a line looked like the old Class System sketch by
John Cleese and the Two Ronnies. Having looked up to Curtly,
I turned and looked down to Dan. He just raised his eyebrows
gently, pursed his lips, let the bowlers walk off, then let out a
delighted *hee-hee*. And he didn't stop smiling all the way home.
I could happily get through the coldness of today's final by shel-
tering in memories like that. As events soon proved, I didn't
need to.

One of the many traditions observed at this famous ground
on a matchday morning is a bell to signal that play will begin in
five minutes, which is always rung by an invited luminary from
the cricketing or wider world. Today that honour was accorded
to Eileen Ash, the world's oldest Test cricketer at the age of 105.
After my year of travelling, inspired by a life snuffed out too
soon, it was refreshing to see someone exceptional being celebrated for their longevity. Whatever happened in the final to
follow, it was unlikely that any of today's players would record
a statistic to eclipse one of Eileen's: she made her Test debut for
England before the Second World War, in 1937. Eileen certainly
wasn't shy about making the most of the day: according to the
Daily Telegraph, she spent the final quaffing champagne in the
President's Box and flirting with John Major. (You're never too
old to make mistakes.)

Eileen's relative obscurity was living proof of the unheralded,
overlooked history of women's cricket, and she must have been
gladdened to see how, albeit belatedly, the balance was shifting.
The moment the penny really dropped for me that something
different was afoot was when I made a dash to the gents' loo
before the start of play: no queue, but also an astonishing
absence of poorly aimed urine soaking the floor. In all my years
of watching top-level sport, that was unprecedented. Once the
players had taken the field, fans of both teams belted out their

national anthems as lustily as you would hear at any international match – but in a dominant register an octave higher than most stadia are accustomed to hearing. There was a majority of women and girls in the crowd, and the air crackled with freshness. Most invigorating of all, this tournament wasn't piggybacking on a men's event. It was a standalone phenomenon in its own right. Over the last few weeks the British public had truly discovered women's cricket. It was climaxing at Lord's, where until as recently as 1998 the MCC refused to admit female members. This centuries-old bastion of British sport was proving it could adapt.

At last the umpires called 'play'. The form book and World Cup pedigree slightly favoured England, but it was too close to call: India had already upset the odds by defeating the home side during the group stage, and batter Harmanpreet Kaur had scored an electrifying 171 not out in their semi-final win over Australia. Both XIs were packed with potential match-winners, and the big question for the near-capacity crowd – give or take the benches in front of the pavilion, the preserve of the MCC egg-and-bacon brigade, which bore some conspicuous gaps – was whether the game could live up to its billing. In fact, by the time the last ball was bowled, I doubt there was any billing that could have lived up to the game.

England batted first, openers Lauren Winfield and Tammy Beaumont steadying nerves in the home dressing room by laying down the foundations of a strong innings. Every four was greeted with a roar of approval from all of us in the Mound Stand, mainly in support of the team but also in gratitude at receiving a new blast from the flame jet behind the boundary, which wafted pleasant bursts of warm air across us that momentarily dispelled the cold. At the end of their 50 overs England had inched their way to a creditable total of 228–7, leaving India to chase down the second highest target ever set at the Women's World Cup. Seeing as they'd smashed 281–4 to beat Australia in the semis, no doubt they fancied it.

The second innings was one of those instances when all the various components of sport combine to make it the most spellbinding spectacle our species has yet invented: drama, skill, athleticism, luck, twists, individual genius, ensemble brilliance – all happening live, unscripted and in real time. In the process something incredibly potent, and also poignant, takes place – it makes you feel more alive. And this, I was coming to understand, was what had helped steer me through two years of grief. This miraculous invention that goes right back to ancient Olympia in the eighth century BC could be medicinal. I'd prescribe it to anyone.

India made a dynamic start, picking off some loose English bowling to rocket towards their target. I had no need to check the scoreboards for their required run rate: the barrage of bhangra drumming five rows in front of me indicated precisely where the balance of power lay. By the time the Indians had reached 191–3 I could have done with some earplugs. Then a breakthrough. Opener Poonam Raut, who'd stormed her way to 86 belligerent runs, was trapped lbw by seamer Anya Shrubsole to pry the door a crack for England. At the same time the heavens did too, causing the climax of the match to be contested through intermittent showers, but the teams carried on regardless. Fifty metres away in the stands, I was having an Andie MacDowell moment: was it raining? I hadn't noticed. Tension and excitement have heating powers of their own.

After the devastation wrought by Raut, a rout from the England bowlers wrestled back the advantage, with Shrubsole producing a predatory spell of 5 wickets for just 11 runs. Now it was the home side who were accelerating to victory and, with India at 218–9, batter Poonam Yadav spooned a high catch straight to Jenny Gunn at mid-off. The trophy was ballooning into Gunn's hands. Time seemed to stop. Why weren't England celebrating? From my vantage point it was hard to see. Then Gunn's body language said it all: she'd shelled it.

Was that England's chance? Would she be haunted for years

to come by those five abominable words, 'You dropped the World Cup'? Pressure does things to people, and after missing an opportunity like that to sup the sweet nectar of glory, you'd be forgiven for spending decades in a search for expiation. Just look at Dick Francis or good ol' Jimmy White. Fortunately, Jenny Gunn had to brood for barely a minute. The very next delivery, the barnstorming Shrubsole thudded a slow yorker into Rajeshwari Gayakwad's off stump, the death rattle putting an emphatic seal on a slender 9-run victory. Shrubsole was mobbed by her teammates. Ecstasy erupted throughout Lord's.

It's stirring to see a trophy lifted, especially when it's a team you support who's doing the lifting. For me and Dan, it was a rare feeling indeed. Now I was among the exclusive club of sports lovers lucky enough to have seen England lift a major world cup on home soil. It had been one of those pendulum-swinging symphonies of fifty-over cricket when it can feel like the most perfect format of the most perfect bat-and-ball game on the planet.

Over the last twelve months I'd been privileged to watch dozens of supreme sportspeople doing their thing: Roger Federer winning his eighth Wimbledon, Ronnie O'Sullivan winning a record seventh Masters, Harry Kane winning . . . my eternal respect for staying so long at Spurs. But in terms of pure sporting theatre that did justice to its occasion, nothing came close to matching the twenty-two women who took the field at Lord's on 23 July 2017. In an ideal world it shouldn't need high-lighting, but as our world isn't ideal, it's worth noting that, of all the events I'd witnessed, it was female sport that had come out top. From start to finish, the final was fought out with supreme skill by players who should already have been household names. If Joe Root ever played a through-the-legs glance shot like Nat Sciver's earlier in the tournament, fans and journalists might well be cooing about it as the 'Shot of the Century' for decades to come. I'd seen ramp shots from Sarah Taylor, metro-nomic bowling from Jhulan Goswami and that destructive onslaught from Shrubsole, whose 6–46 was the most incisive spell I've seen at Lord's in over twenty years of visits, as lethal as Ambrose or Walsh at their best. Since that day, England cricket fans have been spoiled for magnificence, with their men's team of 2019 winning their version of the World Cup for the first time, in ludicrously tight super-over fashion on the same ground. For their stunning triumph, Eoin Morgan & Co. have been rightly immortalised. But raised up to the same pedestal must always be the victorious women of 2017.

It had been a classic day of English cricket, right down to it being cold enough to give you frostbite. The outfield was thronging with officials for the trophy presentation, and I looked down at the empty seat to my side. Then I gazed out across the turf and fixed my eyes on the spot where Dan and I had met Curtly and Courtney all those years ago. I took a deep breath. A rendezvous with a memory, where my best ever friend will always live.

19

The Last Leg

The world comes in all kinds of shapes. The Oval. The Bermuda Triangle. Trafalgar Square. The Pentagon. The Reading Hexagon. Godalming Heptagon. Bolton Octagon. (I've only made one of those up.) Right now, as the calendar flipped over into August, I was seeing circles. First there was football, the inescapable Smaug of sports, which had awoken from its summer slumbers to incinerate anything else from the back pages. Secondly, there was my reacquaintance with singledom, which had made me a boomerang child and looped me full circle to Mum, back home in the nether regions of Croydon, where life for me had begun. (I was born in the town's Mayday Hospital, known by locals as 'May Die'.) And thirdly, the sporting world's cycle had nearly finished a full turn, meaning the journey I'd been on for nearly a year was almost complete. To be a true odyssey, like Odysseus's own, it needed to end with a return, and after visiting forty events across seventeen different sports involving over a hundred separate contests, for my final leg the great fixture list in the sky was taking me right back to my brother. The 2017 World Athletics Championships, featuring many people running around in circles, were coming to Stratford's London Stadium: the beacon that had blazed the Olympics and Paralympics from our city across the globe, and the place where Dan spent his happiest times, to the extent that the little garden outside is definitely not where we illicitly scattered his ashes. I can't emphasise that enough. (You can get fined £5,000 for that kind of thing.) But if we had, it would have been the perfect place for him to be laid to rest, and for this story to end.

Five years had passed since the Games. Since that alchemical period when Britain seemed to forget its frictions and felt, maybe more than any time since VE Day, happy and glorious. But the Olympic site, now renamed Queen Elizabeth Park (after someone or other), still exuded a latent magic. It was as though London had experienced an anti-Chernobyl and this was its ground zero. If you could take a machine there to measure the fallout, a *High-ger Counter*, it would still be clacking away. Track and field is the showcase sport of any Olympiad, and to have the planet's best athletes gathering here again was bound to be significant. You couldn't get closer to recapturing the spirit of 2012 in my lifetime than the World Championships coming here: it was literally a rerun. The emotion of the occasion seemed to be shared by the athletes, because two of the sport's starriest names had decided that this was the right time and place to hang up their spikes. Long-distance legend Mo Farah had announced that this would be his final track appearance, before making a (doomed) switch to the marathon. But even that was small beer next to the most vital news of all: Usain Bolt, the fastest human being in history, had told the world that London 2017 would see his last ever competitive race. Seeing as Bolt had won an unprecedented 'Triple Double' of Olympic gold medals at 100m and 200m and become one of the most famous people on the planet, he had nothing left to prove to anyone. In choosing London for his last hurrah, Bolt confirmed that he too felt a kinship with the place. I knew how he felt. His home straight was going to be mine too.

For the timing to coincide like this had taken a mammoth quirk of fate and some Olympic-level dodgy accounting. All being well, London should have had its World Championship over a decade earlier, because Britain's capital had been awarded the hosting rights for 2005, a full three years before Bolt burst onto the scene. Back then, the plan had been to construct a flashy 43,000-seat arena at Pickett's Lock in the north-east of the city, an inconspicuous spot most famous for being the site of Michael Crawford's audacious roller-skating stunt in the sitcom *Some Mothers Do 'Ave 'Em* (one of Dan's favourite pieces of TV gold). But in a cataclysmic blunder worthy of Frank Spencer, the British government did a whoopsie on the budget and was forced to pull the plug, forfeiting the right to stage the spectacle. It's a minor miracle that the International Olympic Committee awarded London the greatest show on Earth not long afterwards. The Games had put the UK back on the map as a global destination for athletics, making it a natural fit for the second-biggest event in track and field. So another circle, the wheel of fortune, had spun Bolt's last dance to London.

The World Athletics Championships are more than a pale facsimile of an Olympiad. They have a rich history of their own. It was at the Worlds where Bolt registered his unfathomable 9.58 seconds for the 100 metres, and which throughout the 1990s gave rise to some of the most definitive sporting moments of the era: Mike Powell battling Carl Lewis for long jump gold at Tokyo '91; Sally Gunnell's world record for the 400m hurdles at Stuttgart '93; Jonathan Edwards' gravity-defying triple jump at Gothenburg '95, that measured 18.29m or, in old money, a quarter of an inch over 60 feet. With such a roll of honour, it's sad to see that in recent times the biennial showpiece has struggled to maintain its allure, with host city after host city failing to entice enough fans to fill a stadium. At Athens '97 and Seville '99 unsold tickets had to be given away to inflate attendances, while Moscow '13 was blighted by half-emptiness and Edmonton '01 was so funereal as to be lampooned by journalists as 'Deadmonton'. The nadir so far was the horrendously organised Doha '19, which showed a glimpse of the future by inventing social distancing a full six months before the Covid pandemic: it was so ill-attended that at times there seemed to be more people on the track than in the stands. Seb Coe and his chums at World Athletics need to take care, or this oldest of sports could end up like its earliest stadium at Olympia: shadows and dust.

Would London 2017 fall victim to the same malaise? In the weeks leading up to the championships, it seemed touch and go. While I was counting down the days, there was no discernible tingle of expectancy in the press or among friends, and I had to consider whether the rest of the world had just moved on. Thankfully London was being less impatient than me and just taking its time. The Worlds ended up attracting record crowds, but not so much as to prevent a geek like me from snapping up tickets to every night. Once I'd exited Stratford Tube station on Day One to join the mass of people streaming towards the sacred park, my 2012 buzz was firmly back.

It wasn't going to be an easy week, though. So many memories were scattered about this place that it was impossible to pick a way through without stepping on a grief mine. The first detonated before I'd even made it to the stadium. From the Underground the pedestrian route takes you down a piazza lined with family-friendly eateries, and in February 2015 this is where I'd come with Dan and Mum to celebrate my birthday, just a few months before he died. With Lucy and David away on honeymoon, the three of us had arranged to meet up for Sunday lunch, and I'd offered to find us a venue. Knowing that Dan was finding walking difficult, I'd picked a pub in south London which did a good roast and which we could all reach with a minimum of effort. But Dan had other ideas. He lobbied for us to go to Stratford's Café Football, a themed restaurant co-owned by Gary Neville, where we'd taken him for his birthday dinner the previous October. Football, check. Burgers, check. It didn't take Alan Turing to crack his thought process. It made little sense to go back there though, as it was harder for all of us to get to, especially him. Also, it was my birthday and I thought I deserved a say about where we went. But Dan was adamant, and he became upset in a way that surprised even me, demanding that Mum and I agree to Café Football or he wouldn't come. I've been given some ultimatums in my time, but this was one of the weirder ones. Still, I wasn't wedded to any other venue and Dan had a bee in his bonnet, so we went along with it. But before we'd even sat down to eat, that Sunday lunchtime left me with an awful image I'll never be able to shake off.

The three of us met outside Stratford Station and began the short walk to the restaurant, only to be stopped in our tracks by a sudden change in the weather. Out of nowhere a deluge of rain came sheeting down upon us, sending people scurrying for any shelter they could find. Some of the shop fronts had thin canopies, and Mum and I darted for the nearest one. But Dan didn't move. He remained rooted to the spot. I ran back to see what the problem was. He was already exhausted by the short distance we'd walked, and had no energy left even to reach the awning. I did my best to encourage him (carrying him wasn't an option), but no; he said not to worry and to let him be. I didn't want to leave him on his own, but the rain sent me running back to join Mum, and we watched as Dan sagged down on a bench, hoodless, umbrella-less, helpless, shoulders slumped and thick hair sopping, as ill health and the British summer double-teamed him to deliver a soaking. It was one of the saddest things I've ever seen. Almost enough to wash away the technicolour happiness we'd been drenched in here at the Games. Almost.

Two years on from that day, as athletics fans now streamed past me to the stadium, I paused at the spot where Dan had sat. This time it was my turn to be exhausted. The men's 100m final had fallen on the same day as my friend Oli's stag party, and the afternoon had involved a sickeningly rich lunch followed by a speedboat ride down the Thames – definitely the wrong order in which to do those activities. I'd had to wrench myself away from a group Crazy Golf tournament to make it to the athletics.

I caught my breath and parked myself on Dan's bench. Only a few miles away, the stag party was still going on without me, but it might as well have been on another planet. My head was filled with the past: with love, pity and regret, trying to comprehend how the memory of my brother at such a low ebb could reside a mere Olympic sprint away from the site of his happiest days on Earth. It was emblematic of a truth I'd come to understand over the last year. Joy and tragedy are as close to one another as I was to Dan. Life sometimes teeters on a knife-edge between them, and none of us can keep our balance forever.

Since 2012 the Olympic Park complex in East London has been resized and reshaped. The paths still hum with the ghosts of the millions who came here, and its most iconic features are still intact. A three-course feast for the eyes is headed by Zaha Hadid's wave-like aquatic centre, followed by the Space Pringle velodrome. These small, sleek venues are in thrall to the elegant bowl that dominates the park, these days bedecked in the colours of its new tenants, West Ham United (whoever they are), and keen-eyed observers will spot that its signature triangular floodlights have been folded inside the roof where once they pointed skywards in a brilliant crown. Apart from that little has changed. The red iron spaghetti of the Orbit Tower still stands sentry to the east, while the north entrance is adorned by the colossal 22-ton Olympic bell which the world watched Sir Bradley Wiggins ring to commence the opening ceremony. It's the largest harmonic bell in existence and a physical relic of that singular time: its clanging B note still resonates inside me, albeit these days with a more plangent tone, partly for the loss of Dan, partly because of Sir Brad's well-publicised asthma treatments, and partly for the fact that he never actually rang it anyway. He just pretended to: the bell was so big that it had to be chimed by a machine, because no single man would have enough puff to ring it. (Even one who'd been given a Therapeutic Use Exemption.)

One of athletics' charms is that it presents sport at its purest: to take part, all you need is a pair of shoes. (Some, like Zola Budd, didn't even stretch to that.) Reflecting this accessibility was the striking diversity of the participants. Here 205 separate countries were involved, together with five refugees and nineteen 'authorised neutral athletes' from Russia, competing as individuals rather than under their national flag as punishment for state-sponsored doping. (That'll show 'em.) It felt as though every country in the world was represented among the packed crowds as well, which managed to be family-friendly and yet still exuded as much fervour as you'd find at a North London derby. Epitomising the mood was an ebullient man who sat next to me on the opening night draped in a large flag of the Ethiopian Empire, with matching shirt and face paint. To him, this week meant what the Rugby World Cup meant to New Zealanders: everything.

Being there for the whole week enabled me to enjoy the meet on two levels. I could swaddle myself in things I knew well, such as watching Mo Farah storm the 10,000m just as he had done on Super Saturday. His run reminded me of the unique thrill of watching long-distance running in a full stadium, as the athletes are exhorted by a wave of cheering that follows them around the track and gets faster and louder lap by lap, whirring like a centrifuge. But there were times too when I was wowed afresh by a new generation of stars, not least twenty-one-year-old Norwegian Karsten Warholm, who'd made a speculative jump from the decathlon to the 400m hurdles to win gold at his first attempt, in a heavy downpour, shocking himself as much as anyone and screaming with relish as he crossed the finish.

You certainly get your money's worth at an athletics meeting. There are so many events it's hard to know which way to look. Lucky, then, that there was someone to guide us through the action: former Team GB athlete Iwan Thomas, who made for an engaging and inclusive trackside stadium host. There were also idiosyncrasies aplenty, such as the organisers' decision to pipe in a constant soundtrack of tinny dance-pop, which made this site of some of the world's greatest sporting feats feel like a sweaty zumba session down the local gym. Perhaps stirred into some sort of exercise by these 120bpm choons, during the week a streaker decided to invade the track on not one but two occasions. By which I don't mean two streakers, but the same strangely determined bloke *twice*. A portly, middle-aged and scraggly-haired man who looked like the love child of Jay

Rayner and Obelix, with an illegible message scrawled on his chest, he showed a surprising turn of speed that enabled him to give several stewards the slip. (Check out my YouTube channel if you fancy a look.) For services to more family-friendly entertainment, an honourable mention must go to the championship mascot, Hero the Hedgehog, who was unlike anything I've ever seen at a sports event. This dude was nothing like your standard wave-at-the-kids cuddly character. He was a medal-worthy prankster, taking any opportunity to rugby-tackle Iwan Thomas and keeping the crowds laughing between events with a deep bag of practical jokes. He spent the entirety of the final night engaged in a battle with a steward, who I hope for his sake was in on the gag. Whoever he was, actor or not, Hero tortured him with a mixture of balloons, glue and taunting until finally delivering his coup de grâce: a mud pie slammed straight into his victim's unsuspecting face. If the official was feigning his furious reaction, he was doing a brilliant job of making his anger seem pretty damn real. While the British women's 4x400m relay team celebrated winning a fantastic silver medal, behind them the persecuted steward could be seen hunting for a seven-foot-tall orange hedgehog, looking for all the world like he wanted to beat the crap out of it.

For me, everything else that week – including Hero – was only an *hors d'oeuvre* for the men's 100 metres. On the night of Sunday 5 August, for just shy of ten seconds, the eyes of the world would turn back to London. And to one man. In my eyes, in my lifetime, there's no doubt that Usain Bolt is the king. He's the only athlete since Muhammad Ali to assume the mantle of being the Greatest, and to appear entirely comfortable wearing the crown. Only once or twice does a century seem capable of coughing up such an individual, whose genius affords them the ultimate luxury in sport: that on the grandest stage of all they don't just deliver the goods like a common-or-garden brooding victor, they do it with a smile. That's what makes them extra special.

Ali used wordplay to play up his cockiness: 'I done wrestled with an alligator, I done tussled with a whale; handcuffed lightning, thrown thunder in jail; only last week, I murdered a rock, injured a stone, hospitalised a brick; I'm so mean I make medicine sick.' Bolt was too laid back to even bother putting his supremacy into verse. A sublime aura swirled around him merely through anecdotes and swagger. He hadn't only run faster than anyone ever: he claimed he'd done it on a diet of a thousand chicken nuggets. Which is weird because I've tried that diet and it had the opposite effect. Then there was the time he played in a charity cricket match on the opposite side to West Indies star (and self-proclaimed 'Universe Boss') Chris Gayle, during which Bolt clean-bowled Gayle in the first innings and hit him for six for good measure in the second. Immediately before a championship final, his pre-race rituals seemed to include flirting with track officials, on camera, beamed all over the globe. Bolt was Achilles, the great runner, on the Trojan battlefield. There was a touch of the divine about him; he made everything look easy. The world was his plaything. If Usain were to read this, I can imagine him baulking at the comparison. 'Achilles? Nah. I'm way faster.' Now, here he was, returning with nothing to prove but craving one last rodeo all the same. Nigh on the whole world was willing him to win.

Every good story needs a hero, but you've got to have a decent villain too. Lining up against Bolt was America's Justin Gatlin, a one-time Olympic champion and two-time drugs cheat, who'd bafflingly been allowed back into the sport after serving his second ban for using a performance-enhancing substance. Once might be reckless, but twice? If you ask me, Gatlin was taking the piss, 'A' sample and 'B' sample. Seeing as how the rules say a clean runner can be disqualified for a single false start but serial cheats are allowed back, it makes you question their priorities. But Gatlin had served his latest punishment and he was officially free to take part, giving the big race its perfect bad guy.

Beneath an inky sky, the eight finalists walked out onto the track one by one, sparking a standing ovation from the jam-packed stands. It was a pedigree line-up: as well as Gatlin, the contenders included another American, Christian Coleman, who was the quickest man in the world that year; Bolt's Jamaican com-patriot Yohan Blake, the joint-second fastest man ever; and young British tyro Reece Prescod. Gatlin's entrance was signalled by pantomime boos, putting him alongside George Osborne in an elite club of people who've entered this theatre of joy to a chorus of derision. Bolt's arrival was inevitably held back until last, and the crowd exploded in acclaim, with Jamaican fans on all sides holding aloft souvenir scarves bearing his name and face, as if he were Liverpool and they were the Kop. Shoes shimmering bright gold, he pointed with both hands at the name tag taped to his vest, revelling in his legend status, while the giant TV screens flashed up his giant beaming grin at being back on this stage. *His* stage. Usain was a few weeks away from turning thirty-one, and there was the slightest hint that age had started to wither his speed, but it couldn't touch his smile. A mechanical *shhh* sound brought the stadium to order, and the athletes took to their blocks, Bolt's shoulders peeking above those of the mere mortals along-side. Every pair of eyes was drawn to him. Every pair of lungs on their marks to cheer for him. Silence . . . silence . . .

Bang.

A 100 metres final warps time. The start of the race is like the end of a Peter Jackson movie: everything seems to slow down and there are so many plot-lines it's hard to keep focus. As the sprinters blasted from their blocks and strained to hit their top speed, Coleman took a sizeable advantage over the field while Bolt languished back in a sluggish seventh. No need to panic, though. Usain was notorious for having a stodgy first 30 metres. (The mind boggles as to what time he might have posted had he mastered this element of the race like the rest.) Normal ser-vice might yet be resumed. Once a race reaches halfway there's a second warp moment when time catches up with itself, caus-ing the end of the race to seem as though it's being played on fast-forward. Too much to enjoy, too little time to savour it. Again and again throughout his career, this is where Bolt streaked away from his rivals and into the history books.

But this time his trademark acceleration was missing. His long, powerful strides clawed him back into contention, but this was a straining man, not the effortless glider of Beijing or Berlin, and he couldn't reel in Coleman. Worse, out of nowhere had come Gatlin, finding an extra gear in the final 30 metres that surged him past everyone to a third World Championship title. Coleman followed him home for silver and a USA one-two, with Bolt trailing behind them in third.

Third.

Only third.

I say only. He still ran it in under ten seconds: 9.95 seconds (or two Rubik's Cubes, in new money). Just three-hundredths behind the winner. But in this sport, that's an aeon.

A disbelieving pall swept over Stratford; the crescendo of a minute earlier hushed and crushed. Then, once it was clear that Gatlin had won, the vacuum was filled by a fresh round of vociferous booing. Over in the press box there began a hundred post-mortems, up in the stands a thousand more. Was he injured? Was he past it? Was Gatlin running clean? Had Bolt taken bronze? *Bronze?* The greats don't do bronze. Usually when you're in a sports crowd of 60,000, the result leaves one group of fans elated and an opposing set dejected. Tonight everyone seemed to be on the same side, and nobody expected it to be the losing one. But just as striking as the unity of disappointment was the speed at which it dissipated. Bolt began a post-race lap of appreciation, and from his body language it was clear to all that this was a man focused not on the tenth of a second in speed he'd lost but on the ten years of glory he'd always have. He'd surrendered his crown but he was still holding court. Really, he was still king.

As one, the crowd fed off his energy and shrugged off the blow. 'Fuck Gatlin, we love Bolt,' became the unspoken, unanimous verdict, and again the stadium was transformed. Barely a blink ago, this race had been all that mattered. Now it didn't matter at all. Down by the triple jump pit near me, a single image summed up the story: Christian Coleman was in the middle of his own lap of honour, draped in a Star-Spangled Banner and celebrating the biggest night of his life, but he was doing so alone. As far as the press were concerned he was invisible: their cameras were all trained on the bloke Coleman had just bested for silver. Here in a snapshot it was already clear that Usain's legacy far outstripped one defeat. Like Ali's loss to Trevor Berbick in 1981, tonight's bronze medal didn't so much bring down the curtain on the story as remind us of the whole miraculous narrative. I was one of millions who hadn't wanted to see it end like this, but in a way it was a more fitting storyline. Nothing lasts forever.

Still, the world panged for one final flash of the Lightning Bolt and, while the 100 metres had gone, there remained an extra chance to cheer him on. As tradition dictated, the championships were to conclude with the relay races, which brought Usain back as part of the Jamaican quartet for the men's 4x100m final. It took place a week to the day since his shock defeat, and this time I had a seat on the bend before the home straight, offering a prime view of the big guy as he waited to take the baton for the anchor leg. He had the 60,000 of us in his pocket all over again, with nobody caring a jot that his last race hadn't gone to plan. For the crowd he was still the hero; for his opponents he was still the danger. Bolt was only too happy to milk the audience's love one more time and, while rivals to left and right stood still and focused on the track ahead of them, Usain pranced, posed and bowed to his fans. For the next few minutes the spotlight was still his, and nobody has ever known better than a sprinter that every second counts. (Except maybe Paul Daniels in the Eighties.)

Bolt cast such a shadow over the night that it was easy to forget there were three more Jamaicans and seven other teams in the race. Signing off with a gold wasn't going to be easy, because of strong competition from the United States and (dare I say it?)

Great Britain, as well as the ever-present threat of a baton-changing error. On TV, commentator Rob Walker (he of the cheesy snooker intros) declared that 'rarely has there been a greater sense of anticipation ahead of any race in history', a statement that was more over the top than a First World War advance. Even so, we were set for a hell of a race. The leading leg athlete from each team took his marks, the starter's gun fired, and Usain waited.

A sprint relay well-executed is a thing of beauty, a four-act play whose plot unravels only at the final turn, when the staggered lanes even out and the true state of the race becomes plain. After just 27 seconds it was Bolt's turn to take the Jamaican baton, finding himself in third position and sandwiched behind Great Britain and the United States. There was work to do, but victory in sight. Giving chase, his long strides opened out into that unique, beautiful action that has redefined the limits of what a human can do. Pursuit. Poetry. Power . . . Pulling up. Perplexity. Pain. Team GB and the USA were already powering down the home straight, neck and neck, but as they crossed the finish line Bolt wasn't there with them disputing the lead. He was halfway down the track, his left hamstring having chosen this of all times to tear. Unable to run, he winced and hopped for several metres, pushed on by momentum until he finally collapsed on the track, his career concluding in a crumpled heap. Race run. In a horrible irony, Bolt's last leg had ended up being not just a race but a diagnosis. The capacity crowd was so shocked that we barely noticed the other astonishing news: for the first time, Team GB had won sprint relay gold. Do you remember that? No? Exactly. Sorry, boys.

I'd assumed that the World Athletics Championships were going to put a neat bow on my year of sporting adventure, but instead I'd borne witness to an unprecedented home success, and a finale from Mr Bolt that was even more poignant than I could have imagined. It encapsulated how fragile life is; how we should always expect the unexpected; how the very same place can hold the happiest of memories and the bitterest ones too. And it spoke to the fact that sport is what it is because it's unwritten, like life itself. It hits us with our highest highs, our lowest lows, and our dullest nil-nil draws away to Huddersfield Town. Sport can do strange things to us. It can make a grown man cry. Or it can make a grown man shove a lit flare up his arse.

It's often said that sportspeople die twice, with the end of their career tantamount to the end of life as they knew it. Watching Bolt being carted out of the arena in a wheelchair was to see him being ferried into the valley of the shadow of retirement, a desolate place that not all top athletes breeze through as easily as they did their sport. But Usain was already no stranger to bereavement. He'd carried the pain of fresh loss into the stadium as well as out of it. Only months before the world championships, on 20 April 2017, his friend Germaine Mason, a British high-jumper, had died in a motorbike accident at the age of thirty-four. Bolt had been one of the first people on the scene and among the mourners who'd helped to bury his friend. Some speculated that the tragedy impeded his focus and training schedule. Others wondered if it even contributed to his injury: British tabloids had reported that just days before the fateful relay race, he had been pictured out partying late into the night, 'downing rum and cognac, dancing with girls and taking a turn on the decks' at a barbecue held in Germaine's memory. How did the greatest sportsman in the world differ from a sallow, asthmatic couch potato like me? Let me count the ways. But over the course of this week in London, Usain had wanted to rekindle the magic of 2012 and to keep his friend's flame burning.

The stadium emptied. It was time to go home, to bring this odyssey to an end and contemplate what might come next. But first I had to make one final detour. Just outside the London Stadium and overlooked by its western wall lies the Great British Garden, the tucked-away part of the park where Mum, Lucy and I absolutely didn't scatter Dan's ashes on what would have been his forty-fourth birthday. I couldn't leave without stopping by. In my handful of visits, it's never failed to offer a sanctuary from the rivers of fans who routinely teem past, and it resonates quietly, beautifully, with its Olympic history. The garden is divided into three distinct regions, each demarcated on the ground by a large circle: one gold, one silver, one bronze. One of its oaks, the official guide states, was grown from an acorn collected from a tree planted by the founder of the modern Olympics, Baron Pierre de Coubertin, in 1894 to thank the citizens of Much Wenlock for inspiring him. The guide doesn't go on to say that it's since been mulched with the ashes of my brother, which is good, because we've so firmly established that it wasn't. Part of Dan's essence was the ability to always see the funny side, even in death, and he would want me to carry on laughing, carry on regardless, Carry on Up The Khyber, now and always.

Under a pale moonlight and some rather less pale stadium floodlights, I stood on the gold disc and chewed over the freakish end to Usain Bolt's career that had just played out. *It wasn't supposed to happen like that.* There it was in a phrase.

I thought of Daniel John Harvey. How much I missed him. The love we'd shared. What he'd inspired me to do. The joy he'd always miss. How much I missed him. How I'd always be trapped in that loop. But this last year had reminded me that we don't just travel in circles. We're always, all of us, moving forwards on a journey. Life can end in sudden death, and we've engineered sport so it often does too. As painful as the sound of a final whistle can be, it defines everything that went before, whether you're Brazil's greatest ever number 10 or my brother. Sport was born out of death. Sport bottles the lightning of life's unpredictability. Sport equips us for grief.

Selhurst Park. Holmesdale Stand. Block G. Row 26. Seat 133. It had been the end of one story and the start of another. Somewhere along the way I'd reached the point where grief becomes like most people's experience of being a fan: filled with heartache, but we keep picking ourselves up and, as many a manager is now wont to say, we go again. I could never get Dan back. But his soul was so stitched into the enjoyment of sport that, by throwing myself into his beautiful passion, in a small yet huge way I was keeping his spirit alive. And I still am. Whenever I think of my brother, Glad All Over, yes I am.

And after the twists and turns of these last twelve months, what now? Would my sports watching become a more natural, less concentrated affair? Might life become a bit more normal? An email had come through that put paid to that. It was from Tottenham Hotspur. I was eligible for a season ticket. And the new season was starting next week.

Usain Bolt readies himself for his last ever competitive race

Epilogue

At a fork in the main road I halted. Was this the right way?

I couldn't believe I was asking this question. It was a route I used to know so well. It was now Wednesday, 3 April 2019: two years since my last visit to White Hart Lane, and I was surprised to find how the path to the ground had faded from my muscle memory. I had some reconnecting to do. After Spurs had spent the previous two years squatting at Wembley, this unseasonably cold evening would see the club's first competitive match in their new stadium, and it was all over the news: how it had been built from aggregate taken from the debris of the demolished edifice; how the new South Stand was the largest single tier in England; how the bar was the longest in Europe; how the pints filled from the bottom up; how the cost had spiralled beyond a billion pounds; how the pitch could retract; and how the likes of Beyoncé would soon be playing here. (She's a proven trophy-winner. Could she shore up central defence?) For me only one statistic really mattered: it was a quarter of a century since that first Spurs home match against Crystal Palace Dan had taken me to in 1994 for Christmas, and who had the Fixture Goddess deemed worthy of being Tottenham's first opponents in the new arena? Palace. It had to be Palace. I don't think I've ever been this conflicted before a sporting event. I was watching this game for two.

Across the road a small gaggle of people ahead of me were ducking into a nearby park, their navy blue and white bobble hats signalling the right direction. I followed them past Bruce Castle, a grand manor house so unbefitting the area it seemed to have taken a wrong turn of its own. Centuries ago it must have been an imposing sight on the Haringey landscape. Now, though, it was utterly dwarfed. At this distance all I could see was a looming, charcoal-grey smudge behind a few rows of houses and a veil of trees, but it still took my breath away. It was gigantic. I felt like an X-Wing pilot approaching the Death Star: 'Look at the size of that thing . . .'

Impatient to see it, I jogged the last hundred yards to the High Road and there it was, soaring into the sky: the Tottenham Hotspur Stadium. It was as if a mammoth spaceship had landed in London and the visiting aliens had done humanity a favour by picking the least valuable real estate in the entire city to squash. But the unfamiliarity of it was drowned by joy. The air vibrated with chanting. Wherever I looked there were smiles, bathed in blue light from giant new screens that shone the simple message: 'Welcome Home'.

A blast of slanting, squally rain sent me shivering into the new club shop for a scarf and gloves. Except the word 'shop' was an understatement for what confronted me: 23,000 square feet of gleaming superstore, offering a comically vast range of Tottenham-branded memorabilia. There were lunch boxes, Top Trumps cards, PlayStation covers, official shirts (reduced from £90 to a still crazy £77) – I couldn't help comparing it to the equally optimistic gift shop in Jurassic Park. There were even jigsaws, as if Spurs fans haven't had enough of squads being pulled apart and painfully reassembled. And there were official 'half-and-half' scarves featuring the colours and crests of both clubs, a multilateral concept that no self-respecting football fan can ever abide. Except now. On this one occasion there was no choice but to buy one. I had to take a little bit of Dan into the new stadium, even if I stuffed the red and blue half inside my coat.

I rendezvoused with Will, and finally we reached our entrance for the North Stand top tier, the same place Dan had taken me on my *first* first trip to the Lane. Everything was pristine, right down to the new season tickets in our hands. We exchanged a smile, the turnstiles glowed green, and the gates opened.

Me, Dan and Lucy as kids

Dan enjoying the London 2012 Olympics

The Whole Journey

Being a completist and a geek, I thought I'd round off the book with a compendium of fixtures from my two-year deep-dive into the world of sport. It begins with the full results from Crystal Palace FC's 2015/16 season, a historic campaign that started well and ended with Alan Pardew's touchline dancing. Following that comes every event I visited during the 2016/17 sporting season. In the narrative, some of these are mentioned only in passing; others missed the cut completely. (Otherwise the book would have been as long as Ulysses, and my editors told me that would be pushing the odyssey vibe a bit far.) The 'extra' occasions are denoted by being greyed out.

Beyond this list, I'm pleased to report my love of sport is as strong as ever, and it's continued to serve up plenty of strange experiences. Like how I blagged my way into a front-row seat at the World Chess Championship (worth £500) by pretending to be a journalist (a move I call the 'Miles Jupp'). It was mesmerising or stupefying, depending on your point of view. Or like when I spent Tottenham Hotspur's (surely only) Champions League Final at a wedding reception in a theatre in Lyme Regis, where I watched the game in a postage-stamp dressing room along with the only other guest who was a Spurs fan: my girlfriend (now wife's) ex, who I'd never previously met. It was two hours that for both of us combined the twin agonies of sporting agony and extreme awkwardness – a very British combination. But as these episodes happened after 2017, they fell outside the scope of the book.

Crystal Palace Season 2015/16

Premier League

8/8/15 Norwich City 1–3 Crystal Palace
16/8/15 Crystal Palace 1–2 Arsenal
22/8/15 Crystal Palace 2–1 Aston Villa
29/8/15 Chelsea 1–2 Crystal Palace
12/9/15 Crystal Palace 0–1 Manchester City
20/9/15 Tottenham Hotspur 1–0 Crystal Palace
27/9/15 Watford 0–1 Crystal Palace
3/10/15 Crystal Palace 2–0 West Bromwich Albion
17/10/15 Crystal Palace 1–3 West Ham United
24/10/15 Leicester City 1–0 Crystal Palace
31/10/15 Crystal Palace 0–0 Manchester United
8/11/15 Liverpool 1–2 Crystal Palace
23/11/15 Crystal Palace 0–1 Sunderland
28/11/15 Crystal Palace 5–1 Newcastle United
7/12/15 Everton 1–1 Crystal Palace
12/12/15 Crystal Palace 1–0 Southampton
19/12/15 Stoke City 1–2 Crystal Palace
26/12/15 Bournemouth 0–0 Crystal Palace
28/12/15 Crystal Palace 0–0 Swansea City
3/1/16 Crystal Palace 0–3 Chelsea
12/1/16 Aston Villa 1–0 Crystal Palace
16/1/16 Manchester City 4–0 Crystal Palace
23/1/16 Crystal Palace 1–3 Tottenham Hotspur
2/2/16 Crystal Palace 1–2 Bournemouth
6/2/16 Swansea City 1–1 Crystal Palace
13/2/16 Crystal Palace 1–2 Watford
27/2/16 West Bromwich Albion 3–2 Crystal Palace
1/3/16 Sunderland 2–2 Crystal Palace
6/3/16 Crystal Palace 1–2 Liverpool
19/3/16 Crystal Palace 0–1 Leicester City
2/4/16 West Ham United 2–2 Crystal Palace
9/4/16 Crystal Palace 1–0 Norwich City

13/4/16 Crystal Palace 0–0 Everton
17/4/16 Arsenal 1–1 Crystal Palace
20/4/16 Manchester United 2–0 Crystal Palace
30/04/16 Newcastle United 1–0 Crystal Palace
7/5/16 Crystal Palace 2–1 Stoke City
15/5/16 Southampton 4–1 Crystal Palace

FA Cup

9/1/16 Third Round, Southampton 1–2 Crystal Palace
30/1/16 Fourth Round, Crystal Palace 1–0 Stoke City
21/2/16 Fifth Round, Tottenham Hotspur 0–1 Crystal Palace
11/3/16 Quarter–Final, Reading 0–2 Crystal Palace
24/2/16 Semi–Final, Crystal Palace 2–1 Watford
21/5/16 Final, Crystal Palace 1–2 Manchester United

Jon's Ultimate Season Ticket 2016/17

21/09/16 Football: League Cup Third Round, Spurs 5–0 Gillingham, Tottenham Hotspur Stadium

24/09/16 Rugby Union: Aviva Premiership, Harlequins 17–10 Saracens, The Stoop

08/10/16 Rugby Union: Aviva Premiership, Harlequins 20–9 Northampton, The Stoop

29/10/16 Football: Premier League, Spurs 1–1 Leicester, Tottenham Hotspur Stadium

30/10/16 NFL: Washington Redskins* 27–27 Cincinatti Bengals, Wembley Stadium

*Now known as Washington Commanders.

02/11/16 Football: Champions League Spurs 0–1 Bayer Leverkeusen, Tottenham Hotspur Stadium

13/11/16 Rugby League: Four Nations Tournament, England 18–36 Australia, London Stadium

17/11/16 Tennis: ATP Finals, Jamie Murray & Bruno Soares beat Ivan Dodig & Marcelo Melo 6–3, 3–6, 10–6; Milos Raonic beat Dominic Thiem, 7–6, 6–3, The O2, London

27/12/16 Rugby Union: Aviva Premiership, Harlequins 28–24 Gloucester, 'Big Game 9', Twickenham

08/01/17 Darts: BDO World Championship, Martin Adams 3–2 Ryan Joyce, Tom Sawyer 0–3 Paul Hogan, Lisa Ashton 2–0 Sharon Prins, Scott Mitchell 3–0 Mark McGrath, Krzysztof Rtajski 3–2 Willem Mandigers, Lakeside Country Club, Frimley Green

13/01/17 Handball: Men's World Championship, Group D Round-Robin, Sweden 33–16 Bahrain, Denmark 33–22 Argentina, Accorhotels Arena, Paris

16/01/17 Snooker: The Masters, Last 16, Joe Perry 6–1 Stuart Bingham, Alexandra Palace

17/01/17 Snooker: The Masters, Last 16, Neil Robertson 6–3 Ali Carter, Alexandra Palace

19/01/17 Snooker: The Masters, Quarter–Final, Marco Fu 6–2 Mark Allen, Alexandra Palace

22/01/17 Snooker: The Masters, Final: Ronnie O'Sullivan 10–7 Joe Perry, Alexandra Palace

04/02/17 Rugby Union: Men's Six Nations, England 19–16 France, Twickenham

04/02/17 Rugby Union: Women's Six Nations, England 26–13 France, Twickenham

19/02/17 Football: FA Cup Fifth Round, Fulham 0–3 Spurs, Craven Cottage

26/02/17 Football: Premier League, Spurs 4–0 Stoke, Tottenham Hotspur Stadium

12/03/17 Football: FA Cup Quarter-Final, Spurs 6–0 Millwall, Tottenham Hotspur Stadium

19/03/17 Football: Premier League, Spurs 2–1 Southampton, Tottenham Hotspur Stadium

25/03/17 Rugby Union: Aviva Premiership, Harlequins 53–17 Newcastle, The Stoop

25/03/17 Greyhound Racing: Wimbledon Stadium. Winners: A Bit Nippy, Black Alder, Shaneboy Russell, Fweshfromthesesh, Art Of Illusion, Max Diver, Kakantu, Glanmire Prince, Fizzypop Hazard, Ginas Blue, Droopys Acrobat, Glitzy King

26/03/17 Football, FIFA World Cup Qualifier, England 2–0 Lithuania, Wembley Stadium

02/04/17 Rowing: The University Boat Races, River Thames. Men's Blue Boat: Oxford won by 1¼ lengths; Women's Blue Boat: Cambridge won by 11 lengths; Men's Reserves: Isis beat Goldie by 2½ lengths; Women's Reserves: Blondie beat Osiris by 13 lengths

08/04/17: National Hunt Racing: The Grand National, Aintree. Won by: One For Arthur (14/1), owned by Deborah Thomson and Belinda McClung, trained by Lucinda Russell and ridden by Derek Fox. Margin of victory: 4½ lengths

15/04/17 Football, Premier League, Spurs 4–0 Bournemouth, Tottenham Hotspur Stadium

22/04/17 Football: FA Cup Semi-Final, Chelsea 4–2 Spurs, Wembley Stadium

24/04/17 Snooker: World Championship, Crucible Theatre, Sheffield. Second Round, Xiao Guodong 6–13 Mark Selby; Neil Robertson 11–13 Marco Fu; Exhibition: Peter Ebdon 2–1 Dennis Taylor

30/04/17 Football, Premier League, Spurs 2–0 Arsenal, Tottenham Hotspur Stadium

14/05/17 Football, Premier League, Spurs 2–1 Manchester United, Tottenham Hotspur Stadium

28/05/17 Motor Racing: Historic Grand Prix Series, Pau, France

30/05/17 Tennis: French Open, Roland Garros. First Round: S-W Hsieh beat J. Konta 1–6, 7–6, 6–4; A. Murray beat A. Kuznetsov 6–4, 4–6, 6–2, 6–0; J-W Tsonga beat R. Olivo 5–7, 4–6, 7–6, 4–6

03/06/17 Horse Racing: The Derby, Epsom Downs. Won by Wings of Eagles (40/1), owned by Michael Tabor, Derrick Smith and Sue Magnier, trained by Aidan O'Brien, ridden by Padraig Beggy. Margin of victory: ¾ length

13/06/17 Baseball: Major League, New York Mets 6–1 Chicago Cubs, Citi Field, New York

18/06/17 Cricket: ICC Champions Trophy final: Pakistan beat India by 180 runs, The Oval

30/06/17 Motor Racing: A walk of the Grand Prix course, Monaco

05/07/17 Horse Racing, Kempton Park. Winners: Hackney Road, Billesdon Brook, Erinyes, Gibbs Hill, Clowance One, Comprise, Mr Minerals

06/07/17 Cricket: First Test, England v South Africa, Lord's. First Day. England won by 211 runs

12/07/17 Tennis: Wimbledon. Gentlemen's Singles Quarter-Finals: S. Querrey beat A. Murray 3–6, 6–4, 7–6, 6–1, 6–1; R. Federer beat M. Raonic 6–4, 6–2, 7–6

15/07/17 Rubik's Cube: Nations' Cup, Les Docks de Paris. Germany beat Australia in the Final

16/07/17 Rubik's Cube: World Championships, Les Docks de Paris. 3x3x3 tournament won by Max Park (USA) with an average of 6.85 seconds. He also set a new World Record for solving the 3x3x3 cube one-handed, at 10.31 (average)

20/07/17 Golf: The (British) Open, Royal Birkdale, won by Jordan Spieth (USA), -12, victory by 3 shots over Matt Kuchar (USA)

23/07/17 Cricket: ICC Women's World Cup Final, Lord's. England beat India by 9 runs

29/07/17 & 30/07/17 Cricket: Third Test, England v South Africa, the 100th Test at the Oval. Third and Fourth Days. England won by 239 runs

04–07, 10 & 12–13/08/17 Athletics: IAAF World Championships, London Stadium

Sports visited: Football, Rugby Union, Rugby League, American Football, Tennis, Darts, Handball, Snooker, Greyhound Racing, Horse Racing (National Hunt and Flat), Rowing, Motor Racing, Baseball, Cricket, Rubik's Cube, Golf, Athletics

Acknowledgements

There are lots of people I need to thank for helping me to turn this journey into a book and not leaving it trapped in my head as a scramble of thoughts, memories and pain.

I'm so grateful to Cariad Lloyd for inviting me to be one of her guinea-pig guests (and quite possibly the least famous of all) to appear on her wonderful podcast, *Griefcast*, in 2016. It was the first time I'd spoken in public about the loss of Dan, and you gave me confidence to confront bereavement and not let it swallow me up. Thanks to Charlotte Atyeo, who was the first to make me believe this could be a book. You told me it was the only time you'd ever cried on hearing a pitch, and while that reaction might sound like a bad thing, we both knew it was a good thing.

A huge thank you to my book agent, Stan at the North Literary Agency, who didn't just find a home for this project but the best possible home, at Yellow Jersey Press, under the guidance of the magnificent Joe Pickering. Joe, I couldn't have wished for a better editor, and I'm immensely grateful for everything you've done both for me and for Dan. You made me believe in the story and the words, and you put petrol in the engine whenever I felt like conking out. Thanks also to the brilliant team at Yellow Jersey and Vintage: Rhiannon Roy, Ellie Steel and Graham Coster. Matt Broughton knocked it out of the park with his cover design, and Mark Thomas smashed it to all corners with the illustration. Nobody takes better photos than Matt Crockett.

I must say a special thanks to my sporting comrades, who've accompanied me to all kinds of events over the years. James Schad is my oldest friend, and aside from Dan he's racked up more sporting adventures with me than anyone else. He also shares an insatiable appetite for sports geekery, whether it's the highs and lows of Epke Zonderland, or the current form of Northampton's scrum-halves in the Gallagher Premiership. Equal gratitude goes to Will Dixon, my fellow Spurs sufferer. You've taken on the mantle of being my football bezzie (a phrase I know you'll hate), as well as joining me on all kinds of trips from T20 Finals Day at Edgbaston to that fateful afternoon at the Lakeside Darts. Extended thanks to Father Dixon, Luke, for being part of some Glory Glory Nights in N17, Wembley, and beyond.

Big thanks to Tom Walker, for all the support, friendship and fun. And, as if that wasn't enough, for much of the period covered in this book you gave me a home too. Not to mention the receptacle-shaped intergalactic political enterprise that we cooked up at the same time as my sporting odyssey, and which continues to amuse and haunt us to this day.

Some other gallant souls deserve thanks for accompanying me on various legs of the odyssey. Shelley Crofts and Pete James, you were my athletics buddies during Bolt's swan song; David Pitcher, aka Pitch, you shared the wonderful weirdness of Wembley as England played Lithuania; and Matt Parker, you pushed me down the Rubik's Cube rabbit hole, which turned into one of the most memorable excursions of my life. (Cheers to Gregor, for your hospitality and insights at the tournament.)

Thanks to Joanna and Louisa for their wonderful generosity in helping me get tickets to matches I'd never have been able to see otherwise. And I owe inordinate thanks to Jimmy Mulville, not just for letting me into the One Twenty, but for all the insight, empathy, support and laughter. And for giving me that book too.

Nick Newman has been a brilliant support: you gave me an unforgettable weekend when we travelled to Pau in the south of France for an afternoon's motor racing at the historic Grand Prix, followed by a trip up into the Pyrenees. That was going to be a chapter in the book, but it's reluctantly ended up as an unused substitute (until the deluxe 20th anniversary reissue). Even so, it was fantastic to spend a Sunday together quaffing beers, scoffing duck, watching Trabants hurtle into each other and sending scurrilous, satirical tweets. I'll never forget your lap of Pau in a Ferrari. Ok, it was a Fiat 500 with a ropey gear-box, but same difference. Your partners in comedy on Team Dave Podmore have also been a tremendous source of support and fun for many years: Chris Douglas, Nicola Sanderson, Richard Wilson, Lewis Macleod, and of course the incomparable Andrew Nickolds. Yeah, no, as I say, very much so.

I'm indebted to Sarah Hesketh and Charlie Campbell, who both read my early scribblings. Your kindness and encouragement helped get this off the launchpad and into my notepad. Thanks to Dave Hayes, who ran a fine-tooth comb over the golf details from the perspective of someone who knows their stuff. And a big shout-out to radio comedy godfather Ed Morrish, who helped me with my Radio 4 spin-off, *Sudden Death*, which aired in summer 2022 (and which you can find on BBC Sounds).

Thanks to Matt Thacker at The Nightwatchman, for giving me the platform to test-drive my cricket chapter, and to Alison Mitchell at *Test Match Special* for highlighting it on air.

To all of Dan's friends at the Royal Borough of Kensington and Chelsea, I'm so grateful for the love you showed Dan, and for the kindness you showed me and the family. Jon, Steve, Roland, Raj, Abdel, Dave, Tony, Charles, George, Billy, Paul, Richard, Annie, Theresa, Donya, Sheila and Danielle – you all rock. And special thanks too to the twins, Christina and Joanne, for your loving friendship with Dan and for giving him his own piece of Wembley.

The next thank-ees surely won't read this, but I must pay tribute to every sportsperson and fan who contributed to the events mentioned in the book, across the decades, from the straight-laced stars of snooker to the madcap musclemen of World Championship Wrestling. A special mention to Dennis Taylor, Martin Adams, Derek Fox and One For Arthur for being so entertaining and inspirational. And to the late Bob Potter, who passed away in 2023, and who was such a generous and gregarious host.

On behalf of me and Dan, thanks to everyone who helped bring the Olympics to London and who made it such a joyous success, from Seb Coe to the army of Games Maker volunteers. You'll never know how much you enriched two brothers' lives.

Words can't express the love and gratitude I have for my mum, Linda, and my sister Lucy. You've always been a source of strength and support through the highs and the lows that life has brought us. Here's to many more highs to come, with Pitch, Lily, Connie, David and Theresa. Dad, thanks for giving me the desire to write and the belief that I could do it.

To my wife Sarah, and our son Rowan, I love you so much. You've both come into my life since the events of this book, and you've given me so much happiness and so much to live for. I'm so grateful for your long-suffering patience, encouragement, support and smiles.

To all the people who I haven't had space to name-check here, but who've been an invaluable part of my life, thank you.

And to Dan, despite 260-odd pages of trying, I can't put into words how much you mean to me, how much I miss you, and how much I love you. Even though I'm without you, you'll always be with me. I'm so lucky to have known you, and so grateful for how you've inspired me. I'll never be able to repay you, but I can at least say this. For as long as civilisation stands, the British Library will now be forced to hold written evidence that the Grittar Nod is a thing. What would you say to that? 'Too bloody right.'